VALUE
PERSPECTIVES TODAY

"Like the master's pipe, the concept of equilibration is an essential part of him!"

—J. M. Gallagher

(Proceedings from the First Annual Symposium of the Jean Piaget Society, May 26, 1971.)

VALUE
PERSPECTIVES TODAY

*Toward an Integration with
Jean Piaget's
New Discipline in Relation to
Modern Educational Leaders*

JOHN F. EMLING

*Rutherford • Madison • Teaneck
Fairleigh Dickinson University Press
London: Associated University Presses*

Associated University Presses, Inc.
Cranbury, New Jersey 08512

Associated University Presses
Magdalen House
136–148 Tooley Street
London SE1 2TT, England

Other books by JOHN F. EMLING:

Toward a Philosophy of Education
Life Guidance in Secondary Education
*Workbook and Studyguide for Economics
and General Business*
*Workbook and Studyguide for Our Quest
for Happiness*

Library of Congress Cataloging in Publication Data

Emling, John F   1916–
    Value perspectives today.

    Bibliography: p.
    Includes index.
    1. Education—United States—History. 2. Education
—Philosophy—History. 3. Piaget, Jean, 1896–
I. Title.
LA205.E45   370.1′09   75-39114
ISBN 0-8386-1905-3

PRINTED IN THE UNITED STATES OF AMERICA

Respectfully dedicated to

Dr. Ellis A. Joseph
Dean, School of Education
University of Dayton (Ohio)

CONTENTS

FOREWORD

Although values are related to educational processes in many ways, we are still unsure of the nature of values and we are confused about the ways in which educational processes can lead to sound value judgments. Too often we have interpreted values in terms of philosophical systems that have not been verified in terms of satisfaction, and we have settled for educational processes as a way of transmitting cultural mores and have assumed that this will lead to moral behavior.

Prior to these problems, however, there is the question of epistemology. Before we deal with the issues facing us in value theory and educational procedures, we need to learn how people come to know anything at all. For many years, epistemology was the handmaiden of philosophy and led to some odd conclusions about the subject-object relationship. Until recently, we had little concrete information about the relation of the knower to the known, and the genetic epistemology of Jean Piaget, based on scientific procedures, which shows how the knower shapes knowledge in relation to facts and interpretation, is just now becoming known to psychologists and educators.

John F. Emling is among those best acquainted with the research findings of Jean Piaget, and is also a competent educational theorist. *Value Perspectives Today* is an introduction to moral educational theory and practice against the background of Piaget's research findings and in comparison with the theories of other educators.

How education is conceived has much to do with the values that emerge. Emling stresses being creative, inventive, and curious; developing the capacity to be critical, to verify theory by a return to the facts, and to be skeptical of unfounded claims. The emphasis is on students who are active, who find out for themselves, and who distinguish between testing their ideas and accepting any idea that comes along. In this regard Emling repeats two Piagetian slogans: "To understand is to invent" and "In the beginning was the response."

All of this is placed in perspective in the earlier chapters. Emling gives helpful interpretations of the contributions of Horace Mann, William T. Harris, and John Dewey to the development of educational practice, with passing references to Jerome Bruner and Jacques Maritain, so that they may be compared with Piaget. There is also a useful comparison of Kohlberg and Piaget. But the most helpful part of the book, it seems to me, is the interpretation of Piaget, who has written voluminously and is not always easy to understand.

Most educators are aware of Piaget's research on the way children develop mentally, but they do not always see the correlation between biological and mental development. They have applied some of Piaget's findings on moral judgment, but they do not provide the kind of schooling that encourages the development of such moral judgment. They are aware that the student must move toward autonomy, but they provide an examination system that puts a premium on the retention of prior knowledge. They fail to see that unless education is correlated with the findings of genetic epistemology, the effectiveness of the process is effectively stunted.

Without adequate experimentation and verification, we cannot hope for an understanding of how persons learn or of *what* to teach *when* and *how*. This does not come from the "wisdom" of philosophy but from the processes of scientific experimentation. Philosophy cannot tell science what to do, but it can lead to a "wisdom" that is agreeable with science. The scientific approach, on the contrary, can point to the factors in good learning, to the role of the structure of the mind, to the place of logic, and to the powers of adaptation, as one assimilates new facts and interprets them.

Emling describes this process effectively. Against the background of the theories of Mann, Harris, Dewey, and others, he explicates the findings of Piaget for today's education, especially in the field of values, making his book a significant contribution to all of us.

Randolph Crump Miller

Yale University
The Divinity School

PREFACE

The so-called process revolution within the last few decades is resulting in an upsurge of Piagetian studies. Now the major areas of learning experience are clamoring for renewal of interdisciplinary approaches to values. Until recently, the movement has been looked upon as being merely another short-lived reaction to traditional value perspectives—something novel in itself, but without any solid, or even realistic, foundations. For centuries mere stability, not adaptation, has been the permeating basic attitude toward the relevance of values. Since the 1950s, however, the challenging responses to Piaget's new discipline are forcing a reevaluation of this unyielding misconception. The Swiss epistemologist does not hesitate to point out his concern when assessing the educational scene of the past decades:

it is . . . scarcely believable that in a field so accessible to experiments . . . [the teacher] has not organized methodical and sustained experiments, but has remained content to decide . . . [what to teach, when, and how] on the basis of opinions whose "common sense" in fact conceals more affectivity than effective reasoning.[1]

J. F. Emling

Education Center, University of Dayton

15

ACKNOWLEDGMENTS

Grateful acknowledgments are extended to Dr. Daniel L. Leary, his successors Dr. Louis J. Faerber and Dr. Joseph J. Panzer, and Dr. Joseph J. Stander, Vice President.

To Dr. Charles J. Lees, President of Chaminade College of Honolulu, Dr. M. Audrey Bourgeois Grob, Chairman of Department of Educational Foundations, and Dr. Ellis A. Joseph, Dean, special appreciation is due. Without their support this project would never have been realized.

My colleagues, Professors Albert H. Rose, Richard A. Liebler, Edmund L. Rhodes, Clement J. Lambert, Joseph H. Zeinz, and Frank J. Kenney, are given special gratitude for their painstaking critiques.

To Mrs. Mathilde Finch, Editor in Chief of Associated University Presses, Inc., is expressed profound thanks for her personal interest and devotedness in editing.

Finally, to Professor Jean Piaget is extended the thanks par excellence for being the inspiration of this endeavor, and to the Marianists at the University of Dayton for financing the project through their Intercommunity Council.

To the following authors and publishers, for their generous permission to quote extensively from their books and articles, sincere acknowledgment is extended:

17

Denoël-Gonthier, for permission to quote from Jean Piaget, *Six Psychological Studies,* translated by Anita Tenzer, copyright 1967.

The John Dewey Foundation, for permission to quote from John Dewey, *Reconstruction in Philosophy.*

Garrett Hardin, for permission to quote from "Genetics and History."

Harper & Row, Publishers, Inc., for permission to quote from John Gardner, *Self-Renewal*; from James Monroe Hughes, *Education in America*; from Alexander Meiklejohn, *Education Between Two Worlds*; from Mary Ann Spencer Pulaski, *Understanding Piaget*; and from Edgar B. Wesley, *NEA: The First Hundred Years.*

Hodder & Stoughton, for permission to quote from Jean Piaget, *Six Psychological Studies,* translated by Anita Tenzer, copyright 1967.

Holt, Rinehart and Winston, Inc., for permission to quote from Theodore Brameld, *Patterns of Education Philosophy*; from John Dewey, *Logic: The Theory of Inquiry*; and from Irving E. Sigel and Frank H. Hooper, *Logical Thinking in Children.*

Houghton Mifflin Company, for permission to quote from Carlton E. Beck, Normand R. Bernier, James E. MacDonald, Thomas W. Walton, and Jack C. Willers, *Education for Relevance.*

Humanities Press, Inc., New Jersey, for permission to quote from Jean Piaget, *The Child's Conception of the World*; from Jean Piaget, *The Language and Thought of the Child*; and from Jean Piaget and A. Szeminska, *The Child's Conception of Number.*

Interstate Printers and Publishers, Inc., for permission to quote from John A. Stoops, *Religious Values in Education.*

Frank Jennings, for permission to quote from his article "Jean Piaget: Notes on Learning."

The Journal of Philosophy, for permission to quote from Edwin A. Burtt, "The Core of Dewey's Way of Thinking."

Alfred A. Knopf, Inc., for permission to quote from B. F. Skinner, *Beyond Freedom and Dignity,* copyright 1971.

Lawrence Kohlberg, for permission to quote from "Moral Education in the Schools."

Learning Magazine, for permission to quote from Eleanor Duckworth, "Piaget Takes a Teacher's Look."

Horace Liveright, for permission to quote from John Dewey, *The Sources of a Science of Education.*

Longman Group Limited, for permission to quote from Jean Piaget, *Science of Education and the Psychology of the Child.*

Macmillan Publishing Co., Inc., for permission to quote from Hadley Cantril, *The "Why" of Man's Experience,* copyright 1950 by Macmillan Publishing Co., Inc.; from William F. Cunningham, *The Pivotal Problems of Education,* copyright 1940 by William F. Cunningham, renewed 1968 by Zita Sullivan; from John Dewey, *Democracy and Education,* copyright 1916 by Macmillan Publishing Co., Inc.; from J. H. Hayes, *A Political and Social History of Modern Europe,* copyright 1925 by Macmillan Publishing Co., Inc.; from John D. Redden and Francis A. Ryan, *A Catholic Philosophy of Education,* copyright 1942, 1956 by The Bruce Publishing Company; and from B. F. Skinner, *Walden Two,* copyright 1948 by Macmillan Publishing Co., Inc.

Main Currents in Modern Thought, for permission to quote from Jose A. Arguelles, "The Believe-In-An Aquarian Age Ritual."

B. Claude Mathis, for permission to quote from his *Psychological Foundations of Education,* and to Academic Press Inc., owners of the copyright.

McGraw-Hill Book Company, for permission to quote from Philip H. Phenix, *Realms of Meaning,* copyright 1964 by McGraw-Hill Book Co., and from James E. Royce, *Man and Meaning,* copyright 1969 by McGraw-Hill Book Co. Used with permission of McGraw-Hill Book Co.

The National Education Association, for permission to quote from the report of the Educational Policies Commission, *The Unique Function of Education in American Democracy;* and from Horace Mann, *Tenth Annual Report of the Secretary of the Board Covering the Year 1846* (Facsimile ed., 1952).

National Society for the Study of Education, for permission to quote from Nelson B. Henry, ed., *The Fifty-Fourth Yearbook of the National Society for the Study of Education,* Part I.

The New York Times, for permission to quote from John L. Hess, "Piaget Sees Science Dooming Psychoanalysis," copyright 1972 by The New York Times Company. Reprinted by permission; from a review of Jean Piaget, *Six Psychological Studies,* copyright 1967 by The New York Times Company. Reprinted by permission; and from Daniel Yergin, "The Chomskyan Revolution," copyright 1972 by The New York Times Company. Reprinted by permission.

W. W. Norton & Company, Inc., for permission to quote from Jerome S. Bruner, *The Relevance of Education;* from Jean Piaget, *Understanding Causality;* and from John B. Watson, *Behaviorism.*

Oxford University Press, Inc., for permission to quote from David Elkind and John H. Flavell, *Children and Adolescents.*

Michael Polanyi, for permission to quote from *Personal Knowledge,* copyright 1958.

Psychology Today, for permission to quote from Elizabeth Hall, "A Conversation with Jean Piaget and Bärbel Inhelder," and from Mary Harrington Hall, "A Conversation with Michael Polanyi."

G. P. Putnam's Sons, for permission to quote from John Dewey, *Education Today,* copyright 1940, and from John Dewey, *Freedom and Culture,* copyright 1939.

Random House, Inc., for permission to quote from Jean Piaget, *Six Psychological Studies,* translated by Anita Tenzer, copyright 1967, and from Jerome A. Schaffer, *Reality, Knowledge and Value,* copyright 1971.

The Religious Education Association of the United States and Canada, for permission to quote from John F. Emling, "In the Beginning Was the Response"; from Robert Williams, "A Theory of God-Concept Readiness: From the Piagetian Theories of Child Artificialism and the Origin of Religious Feeling in Children"; and from Jeremy Zwelling, "Religion in the Department of Religion."

Routledge & Kegan Paul, Ltd., for permission to quote from

University of Notre Dame Press, for permission to quote from Jacques Maritain, "Integral Humanism and the Crisis of Modern Times."

The University of Texas at Austin, for permission to quote from Hugh C. Black, "The Learning-Product and the Learning-Process Theories of Education: An Attempted Synthesis" (doctoral dissertation).

D. Van Nostrand Company, for permission to quote from John H. Flavell, *The Developmental Psychology of Jean Piaget.*

The Viking Press, Inc., for permission to quote from Jean Piaget, *Science of Education and the Psychology of the Child,* Translation Copyright © 1970 by Grossman Publishers. Reprinted by permission of Grossman Publishers, a division of The Viking Press, Inc., and from Jean Piaget, *To Understand is to Invent,* Translation Copyright © 1973 by The Viking Press, Inc. Reprinted by permission of Grossman Publishers, a division of The Viking Press, Inc.

The World Education Fellowship, for permission to quote from John Dewey, "The Need of a Philosophy of Education."

The Yale Review, for permission to quote from John Dewey, "The Liberation of Modern Religion."

Yale University Press, for permission to quote from Gordon W. Allport, *Becoming.*

VALUE
PERSPECTIVES TODAY

Today, in civilization's struggle to survive, it is timely to make a reassessment and to try to view things in their true relations and relative importance.[1] This is especially true of values, man's humanistic values. In the seven ensuing chapters these values will be clarified, with the expectation that new understanding of the self and of self-fulfillment will result. Through the centuries man has been revitalized by a process of action and reaction, and it is in this perspective that education for values becomes relevant, the more especially when—as here—humanistic responses are integrated with Jean Piaget's new discipline that emphasizes process-and-response.

This newly integrated perspective discloses process as encompassing past, present, and future, and it identifies man personally with the potentials of *values education*. Knowing these potentials, every person can better experience how to appreciate and how to improve himself through more meaningful and more relevant responses in his daily living.

Prologue

INTENT AND OVERVIEW

"Every institution is the lengthened shadow of one man."
Pluralizing this well-known saying bestows the same dignity
on those idea-men who contributed to the establishing of the
great American institution, the common school.

Dynamics of Process-and-Response

Since to understand is to invent and to invent is to understand,
there are no static stages in process-and-response.

Interacting and reacting as it does through a stimulating
personal response to freedom of choice, process is recognized as
the vital key to human values. Man's internalized and externalized dynamics are, in chapter 1 below, challenged, defined,
illustrated, and diagramed to unveil his objective and subjective
worth. Process-and-response, and their dynamics, are values. They
have real significance; they vitalize and transform man's choices;
they become his bread-and-butter issues. These are the learning-
teaching experiences explored here.

Value-education develops in the existential present. Through
the process and response of, and to, an "ever-present past," all

education becomes experiencing. It is in an "I-Thou" relationship to God, to his fellow man, and to nature, that man encounters the beautiful, the good, and the true. In the developmental Piagetian perspective: "In the beginning was the response. . . ."

Evolving Value Perspectives

Today's youth protests and searches for . . . a relevance.

More than three-and-a-half centuries ago, although still under European influence, the pioneers of America originated their own type of meaningful educational activity. From their efforts a cumulative response has sprouted, and the vigorous tree of the American common (or public) school system has blossomed. In *Value Perspectives Today* the search for relevance is seen as characteristic of the learning-teaching process from the earliest times.

As an outcome of the early Pilgrim Fathers' values, the Declaration of Independence initiated a more thoroughly value-oriented education. The influences of religion, naturalism (explaining man and his values by a study of natural science, natural law, etc.), and economic assistance from family and state gradually clarified those values.

How developmental factors are interrelated with value perspectives today in a Piagetian process-and-response approach is the purport of chapter 2 (and the next five chapters), particularly with regard to the public school problem faced successively by the American triumvirate of Horace Mann, William T. Harris, and John Dewey, along with other educational leaders of the nation.

Horace Mann's Nonsectarian Education

The common school is the greatest discovery ever made by man.

The heroic struggle of Horace Mann to achieve a truly

"common" value-education is analyzed in chapter 3. An interpretation of his principles, in contrast to the traditional ones of religious, political, and personal freedom, constitutes the core of this chapter. Through the nonsectarian approach to education during his term as secretary of the Massachusetts Board of Education, he shaped a philosophy of values for the public school.

Mann's achievements won for him the unique title of Father of the Common School System. By his unstinted dedication he preserved and strengthened a mutual reverence between child and teacher. He it was who awakened the people to the supreme importance of value-relationships in the schools of America.

William T. Harris's Secularization of Education

Through education the individual becomes ethical.

As superintendent of the St. Louis public schools, and later as United States Commissioner of Education, Harris aroused a nationwide reaction to Horace Mann's nonsectarianism. In accordance with his Hegelian principles, Harris's church-state interpretation excluded nonsectarianism from education, declaring it to be simply another form of religious instruction. His conservatism presided forcefully over the public attitude toward the nation's schools, both public and private. He succeeded in making the public schools, from kindergarten through high school, predominantly centers of secular learning and values.

Chapter 4 shows how, through his clash with Horace Mann, Harris emerged as both the critic and the criticized of educational responses. By such confrontations, however, he effected the secularization of public education. As is indicated in the chronology of his multitudinous works, he is acclaimed the philosopher par excellence of secularized education.

Challenging their contemporary patriots, Mann and Harris laid the foundation of public education in America. Upon this foundation John Dewey built, and it became the democratic basis of process-and-response, the progressive education of the twentieth century.

John Dewey's Democracy for Education

Education is life. . . . Democracy, an inclusive way of life.

At the turn of the century the country was ripe for a "new" approach to values in education and life. In chapter 5 John Dewey's experimentalism is shown to emerge as the process-and-response reform for perfecting the naturalistic nonsectarianism initiated by Mann. By infusing the conservative educational perspectives of Harris with greater life and relevance, the Dewey movement gradually gained active participants in building a pragmatic social order. Through their efforts in the schools, education was equated with life, and man was seen as the continuum of nature.

In the Deweyan democratic perspective, students become instruments of their own learning. They interact and renew themselves within the same process of continual growth and development. By identifying education with life, youth is taught to discover the fullness of life, to live it in an integral-value relevance of trial and error, and to grasp more fully the socialized educational milieu as his culture. In this manner students experience how the immediate sources of knowledge lie in the self-perpetuating responses to their own needs as further developed today by Piaget.

That perspective has today accorded Dewey the distinctive honor of having created an American philosophy of education. Its core is that of pragmatic values, values constantly in process and unceasingly being tested in the crucible of democratic responses to life.

After Dewey, What?

The future depends on a race between education and catastrophe.

The sixth chapter shows that the post-Dewey enigma merges into a continuing process-and-response to values. Through the relevance of values presently in process, a whole new avenue of value perspectives is emerging—notably those of Jean Piaget's new discipline, of Jerome Bruner's discovery approaches to learning-teaching situations, and of Jacques Maritain's new humanism. Along with other approaches to the real values of man, these are in the process of congealing within a cumulative Deweyan influence. The message of this chapter is the urgency of bringing value-education into the shaping of the future that is now in process.

Further Significant Piagetian Insights

The fundamental question today: *What* to teach *when* and *how?*

Knowledge is no longer a mere product, with moral implications only. Its relevance cannot be divorced from values or from life. In the contrast and integration of the cognitive-moral development of Jean Piaget's model with that of Lawrence Kohlberg's, a meaningful renewal of principles is found to be emerging from the bicentennial observances of the nation, for "What profit would a man show if he were to gain the whole world and destroy himself in the process?"[1] Generalizing the biblical pronouncement to apply to this country, one may say: What will it profit America to gain a world of material existence and destroy itself in the process?

To present an integrated process-and-response perspective for formulating values within the framework of the life and works of Jean Piaget is the intent of this last chapter. In the light of his new discipline, *genetic epistemology,* fundamental process problems of the past are seen in the present and future approaches to knowledge-values. As Piaget writes: "To understand is to invent"—for "In the beginning was the response. . . ."

1

DYNAMICS OF
PROCESS-AND-RESPONSE

There is no possibility of a
    detached self-contained existence . . .
and the whole world conspires to
    produce a new creation. . . .
Continuity in time implies that the
    past determines the present
and the present conditions the future. . . .
    it is when his work is done that
he [man] attains immortality.

—Alfred North Whitehead

(quoted in Robert R. Rusk, *Doctrines of the Great Educators*)

There are no static stages [of process and response] as such.
Each is the fulfillment of something begun in the preceding
one and the beginning of something that will lead to the next.

"Why do you think educators get so enthused [today] about
your work?"
"It's a mystery. I don't know what happened; in Geneva no
one pays any attention," answered the world-famous Jean Piaget.[1]

Thus the renowned Swiss psychologist, affectionately known as "the gracious giant," characterized his reputation, but his new discipline he has marked by the unique phrase, "In the beginning was the response. . . ."[2] He is today's dominant influence in child development.

The traditional Piaget discourse is, by his own admission, abstract, and it rarely concerns classroom applications.[3] His highly theoretical views, however, are simplified in *Value Perspectives Today*, through integrating his insights with values relevant to the educational process.

As a new orientation in a single-process activity, process endlessly expands into response and response into process. What is experiential is no longer in isolation; it now includes the values of past events as being cumulatively effective in the present. According to Piagetian thought, even the future becomes essential to the interaction of any present-past process response:

There are no static stages [in process-and-response], as such. Each is the fulfillment of something[4] begun in the preceding one and the beginning of something that will lead to the next.[5]

Self-Worth

Taking its cue from Jean Piaget's developmental principle "In the beginning was the response. . . ," the accompanying diagrams express graphically the dynamics relevant to values when one is confronted with the concept of self-worth: Who am I? In this framework are found the personal and social relational aspects of the human being upon which Piaget founds his four major stages of growth and development in his new discipline, genetic epistemology. They are the functional bases of the Socratic dictum *Know thyself!*

Within this matrix, all of man's potentialities and competencies as dynamics[6] of the physical, mental, intellectual, emotional, and moral orders affect experiences and satisfactions, to explain what Bess terms man's *rage for awareness*.[7] Arising within the internalized and externalized dynamics of his maturing personhood, man's craving for relevance involves his objective and subjective worth. Diagramed it would be:

Internalized

Man's Personalized Dynamics are   and

Externalized

In responding to conflicts between his maximum objective, and limited subjective worth, man's personal internalized dynamics[8] make actual in process what he possesses potentially. Illustrated, it is:

His Maximum Objective Worth

Man's Personal Internalized   and
Dynamics Involve
His Limited Subjective Worth

Maximum objective worth is man's utmost capacities as a human being—all his endowments. They determine the ultimate to which he can develop and perfect himself as an individual in process, as a member of the human race. Illustrating one's maximum objective worth by a circle varying in circumference, the diameter represents all the natural abilities and talents of his complete personhood as man. Since talents and abilities vary in degree with each individual, the circumference necessarily varies with each person. In reality then, there are as many degrees of maximum objective worth in the world as there are individuals possessing them.

Limited subjective worth, on the other hand, is the person's actual knowledge and appreciation of his own endowments. As personal knowledge,[9] it is the degree to which he knows his maximum objective worth and can evaluate it. To a very great extent, it determines just how much effort he makes in attempting to actualize his full capacities as a human being. Since he cannot develop, perfect, evaluate, or appreciate what he does not know, his limited subjective worth is dependent on his knowledge of himself as endowed by nature—his personal inheritance as a member of the human race. This personalized phenomenon can be visualized by a diagonal within the circle representing his maximum objective worth. It, too, varies in degree with each person:

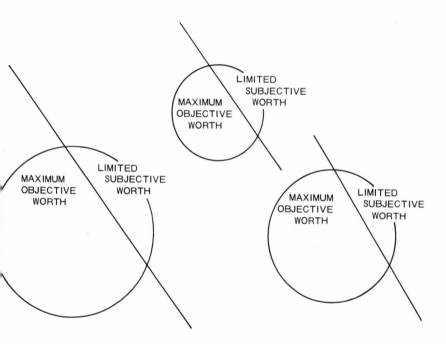

In most of these representations, evidently the limited subjective worth is only approximately one-fourth to one-fifth of what the person's maximum objective worth actually is. Obviously, the more the remaining four-fifths or five-sixths is realized, the richer the person becomes in his personal knowledge and appreciation of his real self. Also the more likely he is to make a better evaluation and use of his potential talents.

History bears witness to thousands of men and women richly endowed with talents. Having learned to appreciate their endowments (limited subjective worth) many, like George Washington Carver and Martin Luther King, put forth heroic efforts to make actual what they knew and appreciated as potential (maximum objective worth) in their own personhood. They thereby achieved phenomenal success and changed the developing world for themselves and their fellow men.

These examples imply reasons why man's internalized dynamics eventually become a responding process of externalized dynamics.[10] In his expressions or repressions, man attains an objective worth that is partially or fully recognized by others. Although always limited, his externalized dynamics are not unlike his internalized ones. They are composed of two main areas:

His Objective Worth

Man's Personal *Externalized*   and
Dynamics Involve

His Subjective Worth

Subjective worth is what the person thinks he achieves both by himself and through the assistance of others in his life at any particular stage of his existence. It can be exemplified by a person who studies mathematics and specializes in teaching that subject.

Objective worth is what others recognize in this particular person as a specialist in teaching mathematics . . . in brief, the achievements and fame he attains as his reputation within his associated society.

In the event that a person's subjective worth (his own appraisal) is less than his objective worth (recognized achievements and reputation), he is rated higher by society than by his own evaluation in life. In the event of the opposite, however, it is possible that he is being deprived of his rightful recognition and reputation in society. In this category belong numerous musicians, poets, inventors, teachers, and other professionals who are not receiving their due for the great services they are rendering humanity.

A contrast for comprehending in a more meaningful way the direct relationship between man's subjective and objective worth and his maximum objective worth is provided in this graphic rise-and-fall indicator, where maximum objective worth is represented by the whole rectangular area:[11]

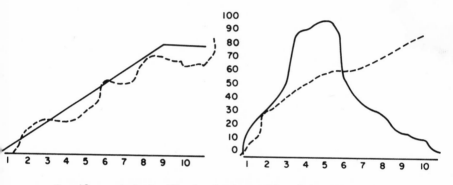

Specific periods in life, beginning with adolescence.

LEGEND: ——Objective worth (what a person actually achieves)
          ——Subjective worth (what others recognize in a
               person's achievements)

Putting it all together, this functional relevance is more completely illustrated in the summary profile below, which answers these questions:

What does it mean for me to have an "exterior" and an "interior," "a without and a within"?—How do I experience the human situation in the world?—How does it affect me with its commonplace, cramping character but at the same time with its hope and impulse towards what is unknown and has not yet been experienced?[12]

Man's
Internalized
Dynamics
(competencies as
endowments)

MAXIMUM OBJECTIVE WORTH is the PERSONAL CAPACITIES AND ENDOWMENTS determining the value, worth, dignity, talent, and ability of each person as a member of the human race. This is independent of any one's knowing it, and it varies greatly in degree with each person.

LIMITED SUBJECTIVE WORTH is the PERSONAL REALIZATION OF ONE'S ENDOWMENTS. It is the person's own awareness and appreciation of his dignity, value, worth, talent, and ability as a member of the human race. No two persons have the same subjective worth.

In general the maximum objective worth is greater than one's limited subjective worth. This is a basic reason why man is striving to know himself better.

Man's
Externalized
Dynamics
(recognized and
honored
achievements)

OBJECTIVE WORTH is the PERSONAL ACHIEVE-MENTS (products, successes, discoveries) determining one's dignity and worth as a member of the human race. These vary considerably with each individual and his opportunities.

SUBJECTIVE WORTH is the PUBLIC RECOGNITION OF ACHIEVEMENTS as one's personal worth and dignity (prestige, respect, acclaim, credit, reputation) in his membership in the human race. No two people ever have the same subjective worth.

In general one's objective worth is greater than his subjective worth, but both are limited. This is a basic reason why man is striving to reach a goal, literally placing himself in process.

Self-Challenging Perspectives

This journey into self, into the realms of darkness and nothing-ness, where there are no precedents, no laws, and no guarantees of safe passage, is not only a retreat from values, but also a process for response to potential growth. It is the perspective of challenge that can make possible a more adequate encounter with truth, beauty, and goodness in life. Thrust back on his own resources, man searches for a creative center. Forced into the situation where he has an unmediated relation with his deepest core values, he enters a sphere of fiery vision.[13] Here is the source of his values, affirmations, and perspectives of conviction.

Certainly this challenging is a state fraught with personal danger and collective risks, a time of extreme anxieties, yet one of hope and excitement in forward-looking thoughts. Reflecting on a similar period of transition, Ralph Waldo Emerson said in his "American Scholar" address:

Our age is bewailed as one of Introversion. Must that needs be evil? . . . I look upon the discontent of the literary class as a mere announcement of the fact that they themself (*sic*) are not in the state of mind of their fathers, and regret the coming state as untried. . . . If there is any period one would desire to be born in, is it not the age of Revolution: when the old and new stand side by side and admit of being compared; when the energies of all men are searched by fear and hope; when the historic glories of the old can be compensated by the rich possibilities of the new era? This time, like all times, is a good one, if we but know what to do with it.[14]

Here is the process-and-response basis for man's liberty to choose. Because of his limited knowledge of himself and others, man today is lacking in relevant choices, with which lack he attempts to cope. In seeking a possible coordination within his dynamics, he often experiences hesitation, uncertainty, frustra-tion, or futility. The rewarding meaningfulness of relevance is absent. As Merleau-Ponty asserts: "Confrontation with man's being [in his internalized and externalized dynamics] can cause dizziness."[15] This is evident from the complexity of the concepts involved in the existential self:

EXISTENTIAL CONCEPTS OF SELF

Self-Fulfillment			Self-Realization	
Conscience Self-	Self-	Self-	Self-	Self-
Knowledge	Determination	Identity	Evaluation	Integration

Confronted with experiences that seem to him inconsistent with his self-structure, man feels threatened. His self-structure becomes more rigidly organized to maintain itself. Out of tune with reality, it must depend upon a spiraling system of defense mechanisms.[16] In this phenomenology, a form of existentialism, the eminent American psychologist Gordon Allport indicates the problems of man's freedom for self-direction:

> Existentialism insists on freedom; much of the psychotherapy now in vogue presupposes it; psychology's new concern with values is at bottom a concern with choices, and therefore revives the problem of freedom.[17]

Choice

Value Perspectives Today grapples with these existential insights. It synthesizes man's struggle for meaning today; it leaves no doubt concerning choices. Despite whatever existentialism is and whichever direction it may eventually take, it is still proving a service to humanity. Disturbing a complacent world, it is entrenching itself in smug self-complacency about society and its values, the individual and his choices.[18]

Man's ways with ideas and his discoveries, in the human experiencing of life, of what he can do and of what he should become, are vital, as Piaget points out in discussing the curricular implications of values and knowledge today. Qualitative judgments in process-and-response education are constantly in the balance. Such judgments bridge the gaps among man's real condition, his human situation, his insights into ideal wisdom, and what his career should be. The importance of a clarification between education and ideas as a process is pointed out by Alfred North Whitehead. As the process philosopher *par excellence,* he stresses, in his presidential address to the Mathematical Association of England, that

> what education has to impart is an intimate sense for the power of ideas, for the beauty of ideas, and for the structure of ideas, together with a particular body of knowledge which has peculiar reference to the life of the being possessing it![19]

In this area of value perspectives, responsible and responsive behavior in process is gaining greater recognition as a distinguishing characteristic of man. Whether mankind does anything significant with it, especially in a free democratic nation like the United States, may very well rest upon the challenging dictum of Pascal: "Thought makes the whole dignity of man and the endeavor to think well is the basic morality." Hugh C. Black sees most human achievements as depending to a great extent on their relevance within the educational process. For such education, he writes,

> enhances the life of the individuals and betters our society in the extent more persons give "better" visions of what man's capacities and potentialities are and what we might become. This entails knowledge of man's capacities as revealed in his "peak" and his "sink" experiences in life.[20]

If Black's analysis is correct, then all education should: (1) involve both personal and social experience; (2) result in personalities who gain insight and wisdom about life; (3) be productive of persons of character and conscience; (4) consist especially of those value experiences worthy of man's *capacities for making choices* in terms of worthy ideals. Therefore:

> Conscience and character, society and education go together [in value relevance]; for social process is involved. Conscience,

for example, is more than the individual's sense or principle for making moral judgments about his conduct and behavior. Derived from *con* (together) and *scire* (to know), "conscience" signifies something known or held in common with others. . . . Leaders in education, then, must be cognizant of man's ideas about conscience [and values] in the interest of better character.[21]

In his book *Reality, Knowledge, and Value,* Jerome A. Shaffer integrates these perspectives, at least partially, when he writes:

I can choose to register or not to register . . . It is a terrible decision. My whole life will be quite different as a consequence of how I decide. . . . But this is clear—that I will have to decide, that no one can make the decision for me, that the consequences of my decision are not entirely predictable, that I will have to face those consequences and live with them, and that I will have to live with myself after I make my decision.

Of course I may not deliberate on this choice, or even consciously make a decision. I may essentially let myself be pushed along. But even then, I have decided to acquiesce; I have still made my choice and I am responsible for it.[22]

By his integration Shaffer compels man to associate himself with the relevance of values, for it is: ". . . the compass which gives man his direction both as to how he should act and what his action is for."[23]

Relevance for Values

A functional application of the Piagetian principles of continuity to learning and teaching indicates a growing conviction that process and response are essential to relevant involvement with values in their tridimensional aspect: truth, beauty, and goodness.

Values, are those aspects of anything which, when recognized and understood, encourage, induce, or incline a person to choose them for his purpose. Like wants, they are practically limitless and the desire to fulfill them, insatiable. In a genuine process of evaluation, for example, any activity, like the product it engenders, involves meaning; any meaning begetting response, however, must, by its very nature, be understood in terms of process. The argument here, not unlike that of the long-debated nature-nurture dilemma, is for the *totality of relevance and interaction*.

In such evolving relationships Piaget sees a twofold aspect impressing and expressing itself as a creative affirmation of the whole person. Within the struggle for self-identity and self-expression toward self-fulfillment, he indicates, man could shut himself off from the world of values. On the other hand, he sees how the values of the world may divorce themselves from man's achieving personhood within society. In either case a process spawning irrelevance occurs.

Man's urgent need of relevance today makes the necessary and the practical paramount for realizing any change of perspective within his future-oriented potential. Durant spells out such a reciprocal effect as an interrelationship of values through what he terms the two phases of the educative process:

> Two processes constitute education and unite with it; in the one, the race transmits to the growing individual its profuse and accumulated heritage of knowledge technics, morals, and art; in the other, the individual applies this inheritance to the development of his capacities and the adornment of his life. In proportion as he absorbs this legacy he is transformed from an animal into a man, from a savage into a citizen, . . . from a simpleton into a sage. Education is the perfecting of life—the enrichment of the individual by the heritage of the race. Let this vital process of transmission and absorption be interrupted for half a century, and civilization would end; our grandchildren would be more primitive than savages.[24]

Need and Response

Coping with the question of value relevance is most difficult, for one should know when process-and-response is relevant. It is no simple problem to surmount; it is not only constantly changing but also growing in complexity. John Gardner seems to put the whole question in sharp focus when he says:

> We want a society that is sufficiently honest and open-minded to recognize its problems, sufficiently creative to conceive of new solutions, and sufficiently purposeful to put those solutions into effect . . . and we all know in our bones that what we do in education . . . has the greatest relevance to building the kind of society we want.[25]

Hardly anyone would question the relevance that Gardner implies is necessary for education; but what kind of educational system can achieve his totality? Certainly clear thinking is not characteristic of contemporary education, as Jean Piaget indicates through his lifelong research in genetic epistemology. Today's preoccupation is breeding a disinclination to think; its offspring is an undeveloped ability to think. Consequently, for more relevant answers, Edith Hamilton recommends a probe into the "ever-present past":

> Is there an ever-present past? Are there permanent truths which are forever important for the present? Today we are facing a future more strange and untried than any other generation has faced. The new world Columbus opened seems small indeed beside the illimitable distances of spaces before us, and the possibilities of destruction are immeasurably greater than ever. In such a position can we afford to spend time on the past? That is the question I am often asked. . . . Yes; that is just what I am doing. I urge it without qualifications. We have a great civilization to save—or to lose.[26]

One of the greatest civilizations of all times was the ancient Greek. It is still challenging civilization today to rival it, and this challenge is necessary. The Greeks, too, lived in a dangerous world. As a small nation, highly civilized, they faced constant dangers from surrounding barbarous tribes. With the greatest

Asiatic power, Persia, threatening them, was not the situation like that of Communist Russia and its conquest of free nations today? It was not the strength of their outside enemies that caused the Greeks to succumb, but rather the disintegrating effects of their own spiritual values and of their own strength. With their high morale they kept Greece unconquered, giving the world a record of art and thought which, in all the centuries of human effort since, is still not surpassed.[27]

The point that Edith Hamilton says she wishes to make is not that their taste was superior, nor that the Parthenon was their idea of church architecture, nor that Sophocles was the great drawing card in the theaters, nor any of the other familiar comparisons between fifth-century Athens and twentieth-century America, but how Socrates (496?–399 B.C.) found on every street corner and in every Athenian people who were caught up by his questions into the world of thought. To be caught up into the world of thought—that is to be educated.[28]

At present there is a strong tendency to make the dominant aim of process-and-response education the defeat of Communism. Genuine relevance in the educative process, however, is possible only when people realize how much it concerns persons rather then movements. Hamilton maintains that it is precisely the absence of the personal aspect that is the problem:

> When I read educational articles it often seems to me that this important side of the matter, the purely personal side, is not emphasized enough; the fact that it is so much more agreeable and interesting to be an educated person than not. The sheer pleasure of being educated does not seem to be stressed.[29]

In their education today too many young people are failing to comprehend personally the immense benefits of the process perspective. To them the question of what factors create and preserve values and their relevance through the ages is confusing. Professor William H. Boyer, in his "Education for Survival," refers to this crucial situation as the paralyzing crises of doubt, confusion, and trouble about the future, increasingly corroding our modern living.[30]

Process Approaches

This paralyzing condition is understandable, for over the centuries the process approaches to humanistic values are multiple; but this span continues to encompass the cumulative relevant values within civilization as they fuse themselves more and more with the personalizing process that is man:

PROCESS-AND-RESPONSE APPROACHES TO MAN

CULTURES	PERSPECTIVES
Ancient	Biocentric
Greek-Roman	Philosophical and Anthropocentric
Judeo-Christian	Theocentric
Renaissance	Humanistic centered
Revolutionary-Political	Liberty vs. License centered
Contemporary-Modern	Democratic-Scientific centered
Ultra	Existential and Phenomenological centered

Even in the Golden Age of Greece, biocentric personalization within society was stressed as integral with its dynamic social and cultural dimensions. At another time, emphasis on a new dimension from the Judeo-Christian culture impressed itself upon man. Then the Renaissance, with its espousal of humanism, presented an exciting new view of life. It was followed by the Industrial, American, and French Revolutions, which resulted in religious, political, and economic freedom. Finally, man almost completely revolutionized the world with modern science, as Livingstone points out:

> the new methods and outlooks of science constituted the earliest steps of a progression which would truly "change the world forever," would shake old beliefs and opinions and arouse new controversies.[31]

During the last century and a half, however, many contributors have merged these process-and-response approaches. They are creating complications in the relevance of educational values through reinterpretations of: (1) Horace Mann, presenting his philosophy of a nonsectarian education; (2) William T. Harris, implementing his mandate for total secularization of education; (3) John Dewey, vitalizing education with his pragmatic experimentalism.

As pioneers, this educational triumvirate first exerted a wide range of influence in the American behavioristic school through J. B. Watson (1878–1958), and exerts it today in the more comprehensive behavioristic technology of B. Frederic Skinner's radical new science of values in process (1904–   ).

At present, however, existentialist phenomenology stresses the role of the operant. It is personalized by Martin Buber (1878–1965) and his contemporaries, especially: (1) Jean Piaget, in his developmental genetic epistemology; (2) Jerome Bruner, in his "discovery" problematic approach to process learning and teaching; (3) Jacques Maritain, in his insistence upon a more complete humanism for the new age of relevance that is just coming to be; (4) Lawrence Kohlberg, in his extensive analysis of moral development.

Educators today are becoming increasingly aware of the crises in values, especially from the Family Life Education Study of the Educational Research Council of America and the Ohio Department of Education:

Months that followed this publication repeatedly illustrated its findings. Incident after incident revealed the discrepancy between stated and applied values. Tensions within our pluralistic society increased as diverse value systems tugged at those values commonly regarded as essential to the survival of the social order. Respect for law and order collided with the right of dissent. Conflict surfaced among the interacting goals of our political, economic, and religious allegiances.

The inability (perceived or real) of the institutions to effectively serve the needs of individuals and diverse subcultures made front-page headlines. Tensions continued to climb between respect for the traditions inherited from the past and the vision held for the future—tensions heightened by a sense of nostalgia and alarm on the part of some, and of urgency and impatience for change on the part of others.[32]

The Commission on Education, aware of both crises and opportunities, established a Task Force on Values in Education in May 1971. After identifying several basic assumptions, the Task Force authorized the development of a position paper in cooperation with the Educational Research Council. As stated, its key objective is:

> That educators (including parents, mass media, administrators, etc.) learn what is involved in a *process approach to values education*, that they become facilitators for students so that students may learn and have the opportunity to practice this same approach with respect to values. This would involve students learning a method to make intelligent, imaginative decisions when faced with value conflict situations and to begin to develop a value system which has meaning for them and which is consistent with the same right of others.[33]

Ever Ancient and Ever New

In spite of the new emphasis on a value system in process-and-response education, there is evidence that the problems of education at the time of Plato's pupil Aristotle (384–322 B.C.) are still the problems of values in response today:

> What should be the character of this public education, and how young persons should be educated, are questions which remain to be considered. As things are, there is disagreement about the subjects. For mankind are by no means agreed about the things to be taught, whether we look to virtue or the best life. Neither is it clear whether education is more concerned with the intellectual or moral virtues. The existing practice is perplexing; no one knows on what principle we should proceed. Should the useful in life, or should virtue, or should higher knowledge, be the aim of our training? Again, about the means, there is no agreement.[34]

These inquiries of Aristotle are practically the same in substance as those currently being asked or proposed for serious study. The designated Father of Psychology, "as the oracle of nature and truth," analyzes the thoughts, feelings, views, values, and opinions of human beings; he tells them the meaning of their own words and ideas long before they are even born.[35]

The changes occurring today cannot be separated from events of the past that are happening again. Many of these developments are the results of a process momentum generated from within the human personality. But many of the fundamental transformations in the *relevance* of values are reflections of *the response,* both personal and collective, to a culture in decadence. This decadence has not only negative characteristics but also positive ones. For decadence in values means that the once-universal norms of behavior and belief, and the institutions of church, family, state, and school that express and reinforce these norms, have ceased to have an influence on large segments of the population.[36]

The authority of these institutions is on the wane. Because their accepted values are deteriorating rapidly, they no longer provide a coherent guide to motivate behavior. When conventional truths are increasingly questioned, or worse, only hypocritically espoused, then the individual discovers that he has no one but himself upon whom to rely in establishing patterns of meaningful existence or relevant values.[37]

At present the introversion of the American people is causing a reaction against those values which are worthy of fulfillment. They are now, however, as in the past, failing to establish the optimum conditions for realization. They seem to be outstripping themselves in constructing roadblocks and barriers to their actualization; of some they remain unaware; to others they give mere lip service.[38] What Emerson voices in his essay on politics is equally apropos of the problems of values-clarification today:

> We think our civilization near its meridian, but we are yet only at the cock-crowing and the morning star. In our barbarous society the influence of character is in its infancy.[39]

To rectify the sterility, new process-and-response approaches to values in education must involve more than a synthesis of the various attempts over many centuries to achieve priorities in values. As indicated in the following chart, they must also encompass the dynamics of the whole person:

EDUCATIONAL APPROACHES OF PROCESS AND
RESPONSE TO THE "EVER-PRESENT" PAST
involve
TRANSMISSION OF HERITAGE
APPLICATIONS OF LEGACY TO LIFE
made relevant
by
CREATIVE AFFIRMATIONS
PERSONALIZATIONS WITHIN SOCIETY

The evolving necessity for relevance, therefore, becomes increasingly evident in the present effect of the interaction of man, society, and the environment within the school:

> [Process-and-Response] Education, then, is not a matter of past answers, impressive structures, or attractive materials. All of these may or may not play a part in truly touching the lives of men. We believe that the leaven of the daily bread of education is relevance.[40]

Educational commitments are increasingly challenging conflicting values and controversial irrelevances of all sorts. Practically every type of society is attempting to perpetuate its own values. Lest the educational process, in becoming anachronistic, lose its impact on the human lives, the approaching impasse demands a process-and-response value-education to meet irrelevance:

Today it is imperative that any unique features of the value crisis be faced squarely by confronting the pertinent issue: man's freedom of choice in the challenges of life. With that in mind, the present dilemmas of the relevance of values within education, and of disintegrating responses to educational relevances

PROCESS-AND-RESPONSE VALUE EDUCATION: *ACTION AND INTERACTION*

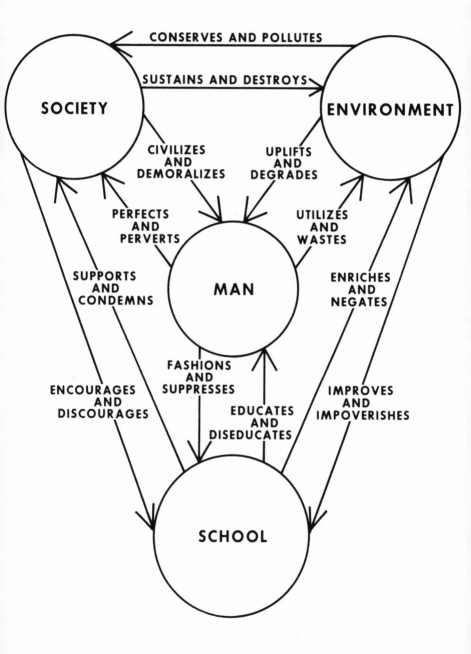

and even irrelevances, along with their pseudo-approaches to truth, beauty, and goodness, constitute the problems in the

> task of human self-education [that] our generation is called upon to begin. But it will be only a beginning. The road to reasonableness goes on and on.[41]

> Humanity is reasonable as well as unreasonable. It is the struggle between these two [value relevances] which defines the course of education. We know what teaching is only as we see and feel what the free spirit of man is trying to do and to be.[42]

To take advantage of these existential perspectives is now opportune. Exposing their processes or procedures will initiate a new thrust into the next era—that of evolving values. In recent years the amazingly prolific observations and theories of Jean Piaget regarding human cognitive development are vying for preeminence in the marketplace of educational perspectives.[43]

SELECT REFERENCES

Black, Hugh C.; Lottich, Kenneth V.; and Seckinger, Donald S., eds. *The Great Educators.* Chicago: Nelson-Hall Co., 1972.

Book, Carlton E.; Bernier, Normand R.; MacDonald, James B.; Walton, Thomas W.; and Willers, Jack C. *Education for Relevance.* New York: Houghton Mifflin Co., 1968.

Cole, Henry P. *Process Education.* Englewood Cliffs, N.J.: Educational Technology Publications, 1972.

Meiklejohn, Alexander. *Education Between Two Worlds.* New York: Harper & Bros., 1942.

Report of the Invitational Conference on Values in Education. Commission on Education, Ohio Council of Churches, 1972.

Shaffer, Jerome A. *Reality, Knowledge, and Value.* New York: Random House, 1971.

The School and the Democratic Environment. Danforth Foundation and Ford Foundation. New York: Columbia University Press, 1970.

The 1970 White House Conference on Children. U.S. Govt. Printing Office, 1970.

Ulich, Robert, ed. *Three Thousand Years of Educational Wisdom.* Cambridge, Mass.: Harvard University Press, 1971.

2

EVOLVING VALUE PERSPECTIVES

Unless the eye catch fire . . .
Unless the ear catch fire . . .
Unless the tongue catch fire . . .
Unless the heart catch fire . . .
Unless the mind catch fire . . .
Unless the spirit catch fire. . . .

—William Blake

Search, rejection, ferment, and revolution: our national heritage.

"We hold these truths to be self-evident, that all men are created equal, that they are endowed by their Creator with certain unalienable Rights, that among these are Life, Liberty and the pursuit of Happiness. . . . That to secure these . . ." is one of the earliest, carefully organized descriptions of value relevance in the historical perspective of America. Today this proclamation is often summarized as simply the right to happiness, in a misunderstanding based on the careless neglect of the meaning of *pursuit*.

54

When Piaget refers to the crises of "pursuit" facing education today, he minces no words. There are many teachers, he asserts, who use archaic methods and alienate their students, who sit passively in classes that they find meaningless, irrelevant, and an outright waste of time. Too much teaching is far from being interesting or challenging. It is like a string of boring facts without any relationship to thought and feeling. What to teach, When, and How remain unpursued and unanswered![1]

In the history of education this confusion is evident in the diversified analyses of the concepts of liberty, equality, and fraternity of the American and French Revolutions. The concepts evolved out of a series of events by which the doctrine of democracy supplanted that of the long-established divine right of kings, and by which the theory of class distinctions eventually gave way to that of social equality.[2] The Revolutions themselves, and the resulting conditions in the schools, however, arose out of the social, political, economic, and religious conflicts of the previous centuries.[3]

The conflicts are still profoundly affecting political and social values. Many current problems of value clarification in education today find their source and impetus in the American Bill of Rights. Adding to the malaise is the failure to distinguish between the cause and the effect of these revolutions. The chafing under the British policy of mercantilism and tax impositions by mandate sparked the American Revolution. Unlike the French Revolution of 1789, the American armed expression of emotional self-dependence ("representation") rested on the virgin soil of a new world without a past history of oppressive centuries such as those suffered by the French; theirs was a revolution of vindictiveness, of escape and rights, and when it is considered alongside the American Revolution for self-determination, we see that France had already previously enjoyed liberty in great measure, but it was now restricted. Lepkowski and Parker aptly express this phenomenon of upheavals:

> Search, rejection, ferment, and revolution: our national heritage. Our forefathers, rejecting European persecutions, settled

a new land and then promptly squabbled among themselves, revolted against England, brawled into a frontier America, fought each other over a Union, squabbled again over unionism, communism, capitalism, and socialism. In short, ours is a nation of protests and choices; it always has been. Today's youth is little different than yesterday's, though faces and issues change. It is, perhaps, the nature of youth to protest and seek change. Today's youth protests and searches for individual relevance. A relevance that will lead to a better people in a better society.[4]

Naturalism in This Revolution

As implied in "The Search for Relevance" (cf. n4), naturalistic humanism today becomes an influential factor when integrating any historical process of value relevance with Jean Piaget's new discipline. In modern times naturalism has given expression to humanistic influences and their values mainly through its first advocates, the radical humanists of the fifteenth century and the Renaissance. Later, Jean Jacques Rousseau (1712–1778), one of its most popular exponents, influenced not only philosophy, science, art, social life, and politics, but also education. As Piaget writes:

> in Rousseau . . . we find a total conception whose value is all the more astonishing today in that it was not inspired by any scientific experiment and that, until now, its philosophical content has too often prevented it from being judged objectively.[5]

Because of Rousseau's convictions about excellence of nature and the perversion of society, Piaget sees him as truly aware of the value of the individual. The age of childhood, Rousseau feels, does have its use, since mental development is regulated naturally by constant laws. Education, therefore, should make use of that mechanism instead of thwarting its progress.[6]

It is from there that Rousseau, Piaget continues, went on to develop an educational theory with the most elaborate refinement of details. It can be accepted as a brilliant anticipation of the "new methods" of education or, on the other hand, it may be challenged, depending on whether one ignores Rousseau's philosophical a prioris or looks upon them as linked to his sociological reforms.[7]

Because of its sociological perversion of society and its fanciful idea of the essential goodness of human nature, it is not possible, Piaget says, to make any full abstraction of Rousseau's metaphysics, for although it is in some ways a precursor of the new methods in education, in other ways it is a compromise, a falling short. Piaget observes that

> observation in itself immediately makes us realize the true novelty of our twentieth-century methods as opposed to the systems of the classical theorists. It is true that Rousseau saw that "each age has its motive force," that "the child has its own peculiar way of seeing, of thinking, and of feeling"; it is true that he provided eloquent proof of the fact that it is impossible to learn anything other than by actively acquiring mastery of it, and that the pupil must reinvent science instead of merely repeating its verbalized formulas; it was even he who gave this piece of advice, for which much will be forgiven him: "Begin by studying your pupils, for assuredly you do not know them at all."[8]

To this appraisal Piaget adds his own critical insights, declaring that Rousseau's intuition of the reality of mental development is no more than a sociological belief, or a polemical weapon. Had he personally studied the laws of the psychological maturing process, he would not have dissociated the development of the individual from the social environment. The notions of the functional significance of childhood, of the phases of intellectual and moral development, of true interest and activity, were already there in Rousseau's work. But they did not truly provide inspiration for the "new methods" until they were rediscovered by authors more concerned with unfevered truth and systematic controls within the present-day (Piagetian) perspectives of What, When, and How to teach.[9]

According to naturalism, the ultimate explanation for the

relevance of all values, even for those of education, is to be found in nature. As a doctrine it asserts the primacy and all-sufficiency of the natural values and holds that man is a product of, and continuous with all-embracing nature. In every phase of his organic life, naturalism maintains, man is subject to nature's laws, which are explanatory of all material reality, the only reality that he can know.[10] To aid in integrating present-day perspectives of education, pregnant in naturalistic humanism, with Piaget's new discipline, its essentials are presented here:

Basic Tenets of Naturalism Today[11]

A. In Its Aim:
   Naturalism seeks the truth about the world in which man lives.
B. In Its Method:
   Naturalism makes use of the empirical way to attain its aim.
C. In Its Resulting System:
   Naturalism builds a picture of the universe through its method of empiricism. Fidelity to its aim and to its method keeps naturalism perpetually adding to, sub-tracting from, and modifying continually whatever it constructs as human.
D. In Its Anthropocentric Perspectives:
   Naturalism spawns Humanism. As a form of Naturalism, Humanism is the understanding of man and his sphere of properly human activities. In this frame of reference, Humanism refers to the sum total of those activities which characterize man as a human being and thus the studies resulting from those activities are termed the humanities.
E. In Its Educational Ferment:
   Naturalistic Humanism revolts against conservative forces in education, stressing personal development, culture and especially freedom. As the rebellion revives, both classical learning and the Greek ideal of liberal education em-phasize individuality, personal self-realization, and self-expression in art, music, literature, and architecture. It even demands societal reforms in moral life and conditions of living. Nature study, physical training, hygiene, and creativity encourage getting the most out of living a fine,

rich, and fully human existence based on a better understanding of the pursuits and activities proper to mankind.

According to Piaget, the forerunner of naturalism is Michel
de Montaigne (1523–1592). His thoughts still affect values in
process-and-response education today. As one of the precursors
in the genesis of the new methods of education, he stands

> against the verbal education and the inhuman discipline of
> the sixteenth century [which] led to some subtle psychological
> intuitions: the true role of interest, indispensable observation
> of nature, necessity for initiation into practical life, distinction
> between personal comprehension and memory ("To know by
> heart is not to know"), etc.[12]

The father of naturalism is John Locke (1632–1704). His
observations, however, are no more than fragmentary. Its theorist is Rousseau. Among the continuators of Rousseau's work are
his disciple, Pestalozzi (1746–1827), and Froebel, a disciple of
Pestalozzi (1782–1852). They may be considered the true precursors of the new methods.[13]

The one who brought naturalism into the school is Johann
Bernard Basedow (1723–1790). He seriously tested Rousseau's
value theories in his experimental school, The Philanthropium.
By reason of his experiments, he has earned the distinction of
being the first in education to establish an institution of learning
with the deliberate intent of setting aside the traditional approaches to the educative process:

> Pupils came to classes dressed like children rather than adults.
> Latin was taught conversationally, and all sorts of games were
> used to make learning pleasurable. Handicraft instruction
> and field trips also helped to motivate interest.[14]

Other Influences

Modern history is not without indication of other varied interactions of naturalism and ever-increasing self-projection which
are helping to shape the present responses in process-and-response

education. Among the influences from the past were the Pilgrim fathers of more than three-and-a-half centuries ago, who initiated their own type of education. They planted an offshoot of the traditional European system, presently growing into a vigorous tree, that of the American school system.[15] This transplant naturally included the rich inheritance from which, in their wisdom and prudence, they selected the good, the beautiful, and the true, then in process of being transmitted through learning and teaching to their own children and their descendants. Not the least significant in their choice of what to transmit was the

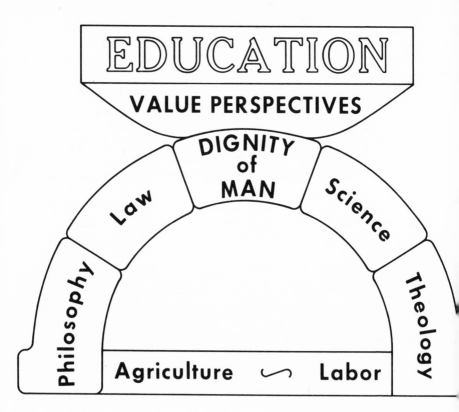

great patrimony of the Greco-Roman philosophy and its natural-law concepts of justice, along with a Judeo-Christian approach to values. These values were almost universally and significantly operative within the increasing population of their day.

Horace Mann's commentary on the Pilgrim Fathers' records reveals the significance of their educational perspectives. The first entry in the public entry book of Boston bears the date "1634, 7th month, day 1." The minutes of public meetings for that year pertain to those obvious values which claim the immediate attention of an infant settlement. Subsequently, in the transactions of one such assembly on the 13th day of April 1635, the following entry regarding education appears:

Likewise it was then generally agreed upon that our brother Philemon Purmont [or Purment] shall be entreated to become schoolmaster for the teaching and nourtering of children with us.[16]

But Purmont was not to render his services gratuitously. Doubtless he received fees from parents. Nevertheless, these same records show that a tract of thirty acres of land, at "Muddy River," was being assigned to him, and that this grant, two years afterwards, was publicly confirmed. About the same time, an assignment was made of a "garden plott" to Daniel Maude, schoolmaster, on the condition of building thereon, if need be. From this time forward, Horace Mann declares, these golden threads are thickly interwoven in the texture of all public records of Boston.[17]

On the educational significance of these early records, Mann, in his tenth annual report as the Secretary of the Massachusetts Board of Education, made the following comment:

It is not unworthy to remark . . . Mr. Purmont was entreated to become a "schoolmaster," not merely for the "teaching," but for the "nourtering" of children . . . which implied the disposition and the power, on the part of the teacher, as far as such an object can be accomplished by human instrumentality, to warm into birth, to foster into strength, and to advance into precedence and predominance, all kindly sympathies towards men, all elevated thoughts respecting the duties and the destiny of life, and a supreme reverence for the charactor and attributes of the Creator.[18]

Gradually,within this evolving mass of activity, there matured a workable basis of unity by which education fostered the rudiments of rational living. Family life and its growth in human culture so interacted as to produce a generally acceptable way of life for learning and teaching in full accord with religious commitments. The schools themselves became one of the best indexes for comprehending the development of value relevance in this country, a fact to which Horace Mann testified just two centuries later:

> The Pilgrim Fathers who colonized Massachusetts Bay made a bolder innovation upon all pre-existing policy and usages than the world had ever known since the commencement of the Christian era. They adopted special and costly means to train up the whole body of the people to industry, to intelligence, to virtue, and to independent thought.[19]

Religion within Process

Although the home was the first school in America, it soon became more like an extension of the religion it fostered. The ministers taught the parents or tutors who, in turn, taught the children to read the Bible and to assimilate the rudiments of religion through their family living, along with application to domestic and civic duties. Actually this moral-spiritual development by the home became the criterion for the whole process of education, precisely because it advanced the all-important cause of the people themselves—religion.[20] Their religious convictions so influenced their philosophy of education that the two came to harmonize well.

Often the ministers were the school teachers. During the early times in Massachusetts, however, where education made greater progress on a wider scale than elsewhere, home and church gave way to town and dame schools. Religion, however, was so inter-woven with education that no one was permitted to attend a dame school without the consent of his minister and parents, who usually defrayed the expenses. The ministers chose the textbooks, which always included the Bible. Probably no single book in use throughout the entire educational process of America has been so intimately and consistently associated with the personalization of values. In learning and teaching, the Bible became a standard symbol of concern for the person in all genera-tions.

As the family and the church continued to exercise their rights in education, they eventually established private religious schools, many of which received state aid.[21] Notwithstanding the multiplication of religious sects, each school seemed sufficiently different from the others to justify its own existence, although the majority were Calvinistic.

Finally there developed the exclusively state-supported and somewhat controlled public schools. They did not in any way monopolize American education; rather, they existed alongside the others in such a manner that the nationwide system of schools became pluralistic. Eventually the system consisted of public, private and church, and parochial schools, with the last dom-inating the educational system of the middle colonies.[22] Ge-ographically, the type of school tended to reflect the preferences, decisions, needs, and even the economy of each section of the country. In all schools, however, religion was practically in-separable from education.

In the South education formed a distinctive pattern along the lines of its peculiar social and economic conditions, consequently tutorial activities in the home or private school were common. Generally schools were available at public expense only to the poor. Resulting from a community effort and servicing poor and rich alike, the old field schools were the most common type.[23] Some parish schools emerged but, since no effective school system had been established, no state supervision was exercised. Due to the demands of agriculture, education was mainly a privilege of the minority. A more or less *laissez-faire, laissez-passer* spirit developed dominating the educational scene. Authorities claim that the effects of this deficiency in the South are still being felt today throughout the nation.

As centers of learning, a system of parochial schools predominated in the middle colonies. In the New York area both supervision and control were entrusted to the Dutch Reformed Church;[24] hence the schoolmaster was always a church official. The schools in the Pennsylvania section were established by different religious bodies, usually with the clergy as teachers. With their approval, however, some private individuals acted as auxiliaries.

By 1635 in New England, Boston had begun its Latin school. In 1639 Dorchester levied a land tax to support a free school. At least until 1640, the country had a totally religious-family sponsored value education solidly rooted in the traditional three R's, in addition to the fourth R, religion. It is no distortion to assert of those living during those early decades that education in process that lacked the fourth R of religion produced an ersatz in the form of another R—rascal. To religion, therefore, more than to any other social influence, was entrusted the noble privilege of fostering and preserving the education of the family.[25]

As a consequence, the early elementary schooling of the colonists consisted in two vital processes of personalization—religion and education. They interacted in such a manner as to fuse, without creating a dichotomy or distinction between religious and educational values. Not that there was a static, unmodifiable, and blind set of absolutes. Far from it. The multiplication of differences within the population evolved with the advancement of science. Through the secular and humanistic processes education was so integrally a vitalization process that the Old-World patterns produced a uniqueness of spirit that has rarely been rivaled in modern times.

Possibly this spirit could be contributory to value relevance today. Such an *esprit de corps* is more readily understandable now because of the important influence of Calvin's city-state at

THE UNITED STATES
1783
SHOWING WESTERN LAND CLAIMS

SCALE OF MILES
0   50 100   200   300   400

Geneva, which embodied the predominating ideal in founding commonwealths whose cornerstone was religion *and* education.[26] History testifies that all education in early America was fundamentally and essentially religious.

By the close of the colonial period three types of educational practices existed in the evolving American school system: (1) in New England a compulsory public school education; (2) in the middle colonies a system of parochial schools; (3) in the South no state supervision except the caring for orphans and children of the poor. There were tutors in the homes and private (tuition charged) schools, often called "old Field Schools";[29] in the Southwest the education of the Indians by the early Catholic missionaries.

Religion became the mother of learning and teaching during colonial times. The education given by the early missionaries to the Indians, notably in the Southwest, played no direct part, however, in the development of the American school system.[30] More religious and political freedom in accord with the all-important ideal of liberty of conscience was the chief purport and fruition of those early educational endeavors.

Ultimately, as a process in historical sequence, the colonists found these principles expressed in the Declaration of Independence, the Constitution of the United States, and the Bill of Rights. The truism that the greater the agreement over ultimates, the more unified society tends to become was confirmed, and still holds true in the present decade. When there is universal concern for relevance of values, there inevitably results a deeply rooted, commonly acceptable way of life; it expands and improves itself constantly by a practical philosophy of education always in process.[31]

Contemporary American society is so different from that of early times that it is often uncertain about the values, in process, upon which the nation rests. Externals, however, cannot disclose the real convictions of the people. Generally, Americans understand their inalienable rights, along with the meaning of their substantive rights. It follows that their educational system should be imbued with commitments to these basic rights.

The difficulty seems to lie not so much in these self-evident truths as in their application and in the quality of education that Jean Piaget is consistently advocating. That the nation is not fully measuring up to the ideal and that it is still the problem-in-process must be faced realistically. The future of these precious liberties and loyalties lies now in the classrooms of the country.[32] Is not this recognition in itself a commitment to process-and-response education for values; is it not, too, a sure indication that the United States is far from becoming a stagnating society; that it is progressing persistently; that it is reformulating itself, ever searching for new adaptations for itself; that it is espousing improvements as indispensable, and that any other course is repugnant?

State within Process

As an educational sponsor in relevance of values, the state had its impact on the What, How, and When of education later than did religion or the home. It was only in 1642 that the officials of the court (legislature) of Massachusetts, upon urgent request from the ministry, enacted the first law in America regarding compulsory education. Through the pen of Horace Mann the practical educational significance of this legal enactment is pointed out:

> In 1642, the General Court of the colony, by a public act, enjoined upon municipal authorities the duty of seeing that every child, within their respective jurisdictions, should be educated. Nor was the education which they contemplated either narrow or superficial. By the terms of the act, the select-men of every town were required to "have a vigilant eye over their brethren and neighbors—to see first that none of them shall suffer so much barbarism in any of their families, as not to endeavor to teach, by themselves or others, their children and apprentices, so much learning as may enable them perfectly to read the English tongue, and [obtain] a knowledge of the capital laws; upon penalty of twenty shillings for each neglect therein." Such was the idea of "barbarism," entertained by the colonists of Massachusetts Bay more than two centuries ago.[33]

The proto-school law of 1642 extended to all children the right to read and understand the Bible, the principles of religion, the laws of the land, and the necessary instruction for profitable employment in the Commonweath.[34] In substance it was a further expansion and direct application of the resolution of the general court from the previous year (1641) that required all families, at least once each week, to teach both their children and their servants the principles of religion. It added the significant phrase "[and the] laws of the land along with the necessary instruction for profitable employment." It thereby incorporated into the educational process a new, enriching dimension. By its application to civilian life, the state gradually became an integral agency of the temporal order. Assuming an additional role in preparing children for their civic responsibilities as well as for their traditional occupations, the law incorporated a new educational objective.

By the same statute, therefore, selectmen and magistrates were empowered to take children and servants from the custody of those parents and masters who, after admonition, were "still negligent of their duty in the particulars above mentioned." They were to bind them out to such masters as they should deem worthy to supply the place of the unnatural parents—boys until the age of twenty-one, and girls until that of eighteen. Here are

> recognized and embodied, in a public statute, the highest principles of Political Economy and of social well-being—the universal education of children, and the prevention of drones or non-producers among men.[35]

From an almost totally Bible-centered religious education,[36] there was initiated a major step toward a civic-centered program of value relevance. The state thereby aided the schools in their sustaining role of preparing children for practical citizenship. In educating, relevance of values was not committed by the family exclusively to the church or to the state as to separate processes; rather, it was but one process in the formation of the complete person.

The principles of process-and-response education for values, which begin with these laws of Massachusetts, were generally acceptable through all of the colonies. Thus did education gradually become a proper subject for legislative action throughout the country:[37]

> Slowly, and to the degree necessary, the state, usually by invitation, lent a hand. Even then the state acted as co-operator, and often as the "servant" of the church, which it recognized as the supreme teacher.[38]

Religion, home, and state began to form constructively but one supporting process of encouragement, direction, and financial as-

THE COOPERATIVE PARTNERS IN EDUCATION

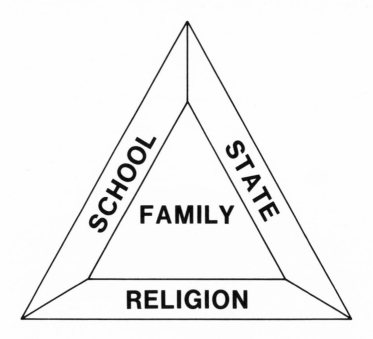

sistance. They walked hand in hand during the critical times when the foundations of the country were under fire and its people were being carefully forged into a united nation with the assistance of their schools.

The pioneering school law of 1647 is an excellent example of this expanding partnership. It required that every town of fifty or more householders support a teacher and provide a school. This law initiated a union without confusion—not a competitive action but a dynamism within the instructional process itself. It likewise encouraged a healthful growth toward effective popular education within each community on the local level, according to its particular needs and aspirations. Even the reasons for the law were not without religious implications and earmarked it as Ye Old Deluder Act.[39] The main purpose in the preamble cannot be misunderstood:

> Since it was the chief purpose of ye old deluder, Satan, to keep men from the knowledge of the Scriptures by formerly keeping them in an unknown language [Latin] so in these days too by persuading from the use of our language.[40]

True evaluation and appreciation of such an enactment came about only two centuries later from the pen of Horace Mann in his tenth annual report to the Commonwealth of Massachusetts. In substance he said that it was not possible adequately to conceive the boldness of this measure, which aimed at universal education through the establishment of *free* schools; that it was one of those grand mental and moral experiments whose effects could not be developed and made manifest in a single generation.[41]

This initiating of a free school system, Mann wrote, appeared still more remarkable when the period in the world's history in which it originated was considered along with the depleted population and poverty of the people who maintained it. In 1647 the entire population of the colony of Massachusetts Bay was approximately twenty-one thousand souls. The scattered and feeble settlements were almost buried in the depths of the forest. The external resources of the people were small, their dwellings humble, and their raiment and subsistence scanty and homely. There was no enriching commerce. The wonderful forces of nature were not then, as now, gracious producers of every human comfort and luxury. The whole valuation of all the colonial estates, both public and private, could hardly have been equal to the inventory of many a private citizen of the present day. The fierce eyes of the natives nightly glared from the edge of the surrounding wilderness, and no defense or succor, save in their own brave natures, was at hand. Yet, as Mann says, it was

> then, amid all these privations and dangers, that the Pilgrim Fathers conceived the magnificent idea, not only of a Universal, but of a Free education for the whole people. To find the time and the means to reduce this grand conception to practice, they stinted themselves, amid all their poverty, to a still scantier pittance; amid all their toils, they imposed upon themselves still more burdensome labors; and, amid all their perils, they braved still greater dangers. Two divine ideas filled their great hearts—their duty to God and to posterity. For the one, they built the church; for the other, they opened the school. Religion and Knowledge!—two attributes of the same and glorious and eternal truth, and that truth the only one on which immortal or mortal happiness can be securely founded.[42]

The church and the home came more and more to recognize the role of the state as absolutely necessary in education. This was owing to many circumstances and modern developments brought about through the increasing demands of popular education, the multiplication of religious sects, even within Calvinism itself, and the gradual expansion of secular knowledge. These brought about a continual advancement of culture throughout the colonies, in addition to a continuing growth in popularity of the modern nationalized state.[43] The many forces throbbing with new life from within the original educational process tended constantly to expand, providing ever-increasing opportunities for a more complete education. They also tended to discourage any of the stagnant or delimiting influences that would keep early instruction solely in the care of the home and the church.

By the close of the colonial phase, the educational process in America still retained the purposes of those early pioneers who chartered the schools into a dynamic and progressive influence for God and country. The "new look" in process was not to exclude religion, but merely to eliminate any sectarianism, while keeping as many religious and moral-spiritual values as were compatible with freedom of worship or would not be violating any of the personal rights and sensitivities of the children or the home.

The close relation between religion and education continued to be so much a part of American life that a visitor to these shores in 1831–33, the noted French observer Alexis de Tocqueville, wrote:

> I have known of societies formed by the Americans to send out ministers of the Gospel into the new Western States to found schools and churches there, lest religion should be suffered to die away in those remote settlements, and the rising States be less fitted to enjoy free institutions than the people from which they emanated.[44]

Relevance of Values in Higher Education

To sow, cultivate, strengthen, render fruitful, and perpetuate those values which reflect and encourage religious commitment in their lives, the Founding Fathers of America's educational system also established a special type of "sectarian" education. It dealt with a highly exclusive form of knowledge particularly necessary for the private and religious schools. In this category Harvard was the first to be founded (1636) to educate men for the ministry, being endowed just two years later for this work by John Harvard, a Charlestown minister.[45] Such theological schools became the chief source of teachers in the religious schools.

Other institutions followed the Harvard pattern. In 1693

the Anglican College William and Mary was established a short distance from Jamestown at Williamsburg, Virginia. Then Yale College was organized in 1701 by ten Congregational ministers to help educate men who would be properly fitted for public employment in both the church and the state. Other colleges followed in rapid succession, among them King's College, now known as Columbia University, which had for its avowed purpose, as announced by its first president, to teach students to know God and to love Him.[46]

In the 1750s, however, there appeared

> a new institution, the academy, offering a range of studies designed to serve a variety of purposes, including a college preparation. Benjamin Franklin (1706–90) in 1749 published his "proposals" for the establishment of an academy in Philadelphia, which opened two years later. He outlined a course of study to include (besides the classics) modern languages, English grammar, rhetoric, literature, history, natural sciences. His announced purpose was to produce a practical, well-behaved, and well-informed man of affairs.[47]

The real breakthrough occurred in 1751. Under the influence of Benjamin Franklin[48] and his associates, the Philadelphia Academy was established as the first nonsectarian college,[49] with its curriculum including the study of morality and religion. Later it was renamed the University of Pennsylvania. In all of these foundations, however, there appeared a process-balanced education, a practical philosophy reflected in Yale's declared purpose ". . . of properly fitting students for public employment *both* in the church and in the state."[50]

Before the Civil War, 207 colleges were established, 180 of them sponsored by religious denominations, 21 state universities, and only 6 either public or semi-public, but not religious schools of higher learning.[51]

In America higher education pointed not to religious fanaticism or sectarian strife, nor even to a totality of the purely secular. Rather, as stated in the charters of Harvard and Yale, it progressed ". . . in the advancement of all good art, literature, and science . . . in knowledge and godliness [encouraging] a willing mind and a righteousness of life that fitted public employment both in the ministry and in the state."[52] With that ideal in mind, Horace Mann, William T. Harris, and John Dewey confronted value perspectives with emphasis on What to teach, When, and How just as Piaget advocates today.

Common School within Process

So many factors—Indian warfare, the Revolutionary War itself, the remissness of parents and master apprentices, an ever-enslaving demand for cheap labor, the colossal needs of poor families, the lessening influence of religion, and the beginnings of industrialization[53]—prevented the Old Deluder Act and almost all other efforts on the part of the state from becoming effective in realizing the ideal of universal education.[54]

Then, in 1789 Massachusetts enacted a law with great enthusiasm, encouraging cities and towns to divide themselves into districts. It proved to be a dubious boon. One of the least desirable results was a sort of segregation of schools into various localities. This often brought about an unnatural balance whereby many of the poor schools became poorer and wealthy ones wealthier. Even Horace Mann in his day considered this early law as unfavorable, as in many instances detrimental to the very cause of the common schools themselves.[55] Other authorities have gone as far as to maintain that this law was largely responsible for the difficulties in the second half of the twentieth century, such as a nationwide challenge over the many issues involved in desegregation. It even seems to be in opposition to what Arnold Toynbee was to state in his 1960 essay "Education: The Long View":

Clearly this educational work [was and still] is a tremendous one. Yet we cannot afford to shy away from it or to exclude any part of the human race from its scope. We have to help mankind to educate itself against the danger of its destroying itself; and this is a duty that we dare not repudiate.[56]

The problem would finally resolve itself by the right of the state to establish a tax-supported public school system, making it the duty of the citizens of the nation to support one.[57]

Now, as a top priority, process-and-response education for values is struggling for fuller realization. In an attempt to analyze the process of this evolution within the common or public schools as they are presently constituted, a strange and extreme complexity is seen, a dilemma in values so paradoxical as to seem irreconcilable. Hardly any understanding in depth of educational crises today is possible without viewing them as a continuing process in the long-range perspective of the common school problem. These crises need to be studied, especially as growing out of the deeply rooted early colonial educational milieu.

The wisdom of Socrates now is reflected in the new discipline of Jean Piaget when he writes that the maieutic process of Socrates is an appeal to the pupil's own activity rather than to his docility[58] and that

it would be impossible to employ a Socratic method without having first acquired some of Socrates' qualities, the first of which would have to be a certain respect for intelligence in the process of development.[59]

That his concepts provide operative vehicles toward integrating the principles of the natural humanists into the modern problem of What, When, and How to teach by cultivating the experimental spirit[60] is evidenced by the following theorists in education:

1302–1374—Francis Petrarch is considered to be the first modern scholar to insist that the best portrayal of the development of human nature is in the classics.

ca. 1466–1536—Desiderius Erasmus advocated study of the nature of the child and proposed more humane and attractive means of discipline.

1533–1592—Michel de Montaigne insisted that education is to

be gained by direct contact with people and their social activities rather than by books alone.

1632–1704—John Locke contributed insights regarding the human mind by rejecting innate ideas and insisting upon the experiences of the senses.

1694–1778—François M. A., Voltaire, encouraged students to think for themselves by testing all things both human and divine by reason.

1712–1778—Jean Jacques Rousseau sought a natural law for education based on three principles: growth, student activity, and individualization.

1723–1790—Johann Bernard Basedow pioneered in the new type of education advocated by Rousseau and deliberately set aside educational traditions.

1746–1827—Johann Heinrich Pestalozzi used his inventiveness and devotion to children to find the way of the heart to the best methods of training intelligence (Piaget, *Science of Education and the Psychology of the Child,* pp. 9, 10, 70, 141–43) .

1776–1841—Johann Friedrich Herbart attempted to adjust educational techniques to the laws of psychology with his process of apperception (Piaget, *Science of Education. . .* , p. 144) .

1782–1852—Friedrich Froebel, in creating the kindergarten, became the champion of a sensory education based on a sensorial phase of individual development (Piaget, *Science of Education. . .* , p. 143) .

1796–1859—Horace Mann used Combe's phrenology with the perspectives of John Locke as the basis for nonsectarian education, by which he directed the public school teachers in developing the physical, intellectual, spiritual, and moral phases of the students.

1820–1903—Herbert Spencer demanded that the new scientific developments be given a major role in schools and colleges.

1832–1920—Wilhelm Wundt established the first psychological laboratory in Leipzig, where Pavlovian reflexology became the basis for learning theories based on the stimulus-response (S–R) bond (Piaget, *Science of Education. . .* , p. 75).

1835–1908—William Torrey Harris as a contemporary and co-patriot of Horace Mann used the perspectives of Hegelianism by which to direct the public schools into the secularization of instruction and of character formation in education.

1859–1952—John Dewey, by fusing the imperatives of science and nature and democracy and humanity, formulated a democratic, science-respecting education that touches in some measure practically every stone in the modern American educational structure today and, according to Piaget, influences education in every country.

1861–1947—Alfred North Whitehead, the father of process philosophy, declared in his *Aims of Education* that any serious fundamental change in educational perspectives must necessarily be followed by a revolution in education.

1882–1973—Jacques Maritain built upon the works of previous naturalistic humanists to propose a "new" humanism of development to end the rift between social and individual claims, the cleavage between religious and secular activity, between work and useful activity and the blossoming of the spiritual and disinterested joy in knowledge and beauty.

1896–   —Jean Piaget, in devoting his life to the biological explanation of knowledge, created a new discipline, genetic epistemology,[61] whereby intellectual development is identified with structures of the human species during four major stages of growth and development, which can aid greatly toward constructive thinking regarding the supreme problem of *When to teach What and How.*

1904–   —Burrhus Frederic Skinner is both a teacher by profession and a learning theorist. His science and technology produced the "teaching machine." To prevent the total destruction of the environment, he proposed a new behavioral approach to education: man directing the development of his environment so effectively as to refashion man *(Beyond Freedom and Dignity)* . In his autobiography *(Particulars of My Life)* he, as potentate of behaviorism, affirms validity for this perspective.

1915– —Jerome Bruner summed up his approach to the human problems of the era by affirming that he was trying to discover how human beings cope. What is it that they require by way of information processing, anticipation, and intention? He is working on a social invention that would make it possible for people to work together on the massive problems of poverty, urban life, and learning by effective use of technology.

1927– —Lawrence Kohlberg has been utilizing Jean Piaget's perspectives in an intensive and extensive analysis of moral development in children. Today Piaget and Kohnberg are two of the most famous researchers and writers dealing with the nature of moral development. They provide the natural basis and framework in education for analyzing teaching strategies to aid children in moral maturity.

Cicero (106–43 B.C.), the renowned Roman statesman and orator, cautioned that to be ignorant of the historical process is to be as a man who has not lived. Failure to grasp his perspective in contemporary life is to risk a gross distortion of the key issues, for he warns: "To be ignorant of the past is to remain a child."[62] The word embodying the study of the evaluative process and its transition to the new epoch is *relevance*.[63]

Jean Piaget sees relevance as the ability to learn from fermentations in the past. Today educators are still concentrating training upon methods and curriculum, without the necessary educational research and experimentation. The reasons are that (1) educators fail to inject new life into training; (2) educators' knowledge of child psychology is shallow and their interest in mental, moral, and emotional development of the child, extremely limited; (3) educators use the antithesis of children's yearning for relevant teaching; (4) educators suppress the natural ferment of childhood energy by expecting students to sit passively in their seats and listen.[64] After epitomizing these faults, Piaget declares that unless

the aim of intellectual training is to form the intelligence rather than to stock the memory, to produce intellectual explorers rather than mere erudition, then . . . education [today] is manifestly guilty of a grave deficiency.[65]

SELECT REFERENCES

Atkinson, Carroll, and Maleska, Eugene T. *The Story of Education.* New York: Chilton Co., 1965.

Baier, Kurt, and Rescher, Nicholas, eds. *Values and the Future.* Glencoe, Ill.: The Free Press, 1969.

Bailyn, Bernard. *Education in the Forming of American Society.* Chapel Hill, N.C.: University of North Carolina Press, 1960.

Beck, Carlton E.; Bernier, Normand R.; MacDonald, James B.; Walton, Thomas W.; and Willers, Jack C. *Education for Relevance.* Boston: Houghton Mifflin Co., 1968.

Black, Hugh C.; Lottich, Kenneth V., and Seckinger, Donald S., eds. *The Great Educators.* Chicago: Nelson-Hall Co., 1972.

Butts, Freeman. *The American Tradition in Religion and Education.* Boston: Beacon Press, 1950.

————, and Cremin, Lawrence A. *A History of Education in American Culture.* New York: Henry Holt and Co., 1953.

Cremin, Lawrence A. *The Genius of American Education.* New York: Vantage Press, 1965.

Cubberley, Ellwood P. *The History of Education.* Houghton Mifflin Co., 1920. *Public Education in the United States,* revised and enlarged ed. Boston: Houghton Mifflin Co., 1934.

Cunningham, William F. *The Pivotal Problems of Education.* New York: Macmillan Co., 1940.

de Toqueville, Alexis. *Democracy in America.* New York: Knopf, 1945.

Hinsdale, B. A. *Horace Mann and the Common School Revival in the United States.* New York: Charles Scribner's Sons, 1900.

Hughes, James Monroe. *Education in America,* 3rd ed. New York: Harper & Row, Publishers, 1970.

Keller, James. *All God's Children—What Your Schools Can Do for Them.* Garden City, N.Y.: Hanover House, 1953.

McCluskey, Neil Gerard. *Public Schools and Moral Education.* New York: Columbia University Press, 1958.

Nevins, Albert J. *Our American Catholic Heritage.* Huntington, Ind.: Our Sunday Visitor, Inc., 1972.

Panoch, James V. and Barr, David L. *Religion Goes to School.* New York: Harper & Row, Publishers, 1968.

Stephens, W. Richard, and Van Til, William. *Education in American Life,* Boston: Houghton Mifflin, 1972.

Sturm, John E., and Palmer, John A., eds. *Democratic Legacy in Transition.* New York: Van Nostrand Reinhold Company, 1971.

3

HORACE MANN'S NON-SECTARIAN EDUCATION[1]

As educators, as friends of the Common School system our great duty is: . . . [to] keep them [the pupils] . . . uncontaminated by . . . [the world's] vices; train them up to the love of God and the love of man; make the perfect example of Jesus Christ lovely in their eyes; . . . give to all as much religious instruction as is compatible with the rights of others . . . leave to parents and guardians the direction, during their school days, of all special and peculiar instruction respecting politics and theology, and at last, when the children arrive at years of maturity, commend them to that inviolable prerogative of private judgement and of self-direction, which . . . is the acknowledged birthright of every human being.

—Horace Mann
(quoted in Neal Gerard McCluskey, *Public Schools and Moral Education*)

The institution of the common school is the greatest discovery ever made by man.

Horace Mann declared forcefully in his First Annual Report that relevance of education in the common school could not be achieved while the school was a proselytizing agency for any religious sect. His objective was ". . . to give every child in the Commonweath a free, straight, solid pathway, by which he could walk directly up from the ignorance of an infant to a knowledge of the primary duties of man; and would acquire a power and an invincible will to discharge them."

In these words Mann, without realizing it, gave expression during his tenure as Secretary of Education in Massachusetts to the then existing, genuinely alarming, educational conditions and abuses, foremost among them being the science of education's failure to determine What to teach, When, and How, as Jean Piaget puts it today, even though, as he declares:

> public educators are civil servants answerable to a ministry that decides not only upon applications but also upon the principle to be applied [in the educative process].[2]

For Mann, one of the greatest violations of the public trust was the irrelevance created by sectarianism. It charged the atmosphere of the common schools with the "calamity of a Calvinistic education" by negating the happiness and character of a "genial, ennobling spirit of liberality."[3]

At the time when Mann was writing, his section of the country was considered the most literate. Certainly it was then the most religious of the nation, but the schools were far from being well organized. Even those proclaiming to be thoroughly Calvinistic in relevance of values were very diverse in their religious teachings:

> A reverence for the sacred history and traditions of their common fellowship caused each group to postpone the definite split in the constant hope that the other would be converted. But, instead of conversion, the lines of demarcation grew more clearly defined largely because of the insistent demands of the Orthodox.[4]

Sectarian differences were so affecting education that they all but threatened to turn learning and teaching into a denominational warfare.

Too many of the small local school districts, attaining the right to autonomy by the law of 1789, were gradually being infiltrated with selfish political interests. The wealthy districts were adamant and refused to help alleviate the educational weaknesses of the others. The poor schools continued to outnumber the richer ones until the ordinary common school district in Massachusetts became extremely weak. By 1825 the poorer schools were so numerous as to cry for reform.

Massachusetts answered the increasingly great need to make the previous compulsory school laws more effective. Specifically, by the law of 1826, the Commonwealth required every town to choose a school committee for the purpose of supervising, and assuming responsibility for the schools' endeavors to form character:

> It shall be, it hereby is, made the duty of the President, Professors, and tutors, of the University at Cambridge, and of the several Colleges in this Commonweath, Preceptors and Teachers of Academies, and all other Instructors of Youth, to take diligent care, and to exert their best endeavors to impress on the minds of children, and youth, committed to their care and instructions, the principles of piety . . . and those other virtues, which are the ornament of human society, and the basis upon which the Republican Constitution is founded.[5]

Notwithstanding the law of 1826, a more highly centralized supervision became necessary to aid the local committees in fulfilling their responsibilities. Local interest in controlling and supporting the common schools was rapidly declining into mere political expediency.[6] To stimulate whatever values remained in the schools, the Commonwealth of Massachusetts created a State Board of Education for improving the whole school system on a statewide basis.

Although the board was simple, too simple today to attract any publicity, that was not true back in 1837. That practically all such boards now do what the first board of education of Massachusetts legislated is ample testimony to its created pattern establishing this new principle: school administration is a branch of public administration. It thus became the prototype, both in its composition and in its functions, for the other state legislatures:[7]

THE 1837 BOARD OF EDUCATION FOR THE COMMONWEATH OF MASSACHUSETTS
COMPOSITION
Eight members appointed by Governor
TWOFOLD FUNCTION
1. To gather information about education in the Commonweath of Massachusetts;
2. To make recommendations to the legislature relative to improving the schools.
SECRETARY OF EDUCATION
The board, furthermore, is empowered to employ a secretary (superintendent) who is:
1. To study the needs of the schools;
2. To point out these needs to the public;
3. To diffuse other information to the public;
4. To help the board of education formulate its recommendations to the legislature of the Commonwealth.

As a result of this new legislation, value relevance in American education entered a more practical phase. This precedent is the first giant step, establishing a pattern within process-and-response education for values that was initiated more than two centuries earlier by the Pilgrim Fathers. This means of bringing order out of chaos throughout the schools of Massachusetts eventually extended to the whole nation.

Mann's Dilemma

In the midst of chaotic heterogeneity, each school had its own special problems of segregation, serious cultural issues, and peculiar difficulties, all of which added to the problem of providing any generally acceptable moral-spiritual values within the educative process itself. In this atmosphere Horace Mann, a former

Calvinist become a Unitarian, was requested to accept the appointment as secretary of the newly formed board of education for the Commonwealth of Massachusetts.[8]

To accept or reject this new position was a difficult decision to make. At the time of his selection for office, he was already forty-one years of age and still feeling the effects of many tragedies in his personal life: the premature death of his father; the drowning of his elder brother, who, according to the strict Calvinist church, had been deprived of heaven; his own rejection by the Calvinists because of his defection from their religious body; and the untimely death of his wife. In addition, other severe crises of a philosophical and psychological nature were causing him to be labeled as anticlerical, antisectarian, and even antireligious. Yet in spite of his ordeals, he gained considerable prestige as president of the State Senate, with a successful career both in the legal world as a lawyer and in the politics of his own state, which assured him a fairly lucrative income.

The new office offered the meager salary of $1,500 a year from the state. To this amount, Mann's friend Edmund Dwight, a wealthy philanthropist and the person mainly responsible for urging him to accept the new position, added another $500.[9] The prospect of future financial embarrassment and the dark, uncharted course of the poorly organized common schools in his own state and in New England in general, made him hesitate. He realized only too well that he could expect at least indirect opposition from the South, where no state supervision of education was exercised, and probably overt opposition from the Middle Colonies, where a system of parochial schools existed under the supervision of the Dutch Reformed Church.

Ultimately Mann overcame most of his doubts and, ignoring the degree of success he had attained, he decided to devote himself to what he considered "the supremest welfare of mankind upon earth."[10] As he later acknowledged, his faith in the perfectibility of mankind and the opportunities of the new position prompted him to use his experience in the common cause of humanity.

First Annual Report

After assuming office in the summer of 1837 as the first secretary of education in the nation, Horace Mann began to familiarize himself with the conditions of the schools. Not the least significant of his tasks were consultations with people interested in improving them. By the new year he had his first annual report ready for presentation to the State Board. It is in its last section that his comments on the difficult status of educational values in the common schools appear.[11]

He observes that whereas formerly the schools had moral-spiritual values evolving from and around those of a particular religious denomination, informing and unifying both the learning and the teaching, now this process is becoming too complicated and exceptionally difficult in its demands on the teachers. In every district he finds coexisting pluralistic groups, each differing fundamentally in religious values and ultimate goals, in both a personal philosophy of life and its application to the educative process.

Toward the end of his report he expressed great concern over the lack of moral instruction, caused by conflicting views of religious sects in so many schools. He viewed this condition with alarm, for such a situation was contrary to his basic philosophical principle that the common school should be as perfect an instrument as possible to help prepare all of God's children for their common citizenship in this great country. Finally he pointed out his vital principle, that of the moral-spiritual.[12]

With determination for improvement in this direction, Mann now began his first all-out effort at reorganization and clarification. He formulated a dynamic values philosophy for American education in the commonwealth schools of Massachusetts and, by implication, in those throughout the entire country. Probably no single undertaking in the nineteenth century until the Civil War was charged with such significant and lasting repercussions.

Through his meetings with members of the Massachusetts Board of Education Horace Mann reached an agreement on the books necessary to teach morality and religious principles common to the different religious denominations in the schools. By September 1838 unanimous approval was extended to:[13] *Lives of Eminent Individuals, Celebrated in American History* (3 volumes); *Life of Columbus* by Washington Irving; *The Sacred Philosophy of the Seasons* by the Rev. Henry Duncan, D.D., of Scotland, adapted by Rev. F. W. P. Greenwood, D.D., of Boston (4 volumes); *Paley's Natural Theology*, adapted for the school library by Elisha Bartlett, M.D. (2 volumes). These selections definitely did not favor any sect, and not even the Christian religion. For example in Paley's works, the words *Christ, Christian, Bible,* and *church* do not appear.

In retrospect these undertakings can be likened to the great cause of the Founding Fathers themselves during the Revolution for Independence, which resulted in the creation of a new nation and the framing of its federal Constitution. So great is the work of Horace Mann that he earned the distinction of being the father of the common or public school system. With the assistance of his board of education, he succeeded in awakening new life by creating nationwide interest in a common school system. He so stimulated the process of educational values in Massachusetts and throughout the country as to bring about "The Great Awakening."[14]

The Great Awakening

In firing practically the entire nation with new enthusiasm for shaping an educational philosophy, Horace Mann encouraged the schools above all to be in harmony with the laws of nature.[15] In so doing, he was reflecting Rousseau's educational philosophy of natural goodness, which was taken over bodily by the naturalists, and Pestalozzi's view of the common school. Jean Piaget sees these as complementing each other when he writes that

it was thanks to this very spirit that Pestalozzi, from the very outset, was able to correct Rousseau on one capital point: a school is a true society, so that the child's sense of its responsibilities and the rules of cooperation are sufficient in themselves to provide its moral training, thereby making it quite unnecessary, in order to avoid harmful restrictions or the danger lurking in emulation, to isolate the pupil inside his own individualism. Furthermore, the social factor has its effect in the sphere of intellectual education as well as in the moral field. . . . Pestalozzi organized a sort of mutual aid teaching system such that the children were all able to help one another with their research.[16]

Through a series of annual reports, widely publicized both in Europe and in America during his twelve years in office, Horace Mann was successful in providing the common schools of Massachusetts with a genuine natural foundation on which moral development and knowledge complement each other. It is not unlike Piaget's genetic principle of developmental epistemology, whereby he insists that mental and moral growth be an extension of the biological.

Even though Mann's orientation and implementation are derived in most part from phrenology, the pseudo-scientific philosophy found in George Combe's *Constitution of Man*, there is a great deal of wisdom to be utilized in applying it to the educative process. Therein science is shown to govern the process of nature and, at least indirectly, of man insofar as he is a part of nature.[17] As Pestalozzi expresses it in *The Evening Hour of a Hermit*:

What man is, what his needs are, what elevates and humiliates him, what strengthens and what weakens him ought to be the most important knowledge for the rulers as well as for the humblest.[18]

Mann envisioned his natural perspective as assisting all professional educators in the work of teacher preparation. Thereby he hoped to help them see their tasks more clearly as a whole amid the frustrating conflicts in an ever-changing world. In his reports he pointed out how, through the philosophy and science of phrenology, a careful analysis of the child in relation to his environment would provide the schools with the proper naturalistic approach for educating the whole person. His laudable objective still exists today, notably in the works of John Dewey, Jerome Bruner, Jacques Maritain, and especially Jean Piaget's. Piaget's developmental experiments in genetic epistemology provide a wholesome natural basis for the learning-teaching process.

One of Horace Mann's practical approaches to relevance of values in his early reports was to show how much of the Massachusetts school system seemed to be vicious. He designated it as unnatural, vicious, and at times preventing the harmonious development of the physical, mental, intellectual, spiritual, and moral character of the child.[19] Through his reports the influence of Johann Pestalozzi (1746–1827) came to this country in the first half of the last century. He contributes immensely to the study of the child and his complete nature by declaring that "all knowledge begins in the senses." Even today Piaget recognizes Pestalozzi in his *Science of Education and the Psychology of the Child* as "perhaps the most illustrious of the pedagogues who were purely and simply educators."[20] For

> Pestalozzi insisted that the natural instincts of a child should provide the motives for learning. He considered cooperation and sympathy, rather than compulsion or physical punishment, the proper means by which to achieve discipline. Influenced by Rousseau, he believed that free expression would allow the natural powers of the child to develop. Since it is nature that gives the drive to life, he maintained, the teacher's responsibility is to adapt instruction to each individual according to his particular changing, unfolding nature as required at the various stages of his development. Pestalozzi looked upon the child as a unity made of moral, physical, and intellectual powers—all of which could be developed harmoniously through education.[21]

Mann makes Pestalozzi's principles the genuine basis of his directives for the learning process. He emphasizes especially how the child is to be considered in relation to his environment so that the body receives the necessary attention in regard to physical health—absolutely essential to such basic needs as security, happiness, and efficiency.[22] Even food and clothing, along with such items as books, studies, lectures, and the school itself, take on moral aspects in the process of education. These, insofar as they are a necessary part of the child's environment, are to be an integral part of the educative process for forming the natural man in the truth, beauty, and goodness of the world as indicated here:

Pestalozzi's Main Principles of Psychological-Educational Developmentalism[23]

1. Moral Instruction	The first among the aims of education should be moral instruction.
2. Social Reform	Education should consist in aiding the individual to help himself and thereby improve society.
3. Practical Activities	On the elementary level learning activities should be utilized whereby the children are led gradually from mere motor skills to vocational competence in farming, trade, and industry.
4. Individual Differences	The teacher should adapt instruction to each individual pupil in accordance with the various stages of his growth and development.
5. Complete Development	The moral, physical, and intellectual are to be developed harmoniously through education.
6. Manipulation of Materials	Sense perception through object lessons furnishing direct contacts with materials rather than reliance on mere books and reading are to be made integral to learning and teaching, such as animals, plants, tools, tec.

| 7. Ultimate Purpose of Education | The social regeneration of the masses physically, intellectually, and morally is the ultimate purpose of education. |

NOTE: It is interesting to recall that these principles of Pestalozzi are well in accord with those of Piaget in their developmental aspects, especially principles 3, 4, and 6.

Mann encouraged the study of Pestalozzi because he challenges all to seek more knowledge about education—knowledge of the what and also the how of the teaching-learning process:[24]

> Anticipating by 100 years Jerome Bruner and his emphasis on the structure of knowledge, Pestalozzi stressed such basic elements of knowledge as number, form, and language. He would urge us [today] to extend his search for knowledge of the fundamental elements and ideas of "each branch of teaching" that it might be brought "to a starting point within the reach of the growing powers of the child." In addition he challenges us to go beyond Bruner and recognize something more than the structure of knowledge. Knowledge must be communicated so as to relate to the children themselves and to their lives [helping] ". . . to awaken a right feeling within them in order to make them active, attentive, and obedient in matters external."[25]

He also saw in Pestalozzi what Piaget refers to concerning the individual efforts of schoolmasters. Their particular inventiveness has enabled them to find their way to the best methods of training intelligence.[26]

Not a few authorities recognize in Mann's humane approaches to early process-and-response education for values an importance in the relevance of values parallel with that of psychology in educating for a better understanding of the whole person. Many of his proposals he culls from Combe's phrenology and Pestalozzi's insights. These he applies to the common schools in order to guide the teachers in basic principles and facets of pedagogy. Updated later through educational psychology, they are put to further work within the educational process through the efforts of William T. Harris. Later Francis Parker, whom John Dewey credits as being the "father" of progressive education, G. Stanley Hall, and especially John Dewey, support these principles.[27] As the father of democratic education during the first half of the twentieth century, Dewey directed the quest for a more meaningful relevance of values in education, seeking to make it naturalistic and always in process.

Moral Education

In Horace Mann's process approach to values in educating the child, the moral-spiritual is as integral to learning and teaching as learning and teaching are to values themselves. In his perspective, for the child to become what he is meant to be, to *be* somebody, he is to realize ever more fully his innermost nature as man. It is the ideal of Pestalozzi's message that he presents to teachers: that through the subject matter of education (such as reading, writing, and arithmetic), the student is to realize his innermost self as a person "who is the same whether on the throne or in a hut."[28]

Within the Pestalozzian perspective, Mann saw the main aim of education as the development of the child's moral and religious character, without any attempt to separate morality from non-sectarian or natural religion. The sectarian, often called the spiritual-religious belief in the supernatural, has no place in the school. He therefore declared that the natural formation of the child's character should be the direct responsibility of the common school, and in this sense the common or public school was the best agency for forming character.

Piaget, however, points out Pestalozzi's limitations:

Generally speaking, Pestalozzi was tainted with a certain systematic formalism, which made itself evident in his timetables, in his classification of the subjects to be taught, in his mental gymnastic exercises and in his passion for demonstrations. His excesses in this direction demonstrate just how little account he took, in detail, of the true development of the mind.[29]

This may explain the antiquated traits persisting in the common schools of Massachusetts; thus, despite those negative influences on the total development of the child's intelligence, Mann maintains that the common school is the antidote to the evils of society. It possesses two grand, fundamental attributes peculiar to itself, which give it its superiority in character development and its most excellent means for reclaiming the world. The first is universality, that is, the capacity to receive and even cherish, like a mother at her bosom, every child who comes into the world; the second is its timeliness in influencing the pliable child, for every effort made in the common school affects the whole life of the child.[30]

Since Mann claims that precisely in universality and timeliness lies the superiority of the common school over all educational agencies, he does not hesitate to proclaim the institution of the common school as the greatest discovery ever made by man. He insists that every child ought to be given the opportunities of its enriching influence, but he permits only as much religious instruction in the common school as is compatible with real religious freedom.

His concern for religious freedom is not without statistical supporting evidence. Clark, in *A Historical Sketch of the Congregational Churches in Massachusetts* (1620–1858, p. 218), lists the number of sectarian churches of 1783 as:

Sect	Number
Roman Catholic	1
Universalists	3
Quakers	6
Episcopalians	11
Baptists	68
Congregationalists	330

He (p. 218) then presents the 1858 statistics, a much more diversified picture in the number of churches within the Commonwealth of Massachusetts:

Sect	Number
Orthodox Congregationalists	490

Episcopal Methodists	277
Baptists	266
Unitarians	170
Universalists	135
Episcopalians	65
Roman Catholics	64
Christ-ians (sic)	37
Friends Meetings	24
Free-will Baptists	21
Protestants or Independent Methodists	20
Second Adventists	15
Wesleyan Methodists	13
Swedenborgians	11
Presbyterians	7
Shakers	4
Unclassified	12

Mann affirms that the school is less likely to favor any one sect when it encourages the generally agreed-upon moral and religious beliefs of Christianity: to love God with all one's heart and one's neighbor as oneself; to do to others as they would be done by; to do justly; to love mercy and to walk humbly with God; to visit the fatherless and widows in their affliction and to keep themselves unspotted from the world; to honor father and mother; to keep the Sabbath holy; not to steal, not to kill, not to bear false witness against neighbors, and not to covet. All these Mann considers as integral to character along the lines of the twenty-fourth chapter of Matthew. For in this chapter of the Bible, he says, there is not a single action or omission for which the righteous are to be rewarded and the wicked punished that may not be taught, inculcated, or warned against in all the schools.[31]

Natural religion means obedience to all God's laws. These include the physical, moral, spiritual, and religious ones, which demand intelligent and virtuous, not sectarian, minds, because the true substance of Chritianity is in the Golden Rule. He therefore concludes that love of humanity, the Golden Rule, and the social betterment of the human race should be the essence of moral education in the common school.

Finally the Bible, without note or interpretation, Mann declares to be the greatest means of realizing the primary aim of the school in process because it breathes God's laws and presents illustrious examples of conduct, above all that of Jesus Christ.[32] In what manner and in what classes the Bible may be used in the schools he leaves to the discretion of local authorities in accordance with the law of 1826.

The Final Report

After twelve difficult years as secretary of the Commonwealth Board of Education of Massachusetts, Mann reminded the people that he had not sought the office, but that the office had sought him, and that he had stayed with it in spite of detriment to his health and fortune. He reminded them also of how some had tried to get him out, but that no one had ever tried to get in. Likewise, he affirmed that, so far as he could determine, he had carried out the avowed policy of the Board. By showing no favor or disfavor to any one political or religious party, he thus helped to establish the principle of nonsectarian education.[33]

In his tenth and last annual report, Mann detailed three propositions describing the broad and ever-enduring foundation on which the common school system of Massachusetts rested:

> The successive generations of men, taken collectively, constitute one great commonwealth. The property of this commonwealth is pledged for the education of all its youth, up to such a point as will save them from poverty and vice, and prepare them for the adequate performance of their social and civil duties. The successive holders of this property are trustees, bound to the faithful execution of their trust, by the most sacred obligations, and embezzlement and pillage from children and descendants have not less of criminality, and have more of meanness, than the same offenses, when perpetrated against contemporaries.[34]

In Retrospect

In fairness to Horace Mann, it is paramount to recognize how, under the conditions of his times, any other compromise regarding the Bible and religious instruction would have meant the almost certain disintegration of the common schools as it is understood today. He kept the Bible in the schools but did not permit the sects to interpret it, and thus allowed it to speak for itself. He encouraged a general, natural, Christian influence to permeate the schools, but any specific sectarian influence, in the form of library books, for example, he eliminated.[35]

Later, during his term as first president of Antioch College in Ohio, he continued to advance a nonsectarian relevance of values based on the Scriptures. There, too, his views on character training and religious education were usually under attack. The difficulty was always the same: the place of religious and moral values in the schools.

His profound and lasting influence in shaping public school philosophy toward a relevance of values in American education, based on a nonsectarian approach to learning and teaching, has no equal. As for his successors, they have meaningful success only insofar as they relate to the new philosophy of the common school education that he initiated during his years as secretary of education. It is becoming increasingly evident that without the following tenets of nonsectarianism that he fought to establish, the common school system would have been strangled in mutual dispute long before the present day:[36]

Basic Tenets of Horace Mann's Nonsectarianism[37]

VALUES	PERSPECTIVES
1. Bible	The reading of the Bible must be without note or interpretation for it is the means par excellence of realizing the primary aim of education. It breathes God's laws. It presents the illustrious examples of conduct, above all that of Jesus Christ.

2. Primary Aim of Education	The development of the child's moral and religious character. There should be no attempt to separate morality and religion, i.e., the "nonsectarian" or "natural" religion.
3. Character Formation	The common school is the most perfect agency for character formation; it is the direct responsibility of the common school.
4. Natural Religion	The true substance of Christianity is the "religion of heaven," i.e., the natural religion as opposed to man-made creedal religions. It means obedience to all God's laws—physical, moral, spiritual, and religious.
5. Religious Instruction	In the common schools as much religious instruction must be given as is compatible with religious freedom. The sectarian spirit is to be shunned by every possible means.

During the first half of the nineteenth century, although many schools were established by religious denominations, they usually had some share of public funds.[38] Sectarianism, however, was widespread during these decades and the fight for funds to help support denominational schools served only to embitter people on this issue. When controversy between sectarian or church-related schools and state-controlled or common schools intensified, Mann became the advocate of the secularized common or public school, with the word *public* standing for the tax-supported and state-controlled common school.[39] Today this controversy, both in public assistance to the denominational and private schools and in the area of moral-spiritual values within the curriculum of the public schools themselves, is intensifying, with Bible reading and prayer being banned from the classroom.

Every new movement in education must run the gauntlet of

bitter opposition before adoption. The impatient public severely blames the conservative party. In Massachusetts, therefore, no more was really achieved by Mann than the purification of public education before the stage of practical experimentation can begin.[40] His co-patriot William T. Harris was correct in stating that Horace Mann was more like a Hebrew prophet of the Old Testament whose predictions were not universally acceptable. For many, his message was so effective as to refute those who accuse Mann of utilizing a stupid and un-American way to meet the sectarian problems within the common schools.

A similar situation may perhaps be recognized with regard to Jean Piaget today, where conscientious teachers, educators, and students of education have been understandably bewildered by the overstated and conflicting claims of Piaget's supporters and detractors.[41] As for the applicability of his ideas of children's mental growth and development within his new discipline of genetic epistemology, they will find, through analyses and duplications of his experiments, guidelines for reaching conclusions of their own with regard to *what, when,* and *how* to teach.

Following Mann's declaration of war on the educational deterioration caused by sectarianism, could his principles of intellectual and moral development ever be satisfactorily applied? This is the question not yet answered—at least in the United States.[42] And, this is the Piagetian challenge of *what, when,* and *how* to teach today.

Chronology of Mann's Works

Manuscripts[43]

The Collected Mann Papers, including Horace Mann's Journal and several thousand letters and papers classified chronologically, are in the archives of the Massachusetts Historical Society, Boston. Robert L. Straker has prepared a 14,000-page typescript that includes copies of many Mann documents in the archives of the Massachusetts Historical Society. The Straker typescript is in the Antioch College Library.

The Minutes of the Meetings of the Massachusetts Board of Education, 1837–48, are in the records of the Department of Education, the State House, Boston.

Books and Articles[44]

"A Bibliography of Horace Mann," in *Report of the U. S. Commissioner of Education for the Year 1896–97*. Washington, D.C.: U. S. Government Printing Office, 1898.

1891   *Life and Works of Horace Mann,* ed. Mary Peabody Mann and George Combe Mann. 5 vols. Boston: Lee and Shepard. (vol. 1: the *Life* by Mary Peabody Mann; vol. 2: *First and Second Annual Reports and Education Lectures;* vol. 3: *Third to Eighth Annual Reports*; vol. 4: *Ninth to Twelfth Annual Reports and Orations*; vol. 5: *Educational Writings*. The *Life* was first published in 1865 by Walker, Fuller and Company of Boston. The 1891 edition was printed four years after Mrs. Mann's death and contains some new material.)

1838–48 *Twelve Annual Reports of the Board of Education* together with the *Twelve Annual Reports of the Secretary of the Board*. Boston: Dutton and Wentworth, State Printers. (The National Education Association issued facsimile editions of the following reports: *Seventh Annual Report Covering the Year 1843* (Washington, 1950) ; *Tenth Annual Report Covering the Year 1846* (Washington, 1952) ; and *Twelfth Annual Report Covering the Year 1848* (Washington, 1952.)

1839–52 Horace Mann and W. B. Fowle, eds. *The Common School Journal*. 15 vols. Boston: March, Capen, Lyon

59314

and Webb. (vols. 1–11, 1838–48; n.s. vols. 1–4, January 1849—December 1852.)

1840 *Lecture on Education.* Boston: March, Capen, Lyon, and Webb.

1844 The Common School Controversy: Consisting of Three Letters of the Secretary of the Board of Education of the Commonwealth of Massachusetts in Reply to Charges Preferred against the Board by the Editor of the *Christian Witness* and by Edward A. Newton Esq. Boston: J. N. Bradley and Co.

Reply to the "Remarks" of Thirty-one Boston Schoolmasters on the *Seventh Annual Report of the Secretary of the Massachusetts Board of Education.* Boston: William B. Fowle and Nahum Capen.

1845 Answer to the "Rejoinder" of Twenty-nine Boston Schoolmasters, Part of the "Thirty-one" who published "Remarks" on the *Seventh Annual Report (of the Secretary of the Massachusetts School Board).* Boston: William B. Fowle and Nahum Capen.

1846 *The Ground of the Free School System.* From the *Tenth Annual Report of the Secretary of the Massachusetts State Board of Education,* 1846. Reprinted as Old South Leaflet No. 109. Boston: Directors of the Old South Work, 1902.

1847 Letter to the Rev. Matthew Hale Smith, in Answer to his "Reply" or "Supplement." Boston: William B. Fowle.

Sequel to the So-Called Correspondence between the Rev. M. H. Smith and Horace Mann, Surreptitiously Published by Mr. Smith; containing a Letter from Mr. Mann, Suppressed by Mr. Smith, with the Reply Therein Promised. Boston: William B. Fowle.

1850 *A Few Thoughts for a Young Man.* Boston.

1861 *Twelve Sermons Delivered at Antioch College.* Boston: Ticknor and Fields.

SELECT REFERENCES

Atkinson, Carroll, and Maleska, Eugene J. *The Story of Education.* New York: Chilton Co., 1965.

Barnard, Henry. *Educational Biography: Memoirs of Teachers, Educators and Promoters and Benefactors of Education, Literature and Science.* New York: Brownell, 1961.

Bestor, Arthur E.; Mann, Jr., Horace; Peabody, Elizabeth; Brownson, Orestes A. *An Unpublished Letter with Commentary.* (Reprinted from the Proceedings of the Middle States Association of History and Social Science Teachers, 1940–41.) New York: Columbia Teachers College, 1941.

Billington, Ray A. *The Protestant Crusade, 1800–1860.* New York: Macmillan, 1938.

Brooks, Van Wyck. *The Flowering of New England, 1815–1865.* New York: Dutton, 1938.

Culver, Raymond B. *Horace Mann and Religion in the Massachusetts Public Schools.* New Haven: Yale University Press, 1929.

Curti, Merle. *Social Ideas of American Educators.* New York: Charles Scribner's Sons, 1935.

Filler, Louis, ed. *Horace Mann on the Crisis in Education.* Yellow Springs, O.: Antioch Press, 1965.

Hegel, G. W. F. *Selections.* New York: Charles Scribner's Sons, 1929.

McCluskey, Neil Gerard. *Public Schools and Moral Education.* New York: Columbia University Press, 1958.

Mann, Horace. *Lectures on Education.* Boston: Ide & Dutton, 1855.

Messerli, Jonathan. *Horace Mann: A Biography.* New York: Knopf, 1972.

Piaget, Jean. *Science of Education and the Psychology of the Child.* New York: Orion Press, 1970.

Stephens, W., and Van Til, William. *Education in American Life.* Boston: Houghton Mifflin, 1972.

Treichler, Jeffie. *Horace Mann.* Encyclopaedia Britannica Press, 1962.

4

WILLIAM T. HARRIS'S SECULARIZATION OF EDUCATION[1]

There is a time for every kind of teaching and we ought to recognize it, and each has its own dangers to be avoided.

—Jean Jacques Rousseau

The common man is destined to participate in the realized intelligence of all mankind.

In announcing how "only a people with universal education can sustain a republican form of government," William T. Harris is reechoing the educational philosophy of Horace Mann:

Where the people are to obey the laws made for them by a hereditary ruling class, it may be necessary that the people shall be taught in the schools so much as will enable them to read and understand those laws. But where the people are to make the laws as well as obey them, what limit can there be to the school education required except the full preparation of the individual citizen to carry on his education for himself?[2]

Perhaps one of the more evident features of William T. Harris's development of the secular is how at present his perspectives resemble those of Piaget by his linking himself with Hegelianism. Harris makes this philosophic science the framework in which to continue Mann's attack on the problems in the schools, today's Piagetian concept of *what* to teach *when* and *how*.[3] In this scientific sociology he, like Piaget in his own genetic epistemology, found an application to the secularizing perspectives of education in his day. Through Hegelianism, Harris was able to infuse new life into the then stagnating and conflicting educational practices. His positions as teacher and then superintendent of the St. Louis public schools, and later as United States Commissioner of Education, were not unlike those of Piaget's positions of teacher at the University of Neuchâtel and the University of Geneva on the faculty of science, his appointment as head of the Swiss delegation to UNESCO, and later his founding of the International Center of Genetic Epistemology in Geneva.

> His [Harris's] most important achievement, however, was to furnish American education with a philosophy which helped the rank and file to adjust their thought and feeling to new actualities without losing the sense of identity with older values and conditions.[4]

When Harris was born, in 1835, American nationality had not yet been consolidated; when he died in 1909, hardly any important group seriously challenged it. At his birth rural America was dominant; at his death urban industrial America was in the saddle. As he began his educational work there was still abundant free land, with something roughly approaching economic opportunities for everyone. As he finished his educational career, the traditional opportunities for the individual, while still existent, were in fact very limited. In 1835 most of the intellectual and social leaders of America believed in a personal God, the freedom of the will, and immortality. In 1909 the advance of science had to a considerable extent changed that. It was his personalized philosophy that aided his fellow Americans, and particularly educators, to accept the new order without entirely repudiating the old.[5] He points out this condition in his work *The Philosophy of Education*:

> Ninety-nine out of a hundred people in every civilized nation are automata, careful to walk in the prescribed paths, careful to follow prescribed custom. This is the result of substantial education, which scientifically defined, is the subsumption of the individual under his species. The other educational principle is that of emancipation from this subsumption. This is subordinate, and yet, in our time, we lay more stress upon it than the others.[6]

Spiritual Values

As an educational leader, Dr. Harris emphasized the importance of spiritual values, both cultural and religious. To his mind philosophy supports the Christian religion. The church, together with the state, civil society, the family, and the school, is a necessary beneficent institution. Yet Harris, unlike Mann, did not wish religious instruction in any form to be given in public schools. The principle of religious instruction is authority; that of secular teaching is demonstration and verification. "It is obvious," he remarks, "that these two principles should not be brought into the same school, but separated as widely as possible."[7]

Harris's Perspective of Instruction

THE SECULAR is based on	demonstration and verification,	and is *separated from*	RELIGIOUS INSTRUCTION, based on authority, which is the exclusive domain of the family and church.

Elementary School Perspectives

In the elementary classes, with a nonsectarian atmosphere for a common, natural formaton of character appropriate to all of God's children, as Mann expressed it, Harris continued to discourage any religious instruction. For elementary education, which must be universal, should give each child the tools with which to participate in the culture of the race—grammar, literature and art, mathematics, geography, and history. Harris called these the "five windows of the soul," claiming that they enabled the individual to appreciate the ideas and cultural values that govern the social organization and civilization in which he shares. As "tool subjects" they assist the child in acquiring further instruments for mastering the entire realms of nature and of mind.

Piaget, however, insists on the importance of children's coming into direct contact through as many senses as possible by handling objects:

> Manipulation of *materials* is crucial. In order to think, children . . . need to have objects in front of them that are easy to handle, or else be able to visualize objects that have been handled and that are easily imagined without any real effort.[8]

In selecting materials the children become conscious of problems and are challenged to look for the solution themselves. The vast technological and business developments that provide libraries and newspapers for the masses, Harris claims, enable the pupil later to master, independently of teachers and universities, the great cultural treasures of the past, even if he goes no further than the elementary school.[9]

Although the most important of the spiritual values in the learning process should comprise the good life, Harris says that religion is not their sole source; higher culture is also fundamental within the philosophy of elementary education. On the material side, he has no heart for a culture ". . . belonging to a class that rests like an upper layer upon the masses below;

who in turn have to spin and to dig for them."[10] In accordance with these convictions, he proceeded to modify the curriculum.

Harris's Expansion of Public Education

Harris reinforced the elementary school first, by adding the kindergarten and encouraging a better sequence of intellectual development throughout the grades. Then he expanded the high school to enable public education to serve the social order better, a policy aimed at helping:

> the poor and unfortunate to help themselves, and . . . [to] elevate them toward human perfection, and the divine ideal. It is this principle, too, that makes clear to us what road leads to the surest amelioration of the evils of poverty and mendicancy. Education is the one sure road to help the unfortunate. Adopt all the cunning devices that social science has invented, and you cannot be sure that direct or indirect help of the poor does not undermine their self-respect and weaken their independence.[11]

In pointing out explicitly that public education in process could more effectively serve the established social order, Harris implicitly defended capitalism against its critics. In greeting the National Education Association assembly of 1894, when the country was enduring labor disorders, he described how the high school provided the people with training in habits of regularity, silence, and industriousness; how it helped to save and preserve the civil order; how the public school was the center of discipline; how the pupil learned to respect the rights of organized industry;[12] how, in the kindergarten, the child of the slum learned self-respect, moral ideals, industriousness, and perseverance—the means, in other words, of conquering natural obstacles.[13]

As an educator, Harris showed great concern for the dangers in the typical rearing of the offspring of the wealthy. He lamented that well-to-do mothers, eager to play a prominent role in "society," often turned over the care of their children to low-bred servants; how they frequently spoiled them and thus deprived civilization of the directive ability that such children very often possess. Believing that the kindergarten could help salvage these pampered children of the rich, he became a pioneer in its behalf.[14]

Development of the Kindergarten

The English-speaking kindergarten in this country became functional in Boston during 1860.[15] The establishment of a training school for kindergarten followed eight years later. Finally in 1873 the first kindergarten in the system of public-school education began at Des Peres School in St. Louis, Missouri, with Susan E. Blow. This was at the request of William T. Harris.[16]

In the course of this evolution, Harris postulated his own image of man's phases of growth and development. Using these four phases, he formulated his rationale for the whole spectrum of public school education:

HARRIS'S IMAGE OF MAN

1. Man needs *higher education*:
   a. To counteract "economic heresies," by a critical and comparative evaluation of human knowledge.
   b. To become a spiritual monitor of society.
2. Man needs *high school education*:
   To participate in the realized intelligence of mankind.
3. Man needs *elementary school education*:
   To obtain "tool subjects" by which to participate in mastering the entire realms of nature and mind.
4. Man needs *kindergarten education*:
   To prevent both wealthy and poor children in society from being spoiled.

A similar approach to learning and teaching is being reconstructed today by Harris on the solid base of Piaget's four stages of mental development: "sensorimotor" stage (pre-kindergarten), preoperational stage (kindergarten), concrete operational (elementary), formal operational (upper elementary and high school). Whereas Harris built his phases on the needs of man in his day as he saw them, Piaget bases his stages directly on the developing intelligence of the child. He begins with what he terms *the sensori-motor* intelligence and continues through the formal operational stage of intelligence to meet these same needs today. This important reversal of history partially explains why the problem of What, When, and How to teach at the present time is still unresolved. With all due respect to these giant pillars of educational development, what would the situation be regarding the What, When, and How to teach today if these two educators had lived in reverse sequence of time? From this perspective Harris would have achieved for public education in St. Louis a system still far superior to that of Horace Mann's in Boston.

Harris's Influence on the Curriculum

His influence on the curriculum is strong. The report of the Committee of Fifteen, his work on other important committees of the N.E.A. (which is the repository of his manuscripts), his impressive contributions to educational literature, his widely read reports while superintendent, and his work as Commissioner of Education are mainly responsible for Harris's sharp impact.

As the utilitarian subjects pressed increasingly for a place in the public school curriculum, Harris did not ignore the new emphasis on hygiene and physiology and the demands for better ventilation and better-lighted schools. Too much emphasis on biological and physiological theories, he cautioned, could lead to undue surrender to the physical nature of man, which should be subordinate to the spiritual or true self.[17] The chief object of physical training as he saw it was to "put will into the muscles." He did not want the intellectual side to be overstressed, however, and therefore he always opposed the movement to abandon the old-fashioned recess, considering it necessary for relaxation.[18]

Higher Education Perspectives

Harris looked to higher education to counteract "economic heresies," and encouraged young Americans to enter college. He favored an adjustment between the public high schools and the higher institutions of learning whereby private school training was no longer necessary to meet college entrance requirements.[19] He expected those in college to gain an insight: ". . . at once to suspect all mere *isms* and one-sided tendencies as socialism and anarchy and anything that has the form of a universal panacea."[20]

Harris viewed college graduates as the future spiritual monitors of society. From them must come social awareness and a deep understanding of existing institutions. They were to check the extravagances of less educated people, who had a fragmented view and were often swept by specious arguments for radical reform into the ranks of the agitators.[21] With these same ends in view, he wrote to President Benjamin Ide Wheeler of the University of California, urging him to accept the presidency of Teachers College:

> The New York Teachers College has done more than any other institution to explore new means and methods by which this [the children of the wealthy], a most important class of our population—important because it furnishes nearly all of the directive power to our industries—can save its children for the blessings of society. Turned in directions of selfish pleasure-seeking, the children of the wealthy do more than any other persons to irritate the masses of the American people and encourage the development of socialism and lines of political obstruction to the large enterprises of capital in the interest of productive industry. . . . In mentioning the great wealth of the trustees I have hinted that a phenomenal endowment of this institution is to be expected when it obtains for itself a universal recognition in the United States for the higher order of work which it will do.[22]

Harris warmly supported the movement for adult education by university extension. In referring to its origin in England he observed that: "There is no movement . . . which has worked for the perpetuation of the power of the upper classes . . . as has this movement of university extension." Since demagoguery increased in proportion to the neglect of the lower stratum of society by the highest, he contended that enlightened selfishness dictated the support of extension work in this country. In view of the demagogic, sensational appeals of popular newspapers, he saw an even greater necessity for adult education to equip the masses with the ability to resist such appeals. Just as earlier educators advocated the free common school to preserve the established social order, so he championed university extension as a double safeguard.[23]

In his relations with educational administrators and teachers, Harris advised that, regarding school affairs, they would find "the conservative business man" their best support in dealing with members who might be classified as cranks, reformers, and demagogues.[24] In his experience, he asserted, he usually found that teachers were the most conservative group in society, with the single exception of the clergy.[25] Therefore:

> The teacher must remember that her lot depended in large measure on her own efforts, that her position would be bettered if she improved her technique, her general culture, and her skill. As in industry, so in the teaching profession, the best from the lowest ranks were certain to rise if they had ability. . . . With the advance of civilization and the increase of productive wealth, he reassured his listeners, the status of the profession in general would improve. Meantime teachers might take comfort in the knowledge that in view of the industrial progress of the country and the "economic law of increased values of vocations that have for their object the protection of culture," the future outlook for teachers' salaries was bright.[26]

Philosopher of Education

Harris is highly appreciated as philosopher of education *par excellence*. Hardly anyone, with the exception of John Dewey, has been more influential in shaping the educational philosophy of the nation's schools as begun by Horace Mann. Harris spoke 145 times at N.E.A.-sponsored national conventions and assemblies alone.[27] As an educator-philosopher his name seems to represent best the last quarter of the nineteenth century in the process of American education, as that of Mann does in the preceding period. By reason of his ability to balance moderately the thoughts and feelings of the common people toward new actualities, his most important achievement was to furnish American education with a conservator who provided a philosophy for educators. This role he fulfilled with no destruction of traditional values, as is evidenced by the applications of his philosophy to education:

HARRIS'S PHILOSOPHY OF EDUCATION[28]

Attributes are	*Application*
1. Moderately constructive	Retaining "status quo" in organization, methods, point of view of schools, and traditional values.
2. Reasonably flexible	Requiring authority, discipline, and application to individual differences.
3. Patriotic in perspective	Encouraging patriotism prudently.
4. Cognizant of man's freedom in equality	Providing minority groups, immigrant population, Indians, and Blacks with equal opportunities of education and civilization.
5. Pregnant with principles of the good life	Establishing the objective of education to be more than religion, so as to include spiritual values, higher culture, moral development, and a more genuinely human life.
6. Responsive to ethical duties	Insisting that education is that process by which the individual becomes ethical.
7. Sensitive to the needs of reform	Approving of instruction in temperance, international politics, art, literature, and philosophy.

8. Universal in their application	Including all social institutions as responsible for education but in different ways.
9. Anthropocentrically oriented	Making the goal of education so apropos as to have the individual assume the responsibility for his own education.
10. Scientifically emancipating	Consisting in the subsumption of the individual under his species and his emancipation from this subsumption.

As the great philosopher-conservator, Harris paid qualified tribute to some educational reformers, such as John Dewey, but opposed the adoption of "fads." Thus he succeeded in keeping the schools fairly rigid in policies of organization, method, and point of view. He was one of the most sturdy champions of the textbook method of teaching (a method not sanctioned today by Piaget), for he thought it peculiarly well adapted to the needs of American children.[29] Harris believed that the Herbartian emphasis on interest as the motivating force in teaching went too far and frequently became a mere craze for novelty. Forgetting that interests are good, bad, and indifferent and should be furthered or repressed in accordance with what the child is to become rather than with what he desires at the moment, he evaluated the Herbartians as failing to appreciate the value of discipline.[30]

Yet, it would be unfair to Harris to overemphasize his role as a conservator of older and authoritarian educational methods and values. If he hesitated to recommend that teachers study "the new psychology" for fear that it would negate ethical and religious convictions, he admitted that this psychology could aid in such instances as determining the best length of study and recitation periods, and in preventing fatigue.[31] Although Harris stood for authority, discipline, and the lock-step method of teaching, he was too much of an individualist to favor the mechanization of the child. Neither did he hesitate to advocate the short-interval system by which the brighter and quicker students were more rapidly promoted and the duller ones given more frequent chances and new incentives.[32] He even anticipated by more than a century the stance of Jean Piaget that pedagogy cannot be directly deduced from psychology, but he was unable to perfect its implications. This torch the Swiss epistemologist is reigniting today.

In the spirit of Gestalt psychology, Harris opposed any unnecessary repetition or fragmentation in methods of instruction. He seemed to have sensed only partially what Piaget observes today:

> The contribution of Gestalt psychology has been, in effect, after having revolutionized the problems of perception in an extremely profound and useful way, to seek in perceptible structures, or "gestalts", the prototype of all other mental structures, including the rational or logico-mathematical ones.[33]

This ideal for learning and teaching Harris applied negatively. He discourages unwholesome analysis as too often resulting in an ". . . absorption in gazing upon adjustments within the machine and not seeing the machine as a whole. . . . For example, the habit of parsing every sentence that one reads may prevent one from enjoying a sonnet of Wordsworth."[34] The discipline and authority that he advocates are rational in character and enable the individual *freely* to subscribe to the law of the social whole to realize more fully his true, spiritual self.[35]

His philosophy of nationalism did not lead him to favor the teaching of the patriotism expressed in the slogan *My country, right or wrong*. Patriotic sentiment, like all sentiment, he said, could not be formally cultivated; it must, like the root of a plant, be well grounded. The teacher must encourage it, by appeals not to blind passion and to sentiment, but to reason.[36]

As superintendent of the St. Louis schools, he upheld the teaching of German, pointing out that when an immigrant population breaks suddenly with its past, there is apt to be a great loss in the stability of individual character. With a Hegelian respect for the ethos of each people, he encouraged the presence of an immigrant population to help promote tolerance, mutual respect, and a high degree of personal liberty.[37] At the same time he warned, so as not to make the country another Botany Bay,[38] against carrying out the idea that America was an asylum for the oppressed of Europe.

Through a personalized education for values, Harris hoped to enable the Indian to achieve more quickly a present higher stage of industrialization. By introducing him to the printed page, the school could help provide him with the ideals of Christianity and of civil society; this in turn would permit him to secure a greater possible freedom in the social whole.[39]

For the black, Harris thoroughly approved industrial training, which inculcates discipline and habits of regularity, obedience, self-control, cooperation, and industry. "The black must teach himself to become a capitalist," he declared. But in addition to industrial training, he insisted that the Negro must be given a cultural education. This would not only fit him for the professions but also introduce him to the roots of civilization and enable him to become better integrated with national life and patriotism.[40] It was, in short, he said, the historical mission of American education to incorporate these and other minority groups into self-government. Unlike European imperialists, universal education must elevate these primitive folk into a superior industrial civilization. For to fail to uplift these less advanced peoples would be to threaten the American ideal by sheer overweight of their number in an essentially undemocratic world.[41]

Piaget sees this problem of the less-advanced peoples as requiring a process of socialization:

The traditional school reduced all socialization, whether intellectual or moral, to a mechanism of constraint. The active school, on the contrary, makes a careful distinction in almost all its achievements between two processes that have very different results and become complementary only with much care and tact: the constraint exercised by the adult and the cooperation of the children with each other. The constraint exercised by the adult achieves results that are all the more considerable in that they answer to very profound tendencies in the child's mentality.[42]

At this point Piaget warns that excessive authority over children tends to suppress initative and self-determination in the development of the child. He sees cooperation among children themselves as having an importance in mental development as great as that of adult action. From the intellectual as well as from the moral influence, such cooperation results in a real exercise of the principles of behavior and not merely in submission to external constraint. Social life introduced into the classroom through effective collaboration implies the very ideals of morality in action. This is the active work of intelligence. It leads to an interrelationship of particular values. Those of justice based on equality and those of "organic" interdependence become of prime concern.[43]

Piaget does not advocate group participation in authority in place of the social action of the teacher. Instead he sees it as achieving a reconciliation. This creates respect for the adult and cooperation among the children. By reducing the constraint exercised by authority, there is a transformation into a higher, more beneficial form of cooperation. To quote Piaget regarding the cooperation of the children with each other, ". . . there exists a whole system of mutual aid based upon a 'special understanding,' as well as a sense *sui generis* of justice."[44]

Mann and Harris

Mann and Harris were kindred spirits steeped in the traditions of the Congregationalists and the Pilgrim Fathers. Both men abandoned their orthodoxy early in life without ceasing to be profoundly religious and influential characters; both advocated the radical reforms and the value philosophy of public school education. Harris's policies toward religion and character development in the public schools made him, like Horace Mann, the center of controversy.[45] The basic problems today within the learning-teaching process are difficult to appreciate in depth if the contributions of these educators to the nation's schools are ignored or misinterpreted. Similarly, the contributions of John Dewey can be evaluated constructively only in the framework and from the perspective of the work of William T. Harris:

Similarities Between Horace Mann and William T. Harris

1. Both were Yankees of Congregationalist affiliation who defected from traditional orthodoxy.
2. Both showed interest in the scientific and pseudoscientific philosophies of their day, especially in phrenology.
3. Both influenced the educational world through a series of masterly reports, prepared in discharging high supervisory offices, which attracted wide attention and are still regarded as models today.
4. Both promoted their educational work on the Atlantic seaboard as well as in the newer West.
5. Both wrote extensively and lectured widely on education and related topics.
6. Both enjoyed the high esteem of their educational contemporaries.
7. Both were centers of controversy in the policies toward religious values and character education they advocated for the public schools.
8. Both were deeply religious and had a profound influence on the American philosophy of the public schools.

In contrasting these similarities with like incidents in Piaget's life, one notes that:

1. Although there is no religious defection in Piaget's life, he nevertheless cuts through all forms of sectarianism, secularization, and nationalities to find the common basis for all orthodoxy in education today.
2. Both as a philosopher and a scientist, Piaget unites into one discipline the perspectives of Mann and Harris to refute the pseudoperspectives of their day.

3. Whereas Mann and Harris reported on child development in education, Piaget reports on his findings that penetrate the child's mind to reveal the stages of his mental development as basic.

4. Piaget's work is no longer limited to the European schools, but has taken on the international scene as its scope of influence, being presently very strong even in the United States.

5. Piaget's extensive writing and lecturing as a genetic epistemologist over the last fifty or more years have led educators to demand that Piaget be an educationalist or at least take up the important educational implications that his discipline defends. Unlike Mann and Harris, therefore, Piaget's contributions are great largely *because* of, rather than in spite of, his being neither an absolute philosopher nor a scientist *per se*.

6. Piaget is enjoying not only the high esteem of his contemporaries, but also profound respect and interest from his critics, opponents, and detractors.

7. Piaget is controversial in both the scientific and philosophical realms today because in his new discipline he is classified in a pejorative sense as a scholar turning from philosophical values and neglecting to appreciate the truly human aspects of the human person.

8. Although Piaget is not directly concerned with the religious aspects of the child, he does respect and provide for moral and ethical development, especially in his studies *The Moral Development of the Child* and *The Child's Conception of the World*, both of which are used extensively today with reference to character formation and moral education in the schools.

These developmental characteristics and attributes contrasting Mann, Harris, and Piaget provoke the following challenging integrations with education today:

MANN AND HARRIS CONTRASTED IN THE LIGHT OF PIAGETIAN CONCEPTS TODAY

It is critically important to realize that whereas Mann and Harris contribute activities for developing the child, Piaget presents his findings on the mental development and thought process of the child.

HORACE MANN experienced what he termed the unspeakable calamity of a Calvinistic education. It led him to abandon Calvinism and to spend his life as a public servant combating sectarianism in all its forms.

In so doing Mann lays the foundation of the American Common School System. He strives toward an oriented, religious-centered, educational philosophy constructed on a nonsectarian program of studies and educational activities.

Jean Piaget (cf. chaps. 7 and 8) experienced a disenchantment with philosophy early in his professional career that led him from would-be philosopher to the career of a psychologist and genetic epistemologist.

He created a new discipline, genetic epistemology. Teaching and learning can now be placed in a scientific perspective of research on a par with other professions.

He established a revolutionary theory of developmental interaction whereby equilibration is the internal regulatory factor: it reveals the child's own mechanisms of intelligence as a self-regulatory activity that begins before language and goes far beyond language.

He developed an operative concept of intelligence presented as thinking in action. Perceptions, as images, as language, are applicable to any content areas of interest. They extend from earliest years in sensorimotor intelligence through the formal operational stage of adolescence and adulthood.

WILLIAM T. HARRIS became immersed in college with the exhilaration of the reformer who sees the evils of the past and knows the true remedy.

He found a natural basis for an inventory of the powers of the mind in Hegelianism and consequently an ideal standard of perfect development. This he utilized as the basis for criticizing all human views and actions.

In applying Hegelianism, he presided over the building and growth of the common school.

MANN AND HARRIS CONTRASTED IN THE LIGHT OF PIAGETIAN CONCEPTS TODAY *(Continued)*

He devoted himself to realizing the unifying value philosophy that has kept the common school system in existence even to the present day.

Mann won the unique distinction of being called the father of the common school, but is considered an iconoclast in his radical reforms.

Intelligence is a general human capacity that biologists call *characteristic of a species.* Originating in the creative, intelligence feeds back from its own general mechanisms of action. Piaget identified the child as constructive and inventive in his responses of thinking and acting.

He developed within a process perspective a provision for individual differences. He recognized laws and stages of mental development within the full range of normal variations. He utilized a developmental motivation for educators to build upon. The child is discerned as possessing an "internal need to know," causing him to seek and select from his environment, with the educator providing but the child deciding.

He proposed the development of the greatest educational resource, the ability and eagerness of each individual to learn, through the active school, instead of stifling him by an inactive school of "cognitive passivity."

Piaget touched the four areas of educational concern—the assessment of intellectual capacity, the structure and sequencing of subject matter, the evaluation of learning outcomes, and the generation of appropriate learning atmospheres.

Harris furnished the common school system with a philosophy of public education. It enabled the poor and middle classes to adjust their perspectives of thinking and feeling to new actualities without retaining the traditional values and beliefs.

Harris devoted himself to such a complete separation between the religious and the secular that public education today is totally secularized.

For his radical reforms he is still considered "The Conservator."

He saw the problem of teacher training as the key problem today. Upon its solution the fate of the schools depends, because teachers must be given more initiative, more freedom, and a better foundation in child psychology with research.

Piaget provided the schools with foundation principles of mental development whereby teachers can now plan better *what* to teach *when* and *how*.

It is Piaget's concepts of the child's thought processes in mental development that must be integrated into American education today—if America will accept them!

Young Harris had caught the radical virus that had contaminated the solidarity and complacency of New England. Having moved on to St. Louis for broader freedom of thought,

> he became converted to phrenology, mesmerism, and the claims and promises of "natural science," repudiated a good deal of the orthodox Congregationalism with which he had been indoctrinated, and turned his back on the authoritarianism of the classics. While he did not, apparently, interest himself in Fourierism or any radical economic doctrines, he was nevertheless a come-outer. Theodore Parker's writings led him to study German philosophy; and he became, and continued to his death, an ardent student of Kant, Fichte, and above all, of Hegel.[46]

Hegelianism and Harris

In 1858 Harris met Henry C. Brockmeyer, who greatly encouraged him to devote himself to the study of German philosophy. This experience resulted in what became the St. Louis Movement and the establishing of the St. Louis Philosophical Society, with the philosophy of Georg Hegel (1770–1831) as the dominant influence in values.[47]

Due to trouble in the German states, many families of German extraction emigrated to the freer shores of the United States. The St. Louis Movement welcomed them with the great opportunities only dreamed of in Europe. It was the Philosophical Society of St. Louis, too, that attracted many of these immigrants and their cultural groups along with the prominent social leaders of the day. John Dewey is credited with obtaining the inspiration for his start from the St. Louis Movement, and with belonging to it in spite of his not thinking so, or even his denial of it.[48]

In 1867 Harris began one of the really great American landmarks in American educational history. He launched *The Journal of Speculative Philosophy*, which he continued to edit for twenty-one years (in *The Journal* John Dewey published his first articles):[49]

The refusal of the editors of *The North American Review* and *The Atlantic Monthly* to publish a criticism of Spencer led Harris, when but thirty-two years old, to found in St. Louis *The Journal of Speculative Philosophy* which he continued to edit through twenty-two volumes, and which familiarized many Americans with German idealistic philosophy, as well as with Greek thought, and their applications to aesthetics and the more practical problems of life.[50]

By popularizing the absolute idealism of Hegel through *The Journal,* Harris provided able and authoritarian support for traditional views:

In fact the Hegelian philosophy which he made the basis of all his social and educational thinking possessed the virtue of being thoroughly optimistic and idealistic in character, infusing the world with a divine purpose and endowing the individual with a noble and immortal destiny by lifting him to a higher plane of self-realization.[51]

In this perspective Hegelianism has its great impact upon American education:

Tenets of Hegelianism Basic to Education

1. Members of the State create the State, its arrangements, and its laws.
2. Possessions of the members of the State are the State's natural resources, its mountains, air, and waters are their country, their fatherland, their outward material prosperity.
3. Achievements of the members of the State contribute to the history of their State.
4. Personal effects of members of the State are what their ancestors have produced. They belong to them and live in their memory. All are their possessions, just as they are possessed by it; for it constitutes their existence, their very being.
5. To the State belongs each of its members; each unit is the Son of his Nation, and at the same time—insofar as the State to which he belongs is undergoing development—the Son of his Age.
6. Duties and rights of the members of the State have the two-

fold aspect that what the State demands as duty should directly be the right of the individual.

7. In education, the State possesses almost absolute power, for it is antecedent to the individual, to the family, to the local community, and to the church. It guards individual and social rights, as well as material goods and culture. Should the autonomy of the State be suppressed, the consequences are certain to retard progress in all elements of civilization.

8. The State is nothing but the organization of the concept of *freedom*. The determinations of the individual will are given objectivity by the State and it is through the State alone that they attain truth and realization. The State is the sole condition for the attainment of any particular end or good.

Gradually *The Journal,* previously the forum for Hegelianism, also became the platform for American philosophers, notably Peirce, James, and Dewey. Through it they exercised their tremendous influence on the philosophy of education and its process of greater growth and development in the schools.[52]

In 1866 the St. Louis Philosophical Society came into existence. It was the actual fruition of a new value-relevance of a previous eight-year influential study that Harris and his friends inaugurated, together with Henry C. Brockmeyer (later Lieutenant-Governor of Missouri and writer of the state Constitution). Through it German philosophy in its special affinity with that of Hegel continued to inject itself into the bloodstream of American culture and education. Even John Dewey admitted being significantly affected by it. In his pursuits, however, Harris seems to have never understood what Piaget terms "the main problem":

The main problem is then that of the "meaning of meaning." I believe that this fundamental concept of "meaning," which is at the center of all contemporary philosophical reflection, hides a no less important ambiguity. . . . In short, a "meaning" and, moreover, "for man" has always at least two meanings, one cognitive and the other vital. It seems to me that one plays a little too easily on words in wishing to combine them into a single concept of "meaning," however close they may be in certain cases.[53]

Harris and Brockmeyer had exceptional appeal for young people, who were attracted to their Philosophical Society. Most of their activities took place in and around the St. Louis public school system.[54] Hegel's philosophy was applied to all the problems connected with teaching and with school management.

One of the chief reasons for the nationwide influence of Harris was the exceptional amount of thought-provoking writing that he performed. His personal view was that any thoughts considered important should be printed and then disseminated, no matter how obscure the publications in which they appeared. He flooded the educational and philosophical world with his material. The Library of Congress Journal of Current Acquisitions (11: 3) indicates that the complete papers of Dr. Harris amounted to about 13,475 items when they were presented to the Library of Congress by his daughter in 1953.[55] There is a striking parallelism here between Harris and Piaget, for both have published a vast amount of information regarding their activities.

Harris mastered Hegel's relevance of values, applied it consistently, and found very little in the line of his own basic principles to alter over the years:

> By the use of the dialectic method of resolving antitheses into higher syntheses, Hegelian philosophy also permitted the exploitation of science for social and economic purposes without sacrificing religion and the concerns of the spirit as ultimate values. In short, the rightwing Hegelianism to which Harris subscribed satisfied religious and idealistic aspirations, paid tribute to the cult of individuality and self-help, and at the same time subordinated the mass of individuals to existing institutions, which included the corporation, the city, and the machine, as well as religion and the national state.[56]

> Thus Christianity was an indispensable institution for securing the proper relationship between the individual and the universal, the temporal and the eternal.[57]

As a Hegelian he emphasized the inevitability of conflicts that ensue when a new and deeper idea emerges.[58] Harris's definition of education gives the clue to his philosophy of education, which he based on the Hegelian concept of institutions. He understood education to be the *process* through which each person becomes ethical, that is, takes on the forms [values] by which he is able to live more humanly in society.[59]

Through the exercise of reason, aided by school discipline and guidance, students acquired ethical habits. By insisting that the natural sciences become the principal burden of the curriculum, Harris envisioned each student as realizing his own limitless moral potential in process within the world of nature. Jean Piaget too points out today that the new methods of education

> seek to encourage this adaptation [of the individual to the surrounding social environment] by making use of the impulses inherent in childhood itself, allied with the spontaneous activity that is inseparable from mental development.[60]

As a countermovement to the radical denials of conservative religious orthodoxy, the St. Louis Movement preserved the traditional values then under attack in the ever-widening conflict between naturalism and idealism within the schools. As defender of philosophical and religious ideals, Harris asserted that right and wrong in moral training rested on the nature of man, the structure of the universe, and all of the sciences, rather than on the so-called freethinking of the times,[61] for

> indeed[,] he was a pioneer in welcoming the application of science to the affairs of everyday life and in urging the introduction of the sciences into the school curriculum.[62]

Harris recognized the inevitability of the "machine age." He was also aware of many of the contradictions of cultural and spiritual values it implied. In addition to the teaching of social studies, fine arts, music, and vocational arts, Harris encouraged a more dynamic approach to character education through an institutional morality.[63] Responsible for broadening manual studies, he expresses sympathy for the establishment of manual trade schools for children "unwilling to carry any further their purely cultural studies." Harris, somewhat in the spirit of Dewey, wished these schools to teach not merely the narrow skills and techniques, but the broader aspects of trade—its place in society and its relation to the traditions and needs of civilization.[64]

Moreover, students in the trade schools, having acquired the tool subjects in elementary school, might through the newspaper and the public library continue to enrich themselves in cultural and nontechnical values.[65]

Viewing man in himself and by himself as an insignificant being, isolated from community and barely able to transcend savagery, Harris maintained that social institutions were indispensable. As a social being, man possessed the potential to achieve a living transformation within himself through the institutions of the family, the school, the state, and the church. All of these provided the necessary guidance to help him realize his rational self, which is the greatest potential of the human race:

By social combination each gives his individual mite to the whole and receives in turn the aggregate gift of the social whole, thus making him rich by an infinite return.[66]

Conservatism[67]

Whereas Harris provided the people with able and authoritarian support for their traditional views, Piaget asserts that Hegel, as an empiricist in the domain of sociology, contributes more to the scientific side:

Whereas the great philosophers of the past all contributed in some way to the scientific movements of their time, or anticipated possible lines of research . . . [so too is it true] with the empiricists in the case of psychology, and Hegel in the case of sociology.[68]

This prudent conservatism of Harris, based on the tenets of Hegelianism, is the more striking because of his realization of what it meant to live in an age of transition. Changes in industry and social conditions compelled him to declare it indispensable that each individual be educated for the power of adapting himself to his particular circumstances and of readjusting in emergencies. Such education would aid each individual in so adapting himself to the social whole that he might realize his true ethical self. Sociology, Harris stated, is "the science of a combination of men into social wholes."[69]

With regard to "social wholes" and the child, Piaget declares that

> it is doubtless true that the child is free to put a greater or lesser degree of interest and personal effort into that work, insofar as the teacher [representing the social wholes] is a good one and the collaboration that takes place between his students and himself will leave an appreciable margin for genuine activity.[70]

In his educational philosophy Harris ranked the school as a bridge between the family and civil society, participating in the nature of both.[71] By forming a socialized transition from the family into civil society and the church, Harris saw the school as conducting a training for the immature, preparatory to constructive participation in all the other complex forms of life.[72]

Harris insisted that other institutions ought to share cooperatively with the school in the vast responsibility of educating.[73] Proclaiming it an impossibility for the school to provide a complete education, he maintained that it could merely teach the person to further his own education by aiding him to understand the printed page and instructing him in the proper use of his social opportunities. Compared to the other institutions, he did not consider the school the most important.

In spite of the technical nature of Hegelianism, he harmonized it with the character of the American scene. Without sacrificing the old American ideals of self-help and laissez-faire, he utilized Hegelianism to stimulate the individual. Surprisingly, Harris justified the existing order by declaring: "*Whatever is, is right.*"

According to Harris's educational philosophy, all social institutions have an ethical duty. The school has the particular responsibility of educating toward the knowledge of truth, appreciation of the beautiful, and the habit of doing good. Consequently,

> as superintendent of St. Louis Schools and as editor of a series of school readers he did a good deal to familiarize American school children with the great literary masterpieces of the past, and he was also an early champion of instruction in art. . . . for the most part he advocated art instruction as a means of cultivating the feelings and curbing the appetites, and of so transcending the beauty of nature as to permit man to realize the divine.[74]

Harris maintained that the immature person is united with his fellows; that he therefore participates in the great work of civilization and culture, and even perfects himself in the image of God.[75] It is this moral imperative that must operate on all levels of education. Harris saw blind faith as becoming transformed into intellectual and moral insight. As Piaget writes:

> The intellectual and moral structures of the child are not the same as ours. . . . But with regard to mental functioning, the child is, in fact, identical with the adult. . . . Just as a tadpole already breathes, though with different organs from those of the frog, so the child acts like the adult, but employing a mentality whose structure varies according to the stages of its development.[76]

Dr. Harris is distinguished as one who fights to preserve what he considers the heritage of humanity. Within the process of public school education, he was always prudently discriminating and slow to accept the untried and the new. By declaring the school a product of civilization and by integrating it with all the forces of society, he gave it less importance in the educative process than the family, the church, the civil community, and

the state.[77] His position of promoting education as a shared
responsibility represents a radical change from the perspective
of his ancestors in Calvinistic New England:

EDUCATION AS A SHARED RESPONSIBILITY
The School in 17th-Century America
FAMILY
CHURCH SCHOOL
[State]
The School in 20th-Century America
FAMILY SCHOOL STATE
[Church]

Therefore,

> unlike Mann and Dewey, he did not expect that the school
> could contribute substantially to the creation of a new order,
> even had he thought one desirable. As an Hegelian, he be-
> lieved that improvement would take place in any case and
> by necessity; that the school was an agent, not for guiding
> the change, but for preserving the values of the past and
> adjusting the individual to society.[78]

Reforms in Education

Harris's struggling with reforms is understandable in the
light of Hegelianism, for Piaget declares that:

> Hegel's dialectic system can be seen as based on sociological
> considerations, in a way foreshadowing the emergence of
> sociology as an independent science.[79]

In applying Hegel's dialectic, therefore, Harris lends his influence to certain reforms:

> An early advocate of co-education, he desired [that] women
> enjoy not only the highest cultural type of learning but
> professional training as well. At the twenty-fifth anniversary
> of Smith College Harris declared that the progress of science,
> the conquest of nature by means of invention, the elimination

of brute strength as a result of mechanical operations, and the achievements of women in higher education assured them of securing their share in the division of labor and in political control.[80]

He also approved the movement for instruction in temperance in the schools. Believing that it would furnish a permanent and active means for disseminating correct views regarding the effects of alcohol on the human body, he wrote: "It may be said that this movement is the most effective one ever devised by the friends of temperance to abate a great evil, perhaps the greatest evil abroad in our land."[81]

In the midst of the knotty problems of evolution as advanced by Darwin, Harris saw in natural selection something only preliminary. He reported that ". . . the study of the totality of its history will reveal to us the purpose—the final cause—the teleology—of the struggle for existence in a living process."[82] Years later he gave evolution its due, stating that science was only beginning to substitute an immanent teleology for the old doctrine. This relevance of process is of even greater importance in education now, when teleology is becoming more and more a chief issue of the identity crisis.

Harris's interest and success in giving a truly international perspective to value perspectives in education can hardly be ignored. What American has with greater emphasis endeavored to elevate to such an idealistic plane the imperialism on which the U.S. embarked toward the turn of the century? At the end of the Spanish-American War expansion was held to be inevitable. "It was, moreover, our duty to show that we could govern backward peoples for their own benefit," Harris declared.

He did not hesitate to use the same arguments in favor of U.S. imperialism regarding the historical mission to help liberate peoples toward self-government. He argued that through universal education primitive folk could be elevated into a superior, industrial civilization. He especially hoped to incorporate the Indians and blacks into the nation. To prevent the sheer overweight of mere numbers among the uneducated from threatening the American ideal in an essentially undemocratic world,[83] Harris insisted that it was necessary to

> teach the Filipinos and Puerto Ricans how to command their physical environment, how to participate in the cultural achievements of the race, and how to further both. To that end we must help not one class of these islanders, but all classes, for the highest ideal of civilization demanded for the lower classes participation in all that was "good and reasonable" and increased self-activity or individuality.[84]

Stressing that imperialism thrust new responsibilities on his countrymen, Harris believed that public education must not be indifferent to them. He welcomed the training that Oxford provided through Rhodes Scholarships to young men capable of becoming administrators in these new territories. He wanted them to be in a position to advance the democratic influence in the councils of the world.[85] Acclaiming that "the new era [is] one of the great portents of American influence on our foreign relations,"[86] he stressed a closer union with Europe:

> We must study foreign literature to understand the basis of foreign opinion and foreign psychology; we must more adequately prepare our young men for the diplomatic service. Our elementary education, however, was not to be altered even in view of the change involved in the emergence of the United States as a world power.[87]

Piaget has also been especially concerned with the international aspects of education:

> In 1929 he was appointed a director of the International Board of Education. After the war he gave generously of his time to UNESCO and became a member of its executive council. . . . Until the summer of 1971 he was the director of his own research institute, the International Center of Genetic Epistemology as well as co-director of the Institute of Educational Science. Students come from all over the world to Geneva to study.[88]

Moral vs. Religious Education

The key to Harris's world outlook in American education is the dictum of Hegel: "The will *wills* will!"[89] His pivotal idea is the universal extension and freeing of man's self-activity. His liberating basis is the existential relationship among art, philosophy, and religion. As they apply to education, he sees philosophy as the piety of the intellect, religion as the piety of the heart, and art as the piety of the senses.[90]

Art, for Harris, is the full realization of the beautiful, an expression under which nations and peoples breathe forth the highest ambitions in their consciousness. In his perspective, art becomes, for values in process, one of the finest products of man's creativity dealing with the beautiful, the good, and the true.

In Harris's philosophy of man, self-actualization receives as much emphasis as self-expression. Because a true consciousness of self is the framework of all knowledge in man, as proposed in the Socratic dictum "Know thyself," Harris makes this real state of awareness a person's chief responsibility. In principle he is reflecting the promptings of John W. Gardner:

> The ultimate goal of the educational system is to shift to the individual the burden of pursuing his own education. This will not be a widely shared pursuit until we get over our odd conviction that education is what goes on in school buildings and nowhere else. Not only does education continue when schooling ends, but it is not confined to what may be studied in adult education courses. The world is an incomparable classroom, and life is a memorable teacher for those who aren't afraid of her.[91]

In his philosophy of moral education Harris stood for strict discipline in the schools. Defining it as a proper balance among intellect and will and emotions within the student himself, he saw how clearly it appealed directly to the will. Because it encouraged self-knowledge, inhibited unruly impulses, and assisted in the acquiring of habits of wholesome self-control, he pointed out that it enabled the student, in his own awareness of himself, to exercise freely and gladly those essentials of moral action necessary in forming his character.

In his position as superintendent of the St. Louis public schools, Harris confronted the great controversy regarding religion. It was the same challenge that Horace Mann found so difficult in his position as secretary of the Board of Education in New England. But whereas Mann encouraged what he considered basic religious principles common to all religions and not distinctive of any single sect, Harris did not. Whereas Mann promoted within the classrooms a general knowledge and love of those very principles upon which all human beings should govern their relationship with their fellow men, Harris did not. Whereas in Mann's philosophy the schools as a public service were to take the initiative in assuming a major responsibility for moral and religious values, including the reading of the Bible, in Harris's they were not.

In accepting the office of superintendent, Harris continued the policy he inherited, which had been inaugurated as early as 1838. With the dedication of the first public school in St. Louis, the people unanimously decided not to have any religious exercises or reading of the Bible in their common schools.[92]

Through the carefully nurtured educational philosophy of Harris, this early position of 1838 continued. Since full reponsibility for a complete education did not rest on the public school but on all the institutions of society in proper hierarchical order, beginning with the family, he carried out the mandate of 1838 conscientiously.

The chief source of trouble in harmonizing so many conflicting views on the place of religion in values education was the failure to discriminate between what Harris called religion and morals. Harris claimed that religion was not morality nor morality religion. His reason was a very simple one, namely, that morality as behavior could be taught and was best taught in school without bringing in any religious instruction. By achieving a complete divorce between religion and the schools, the secular branches of instruction could be taught with greater success.

Since the principle of religious instruction always involves authority, while that of secular instruction involves demonstration and verification, Harris maintained that, to avoid any possible hostility of one toward the other, the two should not be brought together in the school. In view of so many differences in both method and content, he concluded that the school could not be successful in undertaking religious instruction, whereas the church and the home could:

> This doctrine is not based on the denial of the supreme importance of religion, but on the principle that the modern state exists for the realization of one of the principles unfolded by religion and that this moral function can be performed only when the two exist independently.[93]

From his probing of young minds, Piaget provides additional insights today into Harris's tenets of moral education. He finds that

> the essence of morality is respect for a system of rules. . . . Children, particularly after they enter school, develop a strong sense of solidarity with their peer group. They stand united against what they consider "unfair."[94]

The earliest concept of justice, for example, Piaget found to be based on retribution. Morality based on cooperation, however, can develop out of a childhood morality based on parental or teacher authority. Gradually children begin to think of right and wrong in terms of the circumstances of the person involved rather than in terms of "retributive justice" only. When the adult is strong and demanding, the child, Piaget found, feels weak and inferior. Unilateral respect leads for the most part to moral constraint only.[95] The factor essential to moral development therefore is mutual respect and cooperation between children to begin with, and then between child and adult as the child approaches adolescence, and comes secretly at least to consider himself as the adult's equal.[96]

Harris's view of nonsectarian religion, then, was very different from that of Horace Mann. He saw no place for the Bible in the school. He maintained that it was not possible to have any nonsectarian religion that would not be sectarian to some religious denominations.[97] To draw up a list of essentials in religion for the public schools, he advised, "would serve only to impart religious instruction in a new religious denomination and thus, to add another sect to those already existing." Whereas, as R. J. Gabel wrote of Horace Mann:

Mann, who was so bitter toward man-made dogmas, sacrificed no religious conviction in enforcing the elimination of "sectarian" (doctrinal) views that he never believed in anyway. He fought for his own religious belief—the Scriptures as a source of morals—and he secured for the public schools of Massachusetts precisely what his "sectarian" College of Antioch (Unitarian-Christian) advocated, "non-sectarian" religion based upon the Bible.[98]

Apparently Horace Mann never realized that, with his approach to the sectarian problem, others might, with good reason, accuse him of sectarianism. Harris saw in Mann's solution merely another religious sect, and argued that "nonsectarianism" was impossible, and that there was no such thing as a nondenominational religion. Religion and the state schools must therefore be distinct, to safeguard individual liberty and the right to follow the dictates of conscience. There could be but one conclusion: the proper places for religious instruction were the church and the home.

Harris's Justification

Finally, as United States Commissioner of Education, Harris pleaded for the exclusion of religion from all of the nation's schools, regardless of their means of support—private and public and on all levels—in which instruction in secular subjects was given.

All institutions in society, he emphasized, were responsible for character education, but not each one in the same way. The school could be a very effective agent in moral development because of the atmosphere of discipline it created. "This atmosphere is so conducive to moral development and habit formation that it actually has the potential to lay the foundation for religious education imparted by the church." Because of its authoritarian power and sacred surroundings, Harris considered the church alone as being able to teach religious truths effectively, and in this sense too, Bible reading has no place in the school. As a religious exercise, he felt, it required the authority and ceremonial of the church. In the final analysis, any "nonsectarian" teaching regarding religion in the public schools amounted to forming merely another religious sect. The school should, by its very nature, attend exclusively to secular learning and teaching, as based on the following:

Tenets of Harris's Secularization[99]

VALUES	PERSPECTIVES
1. Bible	Bible reading is banned in the schools because only the Church in its authoritative methods and sacred surroundings can properly communicate religious truth. Religious education is assigned exclusively to the Church.
2. Primary Aim of Education	The secular itself is of such vital importance that it must be freed from sectarian bias of every kind. Religion and the state must be separate to secure the highest perfection of each. Education must separate secular and religious "to prevent the weakening of the former and the corruption of the latter," even to such an extent as "almost to secularize our parochial schools."

3. Character Formation	The direct responsibility of the school is to form character. "Whatever separation may be made of religion, morality must be provided for." In this sense the school has charge of moral education developed in and through moral discipline and related concepts of theism from natural law. As integral to this natural base, Harris lists five great duties of school discipline: (1) punctuality, (2) regularity, (3) silence, (4) truth, and (5) industry.
4. Natural Religion	The complete dismissal of nonsectarian or natural religion is necessary in the common schools "to promote a nonsectarian religion."
5. Religious Instruction	The great lesson of history, Harris emphasizes, is that the separation of Church and State is the safeguard of individual liberty. Freedom for all to follow the dictates of conscience is the cornerstone of republican institutions. These can never flourish except upon the conviction that secular instruction itself is of such vital importance as to need separation from religious instruction. Moral instruction, however, must be given.

Because of these secularized tenets in his philosophy of education, Harris's opponents charged him with being a German rationalist, atheist, Deist, free-thinker, agnostic, skeptic, and even an infidel.[100] As an adherent of the Hegelian interpretation of process history and education,

Harris loved to dwell on the peculiar mission of the Hebrews, the Greeks, the Romans, the Anglo-Saxons, and their American offspring. The Hebrews gave the race the realization of a monotheistic God, personal immortality, and divine will; the Greeks, individuality and beauty; the Romans, law, organization, contract, and private property; the Anglo-Saxons, local self-government, which still further emancipated the individual from authority; and the Americans carried on the process by providing the individual with an even greater freedom in local self-government, in public education, and in industry.[101]

The condemnation of Harris by his critics is not dissimilar to that by Piaget's contemporaries in Europe when he published his own account and analysis of his philosophical disenchantment, *Insights and Illusions of Philosophy*. As stated by Furth:

> Philosophers on the continent . . . respond to Piaget's work by classifying him in a pejorative sense as a "positivist," a scholar who has turned from philosophical values and neglects therefore the truly human aspect of the human person.[102]

This stance, however, is far from being universal. In fact, Piagetian psychology became the dominant one of the 1960s and 1970s. As his new discipline, genetic epistemology, has slowly displaced doubt and won admiration and acceptance, its prospects of becoming the outstanding educational discipline of all time are excellent. An amazing attribute of Piaget is his talent for providing an experimental and philosophical principle for every phase or facet of education.

Acclaimed in the selfsame strain in a eulogy of Harris are the tributes of his supporters, such as educators Ella Flagg Young, William Maxwell, James M. Greenwood, W. S. Sutton, Frank A. Fitzpatrick, George P. Brown, and A. E. Winship. James H. Canfield further observed that in his time Harris was one of the best loved as well as the most widely known and influential educators "in this or any other country."[103] In his case, however, what Albert Camus stated in *The Rebel* is equally applicable to Harris as a justification for his conservatism: "Progress, paradoxically, can be used to justify conservatism."[104]

SELECT
CHRONOLOGY OF HARRIS'S WORKS

Manuscripts[105]

The Collected Harris Papers, approximately 13,475 items, are in the Library of Congress, Washington, D.C.

Source material relating to the St. Louis Movement is in the Archives of the Missouri Historical Society, St. Louis, Mo.

Books and Articles[106]

1868–79   The Twelve Annual Reports of the St. Louis Public Schools for the Years 1868–79. (Harris also prepared the Superintendent's Report for 1867.)

1889–1906   Reports of the U.S. Commissioner of Education for the Years 1889–1906.

1867   "Herbert Spencer," *Journal of Speculative Philosophy* 1: 6–22 (preface dated December 1867).

1869   *Hegel's First Principle: An Exposition of Comprehension and Idea* (Begriff und Idee). St. Louis: George Knapp and Co.

1870   "The Immortality of the Soul," *Journal of Speculative Philosophy* 4: 97–111.

"Why Patronize the Public Schools," *American Journal of Education* (St. Louis) 2 (February): 103–4.

1871   "The Theory of American Education," *American Journal of Education* (St. Louis) 4 (January): 3.

"Nature versus Human Nature, or the Spiritual" (unsigned), *American Journal of Education* (St. Louis) 3 (January): 4–5.

"How Far May the State Provide for the Education of Her Children at Public Cost?" (Reprint of address to the National Education Association Meeting in St. Louis, August 23, 1871.)

1872   "Nature and Importance of Moral Training," in the *Seventeenth Annual Report of the Board of Directors of the St. Louis Public Schools for the Year Ending August 1, 1871.* St. Louis: Plate, Oldhausen and Co., pp. 21–37.

1874   "On Hegel's Philosophic Method," *Journal of Speculative Philosophy* 8 (January): 35–48.

"Participation, the Essence of Spiritual Life," *American Journal of Education* (St. Louis) 7 (February): 3–4.

"Church and State," *The Western* (St. Louis) 1 (March) : 113–36.

"The Study of Evolution in Education," *American Journal of Education* (St. Louis) 7 (July): 1.

Edited with Duane Doty. *A Statement of the Theory of Education in the United States of America.* Washington: U.S. Bureau of Education.

1875 "On the Relation of the Will to the Intellect, or the Regulative Principle in Human Life," *The Western* (St. Louis), n.s. 1 (February) : 102–9.

"Moral Education, I," *American Journal of Education* (St. Louis) 8 (October) : 4–5.

"Moral Education, II," *American Journal of Education* (St. Louis) 8 (November) : 4–5.

1876 "Moral Education, III," *American Journal of Education* (St. Louis) 9 (January): 4.

"The Relation of Religion to Art," *Journal of Speculative Philosophy* 10 (April) : 204–15.

"The Division of School Funds for Religious Purposes," *Atlantic Monthly* 38 (August) : 171–84.

1877 "The Idea of the State and its Necessity," *The Western* (St. Louis), n.s. 3 (March) : 206–15.

Moral Education in the Public Schools. New York: E. Steiger.

1881 "Thoughts on the Basis of Agnosticism," *Journal of Speculative Philosophy* 15 (April) : 113–20.

"The Philosophy of Religion," *Journal of Speculative Philosophy* 15 (April): 207–15.

"Kant and Hegel in the History of Philosophy," *Journal of Speculative Philosophy* 15 (July): 241–52.

"The Church, the State, and the School," *North American Review* 133 (September) : 215–27.

1882 "The Education of the Family and the Education of the School," *Journal of Social Science* 15 (February) : 1–5.

"The History and Philosophy of Education," *Chautauquan* 3 (October) : 28–30.

"On the Crime of Educating the People in Free Common Schools," *Journal of Education* (New England and National) 16 (November 2) : 227–28.

1883   "Other Institutions besides the School as Instrumentalities of Culture," *Journal of Social Science* 17 (May) : 133–55.

"Philosophy in Outline," *Journal of Speculative Philosophy* 17 (July): 296–316; (October) : 337–56.

With W. A. Mowry, J. H. Hoose, H. S. Tarbell, and G. S. Hall. "Moral Education in Schools"—Report of the Committee on Moral Education to the National Council of Education, *Education* 3 (September) : 1–14.

1884   "Moral Education in the Common Schools," *Journal of Social Science* 18 (May) : 122–34.

"On the Relation of the College to the Common School," in *American Institute of Instruction Lectures, 1883*. Boston: American Institute of Instruction, pp. 139–71.

1885   "Immortality of the Individual," *Journal of Speculative Philosophy* 19 (April) : 189–219.

"Is Pantheism the Legitimate Outcome of Modern Science?" *Journal of Speculative Philosophy* 19 (October) : 407–28.

"Psychological Inquiry," *Education* 6 (November): 156–68.

Compulsory Education in Relation to Crime and Social Morals. Washington, D.C.

"Emerson's Philosophy of Nature." In F. B. Sanborn, ed., *The Genius and Character of Emerson: Lectures Delivered at the Concord School*. Boston: James R. Osgood and Co., pp. 339–63.

"Emerson's Relation to Goethe and Carlyle." In F. B. Sanborn, ed., *The Genius and Character of Emerson: Lectures Delivered at the Concord*

School. Boston: James R. Osgood and Co., pp. 386–419.

1886   "Religion in Art, 1," *Chautauquan* 6 (January): 190–93.

"Religion in Art, 2," *Chautauquan* 6 (February): 255–58.

"Religion in Art, 3," *Chautauquan* 6 (March): 314–16.

"How I was Educated," *Forum* 1 (August) : 552–61.

"Goethe's Faust." In F. B. Sanborn, ed., *The Life and Genius of Goethe: Lectures at the Concord School of Philosophy*. Boston: Ticknor and Co., pp. 368–445.

1887   "Books That Have Helped Me," *Forum* 3 (April): 142–51.

1888   "What Shall the Public Schools Teach?" *Forum* 4 (February) : 573–81.

"The Present Need of Moral Training in the Public Schools," *Journal of Education* (New England and National) 27 (March 1): 131–32.

"The Church and the State," *True Educator* 4 (April) : 122–23.

1889   "Our Public Schools: Can Morality Be Taught without Sectarianism?" (Symposium) , *Journal of Education* (New England and National) 29 (February 14) : 1.

"Windows of the Soul," *Indian School Journal* 34 (February) : 85–86.

"On the Normal School Course of Study," in *Report of the Alumnae Association, State Normal School, Framingham, Mass.* (July 2) . Boston, Mass., pp. 10–33.

Art Education: The True Industrial Education. Papers on School Issues of the Day, III. Syracuse: C. W. Bardeen.

Morality in the Schools. Register Tract #12. Boston: Christian Register Association.

The Psychology of Manual Training. (Reprint from *Education,* May, 1888 [hand corrected to 1889].)

1890   "Value of School Discipline," *Pennsylvania School Journal* 39 (July): 27–28.

Hegel's Logic. A Book on the Genesis of the Categories of the Mind. A Critical Exposition. (German Philosophical Classics, under the editorship of G. S. Morris.) Chicago: S. C. Griggs.

The Philosophy of Crime and Punishment. (Reprint of paper read before the National Prison Association.) Cincinnati, Ohio.

Thoughts on Educational Psychology. (Reprint of a series of papers in the *Illinois School Journal.*) Bloomington, Ill.: The Public School Publishing Co.

1891   "The Best Works on Pedagogy for Young Teachers," *Journal of Education* (New England and National) 33 (February 26) : 131.

"Dante's Doctrine of Sin," in *Year-Book of the American Dante Society, 1890–91.* New York: American Dante Society, pp. 69–81.

"Vocation versus Culture; or the Two Aspects of Education," in *American Institute of Instruction Lectures,* 1891, Boston: American Institute of Instruction, pp. 1–20.

1892   "Our Educational System: What it is; Why it is; What it Accomplishes," *Chautauquan* 15 (April): 16–20.

Public Schools in the District of Columbia. Report made in compliance with a requirement of the Act of Congress, July 14, 1892; Letter from the Secretary of the Interior. Senate Executive Document No. 12, 52nd Congress, 2nd Session. Washington: U. S. Government Printing Office.

1893   "Herbart and Pestalozzi Compared," *Educational Review* 5 (May) : 417–23.

With F. B. Sanborn. *A. Bronson Alcott: His Life and Philosophy.* 2 vols. Boston: Roberts Brothers.

"In Memoriam: Brother Azarias" (holograph in Harris collection, #320, Library of Congress).

"School Statistics and Morals." (Reprint from the *Journal of Proceedings and Addresses of the National Education Association,* 1893.)

1895   "The Old Psychology vs. the New," *Journal of Education* (New England and National) 41 (May 2): 295.

"Herbart's Doctrine of Interest," *Educational Review* 10 (June): 71–80.

"Herbart's Unmoral Education," *Education* 16 (November): 178–81.

"The Necessity of Five Co-ordinate Groups in a Complete Course of Study," *Education* 16 (November): 129–34. (This is a reply to a criticism of the *Report of the Committee of Fifteen,* and not the same as the similar title in 1896.)

1896   "Is Education Possible without Freedom of the Will?" *Education* 17 (January): 301–5.

"In What Does Spiritual Evolution Consist?" *Education* 17 (March): 413–21.

"Horace Mann," *Educational Review* 12 (September): 105–19.

The Necessity for Five Co-ordinate Groups of Studies in the School. (Reprint from *Educational Review,* April 1896.)

Professor John Dewey's Doctrine of Interest as Related to Will. (Reprint from *Educational Review,* May 1896.)

The Psychological Revival. (Chapters from the *Report of the U. S. Commissioner of Education for the Year 1893–94*). Washington: U. S. Government Printing Office.

1897   The Aesthetic Element in Education. (Address read

before the National Council of Education at Milwaukee, July 1897.)

"George William Frederick Hegel," in Charles Dudley Warner, ed., *A Library of the World's Best Literature*. New York: R. S. Peale and A. J. Hill, 12: 7174–83.

"Relation of School Discipline to Moral Education," in *National Herbart Society, Third Yearbook, 1897*. Chicago. Pp. 58–72.

The Science of Ethics as Based on the Science of Knowledge. Translated by A. E. Kroeger and edited by the Honorable Dr. W. T. Harris. New York: D. Appleton and Co.

1898   *Psychologic Foundations of Education: An Attempt to Show the Genesis of the Higher Faculties of the Mind*. New York: D. Appleton and Co.

1899   "Beauty in Art vs. Beauty in Nature," in the *Report of the U. S. Commissioner of Education for the Year 1898–99*. Washington, D.C., U. S. Government Printing Office.

1901   "Educative Work at Missions," *School and Home Education* 20 (May) : 427–30.

"Isolation in the School—How It Hinders and How It Helps," in the *Journal of Proceedings and Addresses of the National Education Association*, 1901. Washington, D.C. Pp. 357–63.

1902   "Herbert Spencer and What to Study," Educational Review 24 (September) : 135–49.

"How the School Strengthens the Individuality of the Pupil," *Educational Review* 24 (October): 228–37.

"Moral Education in the Common School," *Educational Foundations* 14 (October) : 68–83.

"The Danger of Using Biological Analogies in Reasoning on Educational Subjects." (Reprint from *Journal of Proceedings and Addresses of the National Education Association*, 1902, pp. 215–21.)

1903   "Religious Instruction in Public Schools," *Independent* 55 (August): 1841–43.

"The Separation of the Church from the Tax-supported School," *Educational Review* 26 (October): 222–35.

1904   "A Definition of Civilization," in the *Report of the U. S. Commissioner of Education for the Year 1903–4*. Washington: U. S. Government Printing Office, 1: 1129–33.

"Herbert Spencer and His Influence on Education," in the *Journal of Proceedings and Addresses of the National Education Association*, 1904. Washington, D.C., Pp. 214–23.

"Primary and Secondary Phases of Causality: Natural Science Founded on the Latter and Theology on the Former." (Reprint of an address to the American Philosophical Association, Philadelphia, December 29.)

1905   "Social Culture in the Form of Education and Religion," *Educational Review* 29 (January): 18–37.

SELECT REFERENCES

Atkinson, Carroll, and Maleska, Eugene T. *The Story of Education.* New York: Chilton Books, 1965.

Bardeen, C. W. "William Torrey Harris." *School Bulletin*, 36 (1909) : 65–68.

———— "William Torrey Harris and St. Louis Public Schools." *American Journal of Education*, 30, n.s. 5 (September 1880) : 625–40.

Black, Hugh C.; Lottich, Kenneth V., and Seckinger, Donald S., eds. *The Great Educators.* Chicago: Nelson-Hall Co., 1972.

Blow, Susan E. "In Memoriam, Dr. William T. Harris." *Kindergarten Review* 20 (1909) : 259–60.

———— "The Service of Dr. W. T. Harris to the Kindergarten." *Kindergarten Review* 20 (June 1910) : 589–603.

Brosnahan, Timothy. *Dr. Harris and the Agnostic School House.* New York: Messenger Press, 1903.

Brown, Samuel W. *The Secularization of American Education.* New York: Columbia University Press, 1912.

Clare, Thomas H. "The Sociological Theories of William Torrey Harris." Ph.D. dissertation, Department of Sociology, Washington University, 1934.

Curti, Merle. *Social Ideas of American Educators.* New York: Charles Scribner's Sons, 1935.

Fitzpatrick, F. A. "William Torrey Harris: An Appreciation." *Educational Review* 40 (1910) : 1–12.

Harris, William T. *Report of the Committee of Fifteen on the Elementary School.* Boston: Arno Press, 1898.

John, Walton C., ed. "William Torrey Harris." *Centenary Bulletin* 1936, no. 17. U. S. Office of Education, Government Printing Office, 1936.

Kies, Marietta, ed. *W. T. Harris: Introduction to the Study of Philosophy.* Comprising passages from his writings selected and arranged with commentary and illustrations by Marietta Kies. New York: D. Appleton and Co., 1889.

Leidecker, Kurt F. *Yankee Teacher.* New York: Philosophical Library, 1946.

McCluskey, Neil Gerard. *Public Schools and Moral Education.* New York: Columbia University Press, 1958.

Roberts, J. S. *William T. Harris: A Critical Study of His Educational and Related Philosophical Views.* New York: National Education Association, 1924.

Staub, Edward L. *William Torrey Harris, 1835–1935.* A Collection of Essays, including Papers and Addresses presented in Commemoration of Dr. Harris Centennial at the St. Louis meeting of the Western Division of the American Philosophical Society. New York: Open Court Publishing Co., 1936.

Stephens, W. Richard; Van Til, William. *Education in American Life.* Boston: Houghton Mifflin, 1972.

"William T. Harris" (a phrenological analysis). *Phrenological Journal* 92 (September 1891) : 102–3.

"William T. Harris, his Early Life and his St. Louis Reports." *American Education* 13 (1909) : 308–11.

Winship, A. E. "Friends and Acquaintances: William Torrey Harris." *Journal of Education* 101 (May 28, 1925) : 603–7.

5

JOHN DEWEY'S DEMOCRACY FOR EDUCATION

To Professor Jean Piaget nothing could be more interesting than the discoveries of John Dewey. He shows how ideas of work, based on interest and activity, provide training for thought which were already latently present throughout the whole of the late 19th century psychology.

—Jean Piaget, *Science of Education and the Psychology of the Child*, p. 148.

To achieve socialization of the schools, John Dewey makes his appeal for a democracy for education. This democracy is not a form of government, but a spiritual community based on faith in the social capacity of human nature.

This appeal by Dewey is recognized by Piaget, who declares that the work of John Dewey has influenced education in every country. By contrast with the limited scientific conservation of William T. Harris, the democracy for education that John Dewey presents is an innovation. The meaning of education to Dewey must no longer be limited to mere theory of classroom exercises but must include functions of living.

If man is a continuum within nature, so, too, must be his education. It will include not merely his conduct but all of nature, with the behavior of the universe as well. To realize this full socialization, Dewey proposes as the supreme test the contributions education makes to the all-around growth of every member of society.[1]

Shortly before the turn of the century, satisfaction with Harris's conservatism declined among the school-supporting public. Gradually a more adequate philosophy of education for democratic and scientific living became the clamor of the day.[2] This agitation affected the evolutionary process in American education, which reacted to the needs of the times.

The new demand found a ready exponent and provider in John Dewey. Termed the father of Progressive or Process Education, he succeeded in touching practically every bone in the anatomy of the educational structure. By his pragmatic philosophy of scientific education, he brought to fruition both Horace Mann's dream for a democratic education in America and Harris's desire for its complete social secularization.[3]

Any acceptance of a theory such as Dewey's, for example, appears to depend on its consistency with the thinking of influential educational and social theorists, and more subtly on the *zeitgeist*. For example, Dewey is to Piaget today what Thorndike is to the learning theorists of modern behaviorism, and Piaget's attitude toward education in process may be compared to Dewey's "active learning" and Thorndike's "connective receptive learning." Piaget's position in contemporary education also includes Dewey's wide influence in educational circles as a result of Piaget's reflection of the *zeitgeist*. Thorndike's decreasing influence may be caused by his position's being contrary to the prevailing world view. Therefore,

> the major theoretical difference between Piaget's position and that of behaviorists today is that Piaget's position stresses the "active role" that the subject plays in organizing his experi-

ence. . . . Behavior theory places greater emphasis on the "reactive aspects" of the person's behavior [even though Piaget insists that both active and reactive are important].[4]

Democracy for Education

To perfect the socialization of the schools was Dewey's appeal. *This appeal is for educational democracy, not as a form of government, but as a "spiritual community" based on faith in the social capacity of human nature.* By reason of William T. Harris's preparation for it at the local and national levels during the previous decades, Dewey's "new" education was well received. In this transition Harris became totally immersed. His values philosophy merged so completely with that of Dewey as to lose its identity on the educational scene. This fusion occurred at the time the American school system was being severely challenged to meet the new needs of the modern era.[5]

In this connection, Harris encouraged Dewey to assume the role of leadership. He knew Dewey well after lecturing with him at Concord. Before the turn of the century, there was hardly any opportunity for a layman in the United States to secure a position as teacher of philosophy in higher education because the field was considered a clerical preserve. Upon consultation, however, Harris gave Dewey warm, friendly advice which, according to his own testimony, helped him decide definitely in favor of continuing his philosophical studies. Harris also encouraged him to write his first articles. These he published for him in *The Journal of Speculative Philosophy*. They eventually resulted in the marketing of his first book (in 1886), entitled *Psychology*. The relevance of Dewey's values at the time is evident from the criticism he published in 1887 regarding Spencerian "scientific" ethics:

We believe that the cause of theology and morals is one, and that whatever banishes God from the heart of things, with the same edict excludes the ideal, the ethical, from the life of man. Whatever exiles theology makes ethics an expatriate.[6]

It is because of his early publications that John Dewey is still considered by many American educators a pioneer in psychology as the new science of process behavior. This is particularly true of his application of the method of scientific analysis, which he perfected in educating toward the new democratic ideal. He showed how the task of the school was to stimulate interest in the educative process of the child. This, he stressed, must be in light of the principles of mental activity and patterns of growth evolving from modern psychology.

Piaget insists that all work of the intelligence rests on the psychology of interest, because interest is, in effect, nothing other than the dynamic aspects of assimilation. As he sees it, Dewey demonstrated this with profundity: true interest appears when the self identifies itself with ideas or objects, when it finds in them a means of expression and they become a necessary form of fuel for its activities.[7] Furthermore, an important aspect of both Dewey and Piaget is their contention that human nature is alterable and adaptable, and, therefore, capable of improvement.

The America of Dewey's youth was generally content to react only passively to unexamined terms. Although most of these supposedly stood for entities, Dewey claimed that they were not entities but processes. He even looked at the phenomena of consciousness as activities or processes, and showed a recurrent emphasis on self-realization, human control of fate, and belief in man as a self-determined process. It is in this sense that he viewed education in process as one with growing.[8] From that perspective he pointed out certain important applications to the relevance of values:

> In the first place, the interaction of organism and environment, resulting in some adaptation which secures utilization of the latter, is the primary fact, the basic category. Knowledge is relegated to a derived position, secondary in origin, even if its importance, when once it is established, is overshadowing. Knowledge is not something separate and self-sufficing, but is involved in the process by which life is sustained and evolved. The senses lose their place as gateways of knowing to take their rightful place as stimuli to action.[9]

Deweyan Perspectives of Democracy for Education

MAN is a process	*EDUCATION* must be a process
He performs functions of life.	It must include functions of living.
He is the continuum of nature.	It must be integrated with nature.
He is a social being.	It must be fully socialized.
He is both scientific and democratic in nature.	It must be made scientific and democratic.

EDUCATION IS LIFE, a continuous reconstruction of experiences wherein the individual is the end and society the means.

DEMOCRACY is an "inclusive way of life requiring a continual 'reconstruction of beliefs and standards.' "

The Social Perspective

Since problems of sociology are always uppermost in his mind, John Dewey's approach to the educative process usually centered in and around a social relationship. By his application of pragmatism[10] to American education, under the title *Experimentalism or Instrumentalism,* philosophy became alive and extremely practical whenever and wherever he developed it in relation to education[11] for, as Piaget points out:

> in the first experiments made by Dewey . . . the children were free to work with one another, to collaborate in intellectual research as much as in the establishing of a moral discipline; this team work and this self government have become the essential ingredients of active school practice.[12]

Dewey discerned great social significance in the philosophical aspects of all school subjects. He proclaimed the necessity for all universities to establish a comprehensive foundation for these subjects in their philosophical implications. He insisted that, unless there were thorough university instruction in practical philosophy, centering around its application to social relations in the family, in economics, and in politics, education as a process in itself would continue to become less and less meaningful:[13]

> we are only just now commencing to appreciate how completely exploded is the psychology that dominated philosophy throughout the eighteenth and nineteenth centuries. . . . The effect of the development of biology has been to reverse the picture. . . . The higher the form of life, the more important is the active reconstruction of the medium. The increased control may be illustrated by the contrast of the savage with the civilized. . . . The savage takes things "as they are," and by using caves and roots and occasional pools leads a meagre and precarious existence. The civilized may . . . introduce machinery to till the soil and care for the harvest. By such means he may succeed in making the wilderness blossom like the roses.[14]

Of all the then-existing systems of philosophy, Dewey at first espoused that of Hegel, in addition to that of Plato, who was his favorite.[15] But the new psychology, with its scientific approach to man as a process, was what roused in him the most enthusiasm. By it he utilized a fresh approach to all activities involving the socialization of learning and teaching. He declared it the supreme human interest, that in which all other problems in process came to a climax. In this perspective, Jean Piaget gives John Dewey credit for developing a sociology of education.[16]

In his social-process perspective Dewey was greatly influenced by William James (1842–1910). He even said that his heart was in the great James' program undertaken at Harvard. By returning to the earlier biological idea of the psyche as a stream of consciousness in man, James helped him to discover a new vital force and value for life in action.[17] In it, too, he found a close affinity between his philosophy and the "new" psychology of organisms. Within actual life experiments as they interacted realistically in a unique process, Dewey found practical applications in the theoretical, dualistic interpretations of past centuries that had previously confined many perspectives within Aristotelian concepts.[18]

Although of enormous scope, the essentials of Dewey's social perspectives on education are presented to illustrate why Piaget considers John Dewey, along with Durkheim, as the founder of the discipline of educational sociology:[19]

<pre>
S   S
C   O
H   DEWEY'S SOCIAL PERSPECTIVES ON   C
O   I
O   EDUCATION   E
L   T
                                                     Y
</pre>

1. Education is for a changing social order.
2. Education is to be motivated for meeting life situations.
3. Education should be free so that the child discovers social values.
4. Education should be encouraged through activity movements.
5. Education builds character through social action and interaction.
6. Education should be democratic, not authoritarian.
7. Education should be experimental and subject to social needs.
8. Education should be a social process involving all facets of living.

The School and Society

With the planning of these societal activities, John Dewey's interest in public education began in a formal way three years following his graduation from college. During this time he studied privately in the field of philosophy, which he had already undertaken as part of his college training. In 1884, at the University of Michigan where he taught philosophy with unusual success, he utilized the opportunity to learn much more about public education. As the University itself formed part of the state system and the high schools were regularly visited by the faculty, he often lectured to the teachers at their various assemblies during conferences and conventions. His philosophizing centered mainly on values within process education. According to his own testimony it was here that "other problems, cosmological, moral, logical come to a head."[20]

Dewey acknowledged that representative government, universal franchise, and the freedoms guaranteed in the Bill of Rights, provided the necessary framework within which the democratic social processes could go on. He admitted that they were necessary, but not everything; that they constituted the essential structure, the skeletal form of the social-political body, but were not "its flesh and blood." The flesh and blood, he pointed out, were the attitudes, dispositions, and habits, the beliefs and customs, the ways of thinking and doing—in sum, the intellectual and moral character of the people.[21]

It is in this sense that Dewey saw that ". . . the supreme test of all political institutions and industrial arrangements shall be the contribution they make to the all-round growth of every member of society,"[22] and, in this perspective, education was to be understood as the fundamental method of social progress and reform. All reforms that rested simply upon the enactment of law, the threatening of certain penalties, or changes in mechanical and outward arrangements, he considered transitory and futile. No social order (least of all the democratic) could be built securely unless the school was an active participant in the building of it.[23] It is therefore easy to understand why Piaget has lauded Dewey's leaving the children free to work with one another, to collaborate in intellectual research as much as in establishing moral discipl ne; this teamwork and this self government have today become essential ingredients of active school practice.[24]

Dewey was anxious that an experimental school should become a reality. Then current methods of teaching, particularly in the elementary classes, seemed at odds with the essential principles of child psychology, especially in the area of growth and development, as he envisioned the process. His opportunity came on his acceptance of the position as head of the department of philosophy at the University of Chicago. At his request the authorities agreed to include pedagogy along with philosophy and psychology. This arrangement enabled him to found his experimental school, or "Laboratory School," later known as the "Dewey School," which served the same general purpose for the department of pedagogy as do laboratories in the physical sciences.[25]

The decades joining the nineteenth and twentieth centuries at the University of Chicago mark one of Dewey's most productive periods. Out of them came his most popular book, *The School and Society*, which contains the lectures he gave to raise funds for his experimental school. It was during this time, too, that he turned from Platonic idealism to his naturalistic instrumentalism, a position he retained, as a wholehearted naturalist, for the rest of his life (cf. "Half-hearted Naturalism," *Journal of Philosophy* 24 [Feb. 3, 1927]: 57–64). In this stance, he encountered the friendly differences from the schools of educational thought that merely marked the advance of his progressive movement as a significant process in his democracy for education:[26]

> I have long felt that the construction of a logic, that is, a method of effective inquiry, which would apply without abrupt breach of continuity to the field designated by both of these words (science and morals), is at once our needed theoretical solvent and the supply of our greatest practical want. This belief has had much more to do with the development of what I termed, for lack of a better word, "instrumentalism," than have most of the reasons that have been assigned.[27]

Paralleling this theme, Jean Piaget updates this work of John Dewey in recognizing it as an aid in establishing an outline for "genetic logic."[28] For, he says,

> what is true regarding language—means of expression for collective values—is also true for these values themselves, as well as the rules applicable to them, beginning with the two most important systems of values and standards for the later adaptation of the individual to his surroundings: logic and ethics. . . . [Since] . . . logic is not innate to the child . . . it fol-

lows that the first task of education is to form reasoning . . .
and the right to an ethical and intellectual education implies
more than a right to acquire knowledge or to listen, and more
than an obligation to obey: it is a question of a right to forge
certain precious spiritual tools in everyone, which requires a
specific social environment, not made exclusively of submissive-
ness.[29]

Because of the difficulties of working harmoniously under the
conditions imposed upon him by its president in the experimental school he established, Dewey resigned from Chicago University. In 1904 Nicholas Murray Butler, then president of
Columbia University, offered him a professorship on the faculty
of philosophy. His acceptance inaugurated for him nearly half
a century of association with Columbia University and its Teachers College. It proved to be one of the longest periods of influential educational activity ever witnessed in America by
teachers. From Teachers College at Columbia, Dewey's pragmatism informed the whole educational system as a process,
profoundly affecting the entire world.

The Continuum of Nature

As his prime educational objective, Dewey advocated the mod-
ification of the existent world and man's relationship with it.
In the process he intended to discover more fully the means of
arriving at, and of clarifying, the meaning of all programs of
behavior. Central to his philosophy is the concept that man is
the continuum of nature, that a strict genetic continuity is integral to the dynamism that pervades all human understanding.

By his pragmatic approach to man, John Dewey made the
distinct shift from the philosophy of essence to the philosophic
view of man as process.[30] He referred to this energetic perspective
as a breakthrough from an intelligence that merely shapes things
for the now to one that would continue to effect a progressive
interaction of shaping and of being shaped.

For Dewey, knowledge is more than a mere possession, it is a *doing,* and actual knowing is the outcome of the doing. In this process, therefore, any intellectual element is just what man does with his "ideas." It consists in how he uses them in the problematic situations in which he finds himself as an integral part of the world of nature. For Dewey, all thinking becomes problem-solving and is sound psychology:[31]

> Thinking begins in what may fairly enough be called a forked road situation, a situation which is ambiguous, which presents a dilemma, which proposes alternatives. . . . When there is no question of a problem to be solved or a difficulty to be surmounted, the course of suggestions flows on at random.[32]

It is evident that this philosophy of instrumentalism or experimentalism has relevance to the values of life. It provides a design for life and for full participation in present living. Nowhere is this so evident as in the definition of education that Dewey expressed very simply in the word *life.*[33] For him life is the real force within all societal processes. His experimentalism forged his educational philosophy of values. The gradual bringing of a new education to birth out of the agrarian conservatism of Harris, which had been lodged in the traditional, Old-World patterns of Horace Mann, is his unique achievement. His radical departure arose naturally from new relations, new demands, and new conditions, evolving from the needs and spirit of the new age.

Even though Piaget has not dealt directly with education in his new discipline, his theories are eminently relevant to educational practice. Not unlike John Dewey who preceded him, Piaget encouraged many changes within the learning-teaching process. He has established an active psychological approach to teaching, based on how (1) the young child is very different from the adult in his methods of approaching reality, in his views of the world and the environment in which he lives, and especially in the language he uses; (2) children learn best from concrete activities, such as manipulation of objects and exploration of a wide variety of potentially interesting projects, so that active learning is encouraged through the self-activity of the learner; (3) action and interaction are essential to each classroom situation, so that interest and learning are facilitated by the experience, which is presented in relation to what the pupil already knows and yet is sufficiently novel to encourage interest; (4) the teacher must tailor the curriculum to the individuals involved in the learning situations, to enable the children to have sufficient opportunities to learn and to want to learn; (5) there are some things that the child can not be taught because he can not learn them at any level, regardless of the method advanced; (6) finally, there are at each stage of the child's mental development certain things that he can learn, forms of thought that he can develop regarding the nature of reality.[34]

If there must be a departure from the past in the process of education for the nation, it is not for the sake of novelty, nor just for being different. Rather it is because the conditions of the newer times seem not only to welcome but also to call out for change on all sides.

Dewey believed that above all else this nation needed his experimentalism rather than traditionalism, which could have very little influence in a country just coming to birth. The behavior of the human being needs to be the primary object of a directed, intelligent, trial-and-error, developmental process in education.

As for Dewey's experimentalism, Piaget agrees that the conception of compulsory school work of the passing generation is an anti-psychological anomaly. Experimentalism supports the central problem of the new education that the great classical educators and Piaget himself questioned: Is childhood capable of this activity so characteristic of the highest forms of adult behavior, of diligent and continuous research springing from a spontaneous need?[35]

New times demand new methods. For what prudent man, Dewey says, cannot see how the lever that shakes the educational world needs a new fulcrum? Man's home is nature; his purposes and aims depend for execution on natural conditions; the things that exist around him, what he touches, sees, hears, and tastes, are interrogations for which answers must be sought.[36]

Dewey belongs to that category of process philosophers who designate themselves philosopher-moralists. His distinctive feature is a vision of ultimate ethical value, realizable in all branches of philosophy, which would give life true personal fulfillment within a social dimension. He assumes that a self, which accepts the guidance of intelligence and is thus provided with sound moral criteria, is a socialized self—that is, one that fulfills itself in the social relationships of family, school, neighborhood, vocation, and the entire human community.[37]

In this perspective Edwin A. Burtt states what becomes the *key* to Dewey's way of thinking:

> I think the answer is clear and simple. The central principle is that of *responsibility*—not, of course, in the limited meaning this word has in the philosophy of law or even in the traditional moral philosophy with its separate fields of problems, but in the meaning it might convey when applied by a reflective moralist to all philosophical issues . . . that *all human action, including thinking as an important part of action, has consequences; and that the vital difference which men in general and philosophers especially are concerned about is whether responsibility for those consequences is accepted or not.*[38]

In Dewey's view, the consequences, whether or not man wants it to be so, are within every act; the act in being performed brings its consequences into being for the actor; therefore, he cannot escape responsibility for them: "We are responsible for our deeds because they are ourselves. . . . I am myself, I am conscious of myself in my deeds, I am responsible, [these] name not three facts, but one fact."[39]

Interaction and Renewal

The basic principle in Dewey's teaching is that the life process constantly renews itself. This renewal he applied to those situations which grow directly out of the school itself so that classroom

activities give birth to new life by becoming as perfectly conformable as possible to life situations.[40] Dewey ruled out such
artificial situations as those gleaned from a textbook in morals,
whereby the student learns moral rules and directives by making
merely purely theoretical distinctions. This is a sure way, he
cautioned, in which to destroy the scientific method and to
achieve within the educative process the destruction of its
scientific aim.[41] He declared that

> the major task of human life is to develop power of intelligent
> foresight of consequences in every kind of situation; the es-
> sential task of philosophy is to clarify the conditions that such
> foresight involves, so that men will understand what it means
> to be responsible in every phase of life and how that respon-
> sibility must be carried out.[42]

Dewey frowned upon any approach to moral education that
assumes that theory is all right in itself but out of place in the
classroom. Life is one, and what is characteristic of life must
also be characteristic of the schools.[43] The emphasis of the traditional training in moral precepts needs to be supplanted by an
empathy between teacher and learner as an active value for all
human behavior. In this behavioral value of action Piaget discerns the various stages of moral development overlapping and
even envisions the same child as being in different stages simultaneously, because (1) the stages of morality and the course of
their development are not clearcut; (2) the learning theory of
morality is moot; (3) egocentric thought in children is inevitable
in relation to their unilateral respect for adults; (4) much more
experimentation and theorizing on real life values must take
place concerning moral judgment and behavior.[44]
Dewey asked whether it was not relationships in the complex
world of which the students are members that they need to experience, rather than any particular subject as ethics? Here he
emphasized effectively how there could be two sets of studies,
one for learning in the school and another for living outside of

the classrooms. Since life is one, studies should be one with life. For him, genuine education was life; without life there could be no education.

Man must learn to live his life, Dewey maintained, as an integral, unified being in society. Since all education takes place in direct proportion to the fullest participation in the social consciousness of the race, he concluded that society itself encompassed all of mankind's values. To achieve the societal is to assure a real values education in process.[45] The school then becomes a miniature community or society, instead of being merely a pause during which lessons are learned with the possibility of living them only in the future. He listed two criteria for determining an educative experience: continuity and interaction.[46] By their union they would provide the measure of educational significance and value relevance of an experience; in this relationship, Dewey affirmed, any experience could be judged to be educative or noneducative on the ground of what it moved toward and into.[47]

In creating lifelike opportunities to learn through directed living, not only do teachers teach morals in character training but they do so every moment of the day during the school week: "Character denotes this complex continuum of interactions in its office of influencing final judgment."[48] Thus, only when social life and values are one within the learning-teaching process itself can all aims and values that are desirable in process education become, in themselves, moral.

Personality characteristics such as discipline, natural development, culture, social efficiency, and personal refinement, Dewey affirmed, are all worthy of that society wherein the individual as a student is becoming a full-fledged member. Likewise, he acquires morality. In consequence, education is no longer a mere means to moral development, but is transformed into such a life, becoming relative to nothing except more education, just as change is relative to more change and interaction.[49] He therefore maintained that since we live only at the time we live, we can be prepared for living in the future only by extracting the full meaning from each present experience. This means that attentive care must be devoted to a whole-while meaning. The educator who has achieved maturity and best sees the connection between the pupil's present and future is responsible for an ever-present process. He is responsible for instituting the conditions for the kind of present experience which has a favorable effect upon the future.[50]

In other realistic approaches and principles, John Dewey challenged practically every tenet of the so-called traditional philosophy of education. His philosophy of education presupposed, in addition to a set of values and a theory of instruction, a particular image of the child that dominates the components of each philosophy. On the other hand, however, Piaget's impact on educational philosophy is owing to his unique image of the child that his works project: (1) the prerequisite for educating is to develop effective modes of communication with the learner, i.e., to comprehend what children are saying and to respond in the same mode of discourse; (2) the child is always in a state of activity, i.e., he is always learning something new at the same time that he is unlearning and relearning. Therefore the scope of education should be broadened to modify the child's existing knowledge; (3) the child desires, by his very nature, to know, hence his education must be so directed as to insure that he does not dull his eagerness to learn at his own pace and rhythm of learning.[51]

Through his pragmatism, Dewey is today still stimulating people to take a deeper look at their own commitment to first principles and to reevaluate those which, up to his time, had rarely if ever been questioned. Is education for values coming into a process that is no longer based solely on the philosophy of "fixation"? As Henry P. Cole notes:

The acceptance of the learner's need to explore and create his own meaning, as well as the observation that he must be

allowed much freedom to do so, is an assumption made by
many who have studied human behavior and have become
involved in education.[52]

Cole singled Dewey out for special mention, and also Jean Piaget,
for in his equilibration theory,

> Piaget assumes that a child conceptualizes the world through
> the assimilation of information derived from experience into
> "his" previously existing logical schema. However, the logical
> schema, which is never adequate for the assimilation of the
> new experiences the child continually encounters, is forced to
> accommodate itself to include this new information. Thus, the
> child's perception of the world at any given instant consists
> of a series of "creative products" which have resulted from
> the interaction of the existing schemata of the child with the
> stimuli of the environment. Since both the child's schemata
> and experiences are unique, the "creative products" of each
> child are also unique.[53]

Continuous Growth

Dewey's idea of "democracy for education" is now being characterized as that worldwide process by which the greatest intellectual and moral readjustments in history are occurring. His
experimentation in education is enriching the "here and now"
of society, supplanting the exclusive long-range objective of the
other worldly-centered perspective of early colonial days.[54] It is
making the teleological possible within the present, as found in
the beauty, goodness, and truth that are nature's own to bestow.

These values are contingent upon being discovered and rediscovered by man through scientific investigations within the educational activities themselves. Dewey's principle sees all reality
as in continual process. His method is a perpetual wellspring for
a richer life, one enriched by nature. Eeach person is to realize
these riches through learning that directs his personal living.
The "learning-living" process is thus pregnant with Dewey's
dynamic insights, which offer a more intelligent and personalized

relevance of values that constantly perfect society as man continually perfects himself. As Piaget writes:

> The right to education, therefore, is neither more nor less the right of an individual to develop normally, in accord with all the potential he possesses, and the obligation that society has to transform this potential into useful and effective fulfillment.[55]

This view of change is at variance with most concepts previously advanced. In his unique approach, John Dewey found a place for every individual and the means for each to attain his position as integral to society. A conservative who desires to follow his own point of view is likely to seem reactionary to another, or to a group within society. Dewey merely exhorts him to choose intelligently, but only after a careful assessment of the situation, coupled with a conscious anticipation of its consequences.

Dewey saw democracy as identical with the moral-social, not alone the political structure, and saw the democratic process itself as eventually to be absorbed by society with some sort of transformation of values.[56] This would provide the means by which each man would gradually shed the mortality of his own nature and live in the universal, becoming one with whatever is good, beautiful, and true.

Motivated by the sincere desire of forwarding the best interests of humanity, John Dewey interwined science and philosophy in his democratic ideal, and asked: Is it expecting too much to say that the institution of a happy marriage between theory and practice should be the objective and the chief meaning of a science of education and a philosophy of education? For, he writes:

> The science and philosophy of education can and should work together in overcoming the split between knowledge and action, between theory and practice, which now affects both education and society so seriously and harmfully. Indeed, it is not too much to say that [the] institution of a happy marriage between

theory and practice is in the end the chief meaning of a science and a philosophy of education that work together for common ends.[57]

In the dynamics of Dewey, fulfillment is always sought but never fully attained. Values are worthwhile, but they are values simply because they lead to new likings and new values. The continuum is without beginning or end in its process; as Dewey puts it: "What I have tried to show is that the ideal itself has its roots in natural conditions; it emerges when the imagination idealizes existence by laying hold of the possibilities offered to thought and action."[58]

Piaget interprets Dewey's active school as simply asking that the laws of intelligence be respected:

> Even in the adult the intellect cannot function effectively, cannot provide an opportunity for an effort on the part of the entire personality, unless its object is assimilated by that personality instead of remaining exterior to it.[59]

Then Piaget reasons that this assimilation is even more applicable in the case of the child. In the child, assimilation is not in equilibrium with the processes of accommodation to things. A continuous play-exercise process is required along with the adaptation proper,[60] so as to achieve equilibrium in the maturing person.

In Retrospect

Basically, Dewey showed that the logic of science and philosophy was the "instrument of human progress." Like Jean Piaget in his new discipline, he actually demonstrated that its influence on knowledge and values was almost unequaled in variety and scope. Practically every person in the United States today finds his education and the relevance of his values profoundly affected by John Dewey's ideals of logical democratic living. Dewey's "process" philosophy of education, however, is not limited to this country. Through his "democracy for education" he brought about "a profound revolution in education, not only in America, but also in much of the rest of the world."[61]

Among the American pragmatists who revolted against what many considered a sterile intellectual tradition in America and useless speculative metaphysical traditions then flourishing in Europe, were Charles Peirce, William James, and John Dewey. They studied pragmatism as a point of view, based it on definite postulates, and expressed it in a distinctive way with regard to mental life and conduct; then, extending its utility to solving intellectual problem, they furthered man's progress in the new age. They react positively against the "otherworldliness" of the early American puritanical ethics with a philosophy that is practical in relation to the values of this world.[62]

In reading James and Dewey especially, Piaget discovered that the psychology of the twentieth century was an affirmation that the life of the mind is a dynamic activity. As he writes:

> in the field of scientific observation proper and in the reaction of experience itself against an oversimplified mechanistic view of psychology, we find a widespread effort to develop both qualitative and quantitative methods aimed at achieving a more accurate vision of that authentic process of construction that is the true development of the mind.[63]

John Dewey's "democracy for education," commonly referred to today as Experimentalism or Instrumentalism, was a highly developed form of pragmatism that had for its aim the creating of a freer and more humane experience in which all would share and to which all would contribute. "Upon the whole," Dewey confesses, "the forces that have influenced me have come from persons and from situations more than from books."[64]

To Charles S. Peirce (1839–1914) Dewey attributes the credit for introducing pragmatism into the United States. At first Peirce's specific purpose was merely to clarify, and in some cases to eliminate as meaningless, traditional metaphysical questions; but when he developed his theses in his more mature writings, his pragmatism formed part of a highly systematized theory of logical values that Dewey utilized as having important bearings on all educational philosophy in America.[65]

It is significant, however, that during Dewey's earliest years of developmental logic, Peirce seems to have had little, if any, influence on him. But in 1938 Dewey did not hesitate to write:

The readers who are acquainted with the logical writings of Peirce will note my great indebtedness to him in the general position taken. As far as I am aware, he was the first writer on logic to make inquiry and its methods the primary and ultimate source of logical subject-matter.[66]

Dewey called Peirce the father of American pragmatism, which evolved during the post-Civil War period from the philosophy of empiricism of the nineteenth century. Through his efforts, it attained its place between the two extreme traditional positions: sensism and idealism. Dewey is also credited with formulating the idea generally referred to as Peirce's Principle and with applying the word *pragmatism* to this idea.[67] He nullified denotationalism and nominalism by his most famous statement regarding pragmatism:

Consider what effects that might conceivably have practical bearings, we conceive the object of our conception to have. Then our conception of these effects is the whole of our conception of the object.[68]

After Peirce, it was William James who had the profoundest impact on Dewey's pragmatism. According to James, the principle of pragmatism lay dormant for about twenty years. Then, in 1898, in a lecture at the University of California, he reintroduced the term. By that date he judged the time to be ripe for its reception; thus he referred to the method of pragmatism as "a new name for some old ways of thinking."[69]

Peirce's most eminent and most generous colleague was the

renowned American psychologist of Harvard University, William James (1842–1910). Originally he trained to be a physician. In the course of his profession, however, he formulated pragmatism around the unique subject of man's mental processes, defining the vital life principle as the stream of consciousness within the human being. Like Peirce, by whom he was profoundly influenced, he became a scientist, but his approach he derived directly from the personal subjectivity of man based on the principle that the unknowable may only appear to be unfathomable. Since his approach, although ethereal, made such distinct demands upon man's activities, James concluded that "we surely are not ignorant of its [the unknowable's] essential qualities, and in order to attain new knowledge we must go on experiencing and thinking beyond the evidence of experiences."[70] In his unique approach, he taught what John Dewey espoused wholeheartedly in his experimentalism: that there is only one undeniable truth— the present phenomenon of consciousness and how this personalized process within man is the gateway to learning.

Applying this vitalistic approach of James to the problem of man's nature in process, Dewey points out how it is from James that he learns to think of life in terms of "life in action". He wrote to James that, so far as he was concerned, he was simply rendering back in logical vocabulary what was already his own.

Piaget, however, extols John Dewey as a great name in psychology, the founder of schools and an inventor of exact educational techniques. He associates him especially with William James and Baldwin, declaring that with them psychology from the outset and in all its aspects is *an affirmation and an analysis of activity*.

Dewey, however, by varying, transforming, and selecting from James's pragmatism, makes it different and new under the form called *instrumentalism*.[71] Such revitalization brings pragmatism to its unique applicational development in American education. By insisting that what the students do in school liberates them in such a way as to enrich "their subsequent stream of experience," he presents the key for discovering how they grow in dedication to the values of the human spirit. These can be schematized (to verbalize):

Tenets of Dewey's Democracy for Education[72]

VALUES	PERSPECTIVES
1. *Bible*	As a "scientific" substitute for the traditional source of the Bible in the concept of religion in education, Dewey gives educational democracy, not as a form of government, but as a "spiritual community." Faith in the social capacities of human nature is his foundation of democracy, Dewey's substitute for the Bible.
2. *Primary Aim of Education*	The school is to view education as above all else the handmaiden of democracy, in which "every child is a potential member of the democratic church, and it is the function of education to actualize his membership and to widen his powers of participation." In this way the primary aim of education is growth; the norm for growth is always the social one—"growth in shared experiences," "growth in associated living," "growth in the good society" so that "an individual apart from social relations is a myth or a monstrosity."
3. *Character Formation*	This standard is democracy as the way of life, a pragmatic approach. By providing it as the moral rule for personal conduct, the school makes realizable, through education, a dynamic, viable, socialized, and progressive life in nature. In this system traditional moral and spiritual values are replaced by civic and social values.
4. *Natural Religion*	Dewey is at one with Mann in opposing sectarian religion in the public school and one with Harris against any form of supernatural religion in its classrooms. He goes beyond both, however, in placing ultimate faith in values verifiable in experience. He sees the religion of education the natural religion that could realize itself through science alone.

5. *Religious*   Dewey rejects the dichotomy between
   Instruction   moral training in the school and reli-
                      gious instruction in the Church.

Toward a Synthesis

Although John Dewey died in the late spring of 1952, his progressive spirit lives on in the philosophy of process, which his writings and disciples continue to inject into the bloodstream of civilization. Among the foremost philosophers of American education, he published no fewer than thirty-eight books and eight-hundred-and-fifteen articles and pamphlets.

A controversial figure, Dewey lived to see his influence felt in such diverse areas as teaching methods and jurisprudence, psychology and ethics, logic and law, aesthetics and international relationships, religion and economics, philosophy and sociology. His contributions are still paving the way for a whole new approach to value relevance in its most pragmatic sense.[73]

The consensus today among historians of education and students of social thought clearly indicates three leaders who contributed effectively in creating and developing the present philosophy of values within American public schools: Mann, Harris, and Dewey. These prominent educators span the history of the American public school and are aptly termed its triumvirate of value proposals.

Penetrating and integrating the work of this triumvirate today is Jean Piaget with his genetic epistemology and its repercussions in the mental development area of process-and-response values.

To John Dewey, America's most influential and controversial thinker,[74] the creation of the first and only system of philosophy native to America is attributed. It is as comprehensive in its tridimensional principle and application to relevance of values as it is to life itself:

The Tridimensional Principle in Dewey's Experimentalism[75]

EXPERIMENTALISM	Scientific and Technological	consist in a critical, experimental procedure of reconstructing in its methods of testing the whole of reality through experience, whereby knowledge is considered true only when it is the outcome of experience and has been tested by experience; this results in education's providing for greater intellectual independence and initiative on the part of the learner, because it is through his own experiences that the individual can interpret the whole of reality.
	Sociological and Institutional	present the actual basis to integration of science with industry and democracy, these become the foundation and source of all effort with work and industry. They are carried on in the interests of the group, in conformity with group desires that set the norms of morality. The consequence is that only in a living school, a school in which life is experienced, and in which education is conceived as life itself, can the child learn to face the continuous changes in modern complex society.
	Ethical	constitutes the good, to be tested by the consequences of experience and whether they prove beneficial to the individual in his natural and social environment. The ethical consists in growth as the summum bonum, nothing being relative to growth but more growth in experience. Therein is recognized the worth of man as being solely social and established in supreme optimism and belief that human powers and possibilities may be infinitely perfected by such education.

> Growth, then, is the richest reward for
> the individual when, in concert with all
> others, he brings intelligence and good
> will to the shared task of creating values
> for which his culture is to strive. This
> does not consist in eliminating differ-
> ences but in deliberately using them to
> facilitate the continuous and cooperative
> reconstruction of values.

Piaget is now in the front line of furthering Dewey's liberating challenge.[76] Still, he stands apart as not being himself a teacher or a social reformer. He is therefore able to study the child's development of intelligence in an analytic and detached manner as no person can who is busily involved in everyday practice:[77]

CHRONOLOGY OF DEWEY'S WORKS[78]

1882   "The Metaphysical Assumptions of Materialism," *Journal of Speculative Philosophy* 16 (April) : 208–13.

"The Pantheism of Spinoza," *Journal of Speculative Philosophy* 16 (July) : 249–57.

1884   "Kant and Philosophic Method," *Journal of Speculative Philosophy* 18 (April) : 162–74.

"The New Psychology," *Andover Review* 2 (September): 278–89.

1886   "The Psychological Standpoint," *Mind* 11 (January): 1–19.

"Psychology as Philosophic Method," *Mind* 11 (April): 153–73; *Psychology* (New York: Harper and Brothers).

1887   "Ethics and Physical Science," *Andover Review* 7 (June): 573–91.

1888   "The Ethics of Democracy," in *University of Michigan Philosophical Papers*, 2d s., no. 1 (Ann Arbor: Andrews and Co.).

1889   "Ethics in the University of Michigan," *Ethical Record* 2 (October): 145–48.

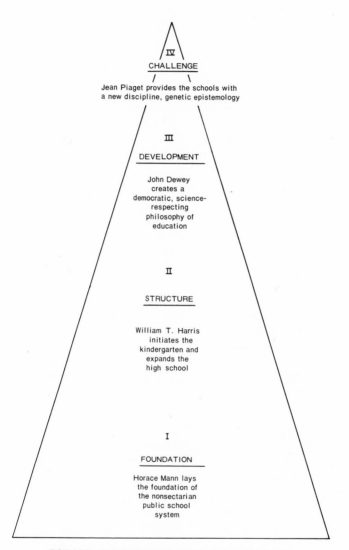

TOWARD STRUCTURING PUBLIC EDUCATION

1891 "Moral Theory and Practice," *International Journal of Ethics* 1 (January) : 186–203.

Outlines of a Critical Theory of Ethics (Ann Arbor: Register Publishing Co.).

1892 "Green's Theory of the Moral Motive," *Philosophical Review* 1 (November): 593–612.

"Two Phases of Renan's Life: The Faith of 1850 and the Doubt of 1890." *Open Court* 6 (December 29) : 3505–6. (Reprinted in *Characters and Events* [1929], 1: 18–23, "Ernest Renan.")

1893 "Renan's Loss of Faith in Science," *Open Court* 7 (January 5) : 3512–15. (Reprinted in *Characters and Events* [1929], 1: 23–30, "Ernest Renan.")

"Self-Realization as the Moral Ideal," *Philosophical Review* 2 (November) : 652–64.

"Teaching Ethics in the High School," *Educational Review* 6 (November) : 313–21.

1894 "The Chaos in Moral Training," *Popular Science Monthly* 45 (August) : 433–43.

The Study of Ethics: A Syllabus (Ann Arbor: Register Publishing Co.) .

1896 "The Metaphysical Method in Ethics," *Psychological Review* 3 (March) : 181–88.

1897 "Ethical Principles Underlying Education," in *National Herbart Society, Third Yearbook, 1897* (Chicago: University of Chicago Press) , pp. 7–34.

My Pedagogic Creed (New York: E. L. Kellogg and Co.) .

1898 "Evolution and Ethics," *Monist* 8 (April) : 321–41.

Review of William Torrey Harris, *Psychologic Foundations of Education, Educational Review* 16 (June) : 1–14.

1900 *The School and Society* (Chicago: University of Chicago Press) .

1902 "The Evolutionary Method as Applied to Morality: I—Its

Scientific Necessity," *Philosophical Review* 11 (March): 107–24.

"The Evolutionary Method as Applied to Morality: II—Its Significance for Conduct," *Philosophical Review* 11 (July) : 353–71.

The Child and the Curriculum (Chicago: University of Chicago Press) .

1903   "Psychological Method in Ethics," *Psychological Review* 10 (March) : 158–60.

"Emerson—The Philosopher of Democracy," *International Journal of Ethics* 13 (July) : 405–13. (Reprinted in *Characters and Events* (1929), 1: 69–77.)

The Logical Conditions of a Scientific Treatment of Morality. University of Chicago Decennial Monograph, 1st s. 3 (Chicago: University of Chicago Press) : 113–39.

"Religious Education as Conditioned by Modern Psychology and Pedagogy," in *Proceedings of the First Annual Convention* (Chicago: Religious Education Association), pp. 60–66.

Studies in Logical Theory (Chicago: University of Chicago Press).

1904   "The Philosophical Work of Herbert Spencer," *Philosophical Review* 13 (March) : 159–75.

1908   "Religion and Our Schools," *Hibbert Journal* 6 (July): 796–809. (Reprinted in *Characters and Events* (1929), 2: 504–16) .

With James H. Tufts, *Ethics* (New York: Henry Holt and Co.).

1909   "Is Nature Good? A Conversation," *Hibbert Journal* 7 (July): 827–43.

"The Dilemma of the Intellectualist Theory of Truth," *Journal of Philosophy* 6 (August 5) : 433–34.

Moral Principles in Education (Boston: Houghton Mifflin).

"The Moral Significance of the Common School Studies," in Northern Illinois Teachers' Association, Program of Meeting, November 5th and 6th, 1909, pp. 21–27, Elgin, Illinois: N.I.T.A. (Eastern Section).

1910 "Some Implications of Anti-Intellectualism," *Journal of Philosophy* 7 (September 1) : 477–81.

Educational Essays by John Dewey, ed. J. J. Findlay (London: Blackie and Son, Ltd.).

How We Think (Boston: D. C. Heath and Co.).

The Influence of Darwin on Philosophy and Other Essays in Contemporary Thought (New York: Henry Holt and Co.) .

1913 "The Problem of Values," *Journal of Philosophy* 10 (May 8): 268–69.

Interest and Effort in Education (Boston: Houghton Mifflin Co.).

1915 *German Philosophy and Politics* (New York: Henry Holt and Co.) .

1916 *Democracy and Education: An Introduction to the Philosophy of Education* (New York: Macmillan).

Essays in Experimental Logic (Chicago: University of Chicago Press).

1917 "H. G. Wells, Theological Assembler," *Seven Arts Magazine* 2 (July) : 334–39. (Reprinted in *Characters and Events* (1929), 1: 78–82.)

"Duality and Dualism," *Journal of Philosophy* 14 (August 30) : 491–93.

1918 "The Objects of Valuation," *Journal of Philosophy* 15 (May 9) : 253–58.

1920 *Reconstruction in Philosophy* (New York: Henry Holt and Co.).

1921 "Classicism as an Evangel," *Journal of Philosophy* 18 (November 24) : 664–66.

1922 "The American Intellectual Frontier," *New Republic* 30 (May 10): 303–5. (Reprinted in *Characters and Events* [1929], 2: 447–52.

"Education as a Religion," *New Republic* 32 (September 13): 63–65.

Human Nature and Conduct (New York: Henry Holt and Co.).

1924   "Kant after Two Hundred Years," *New Republic* 38 (April 30) : 255.

1925   *Experience and Nature*. Lectures on the Paul Carus Foundation, 1st s. (Chicago: Open Court Publishing Co.).

1926   "Church and State in Mexico," *New Republic* 48 (August 25) : 9–10. (Reprinted in *Characters and Events* [1929], 1: 352–57).

"Bishop Brown: A Fundamental Modernist," *New Republic* 48 (November 17) : 371–72.

1927   "Half-hearted Naturalism," *Journal of Philosophy* 24 (February 3) : 57–64.

"Anthropology and Ethics," in *The Social Sciences and Their Interrelations*, ed. W. F. Ogburn and Alexander Goldenweiser (Boston: Houghton Mifflin Co.), pp. 24–36.

1928   "Personal Immortality: What I Believe," *New York Times*, April 8.

"The Direction of Education," *Teachers College Record* 30 (October) : 7–12.

1929   With Albert C. Barnes, Laurence Buermeyer, and others. *Art and Education* (Merion, Pa.: Barnes Foundation Press) (articles by Dewey: "Experience and Nature and Art," pp. 3–12; and "Individuality and Experience," pp. 175–83.)

Characters and Events: Popular Essays in Social and Political Philosophy, ed. Joseph Ratner. 2 vols. (New York: Henry Holt and Co.) .

The Quest for Certainty (New York: Minton, Balch and Co.).

1929   *The Sources of a Science of Education* (New York: Horace Liveright) .

1930   "Credo," *Forum* 83 (March) : 176–82.

"Religion in the Soviet Union," *Current History and Forum* 32 (April) : 31–36.

"From Absolutism to Experimentalism," in *Contemporary American Philosophy*, ed. G. P. Adams and W. P. Montague (New York: Macmillan) , 2: 13–27.

Individualism, Old and New (New York: Minton, Balch and Co.).

1931 *Philosophy and Civilization* (New York: Minton, Balch and Co.) .

1932 "Education and Birth Control," *Nation* 134 (January 27) : 112.

"Monastery, Bargain Counter, or Laboratory?" *Barnwell Bulletin* 9 (February) : 51–62.

1933 "A God or THE God?" (Review of *Is There a God?: A Conversation*, by Henry N. Wieman, Douglas C. MacIntosh, and Max C. Otto) , *Christian Century* 50 (February 8): 193–96; (March 22) : 394–95.

1934 *Art as Experience* (New York: Minton Balch and Co.) .

A Common Faith (New Haven, Conn.: Yale University Press) .

"Education for a Changing Social Order," in *American Association of Teachers College, Thirteenth Yearbook* (New York) , pp. 60–68.

"Liberation of Modern Religion," *Yale Review*, n.s. 23: 751–70.

1935 "Religions and the 'Religious' ": A Letter, *New Republic* 82 (March 13) : 132.

"Intimations of Mortality" (review of Corliss Lamont, *The Illusion of Immortality*) , *New Republic* 82 (April 24) : 318.

"Bergson on Instinct" (review of Henri Bergson, *The Two Sources of Morality and Religion*) , *New Republic* 83 (June 26) : 200–201.

1936 "One Current Religious Problem," *Journal of Philosophy* 33 (June 4) : 324–26.

"Religion, Science and Philosophy," *Southern Review*, 2d s. 1 (Summer) : 53–62.

"Horace Mann Today," *Social Frontier* 3 (November): 41–42.

1937   "Education, the Foundation for Social Organization," in *Educating for Democracy, A Symposium* (Yellow Springs, Ohio: Antioch Press), pp. 37–54.

With W. H. Kilpatrick and others. *The Teacher and Society.* First Yearbook of the John Dewey Society (New York: Appleton-Century Co.).

1938   "Does Human Nature Change?" *Rotarian* 52 (February): 8–11, 58–59.

"The Relation of Science and Philosophy as the Basis of Education," *School and Society* 47 (April 9) : 470–73.

"Determination of Ultimate Values or Aims through Antecedent or A Priori Speculation or Through Pragmatic or Empirical Inquiry," in *National Society for the Study of Education, Thirty-seventh Yearbook,* pt. 2 (Chicago), pp. 471–85.

Experience and Education (New York: Macmillan).

Logic: The Theory of Inquiry (New York: Henry Holt and Co.).

1939   "Experience, Knowledge and Value: A Rejoinder," in *The Philosophy of John Dewey.* Volume 1 of the *Library of Living Philosophers,* ed. Paul A. Schilpp. (Evanston, Ill.: Northwestern University Press), pp. 517–608.

Freedom and Culture (New York: G. P. Putnam's Sons).

Intelligence in the Modern World, ed. Joseph Ratner (New York: The Modern Library).

1940   "Nature in Experience," *Philosophical Review* 49 (March): 244–58.

Education Today, ed. and with a foreword by Joseph Ratner (New York: G. P. Putnam's Sons).

1942   "Ambiguity of 'Intrinsic Good,'" *Journal of Philosophy* 39 (June 4) : 328–30.

1943   "Valuation Judgments and Immediate Quality," *Journal of Philosophy* 40 (June 10) : 309–17.

"Further as to Valuation as Judgment," *Journal of Philosophy* 40 (September 30) : 543–52.

1944   "Democratic Faith and Education," *Antioch Review* 4 (June) : 274–83.

"Some Questions about Value," *Journal of Philosophy* 41 (August 17): 449–55.

1945   "Ethical Subject-Matter and Language," *Journal of Philosophy* 42 (December 20) : 701–12.

"Democratic Faith and Education," in *The Authoritarian Attempt to Capture Education*: Papers from the Second Conference on the Scientific Spirit and the Democratic Faith (New York: King's Crown Press) , pp. 1–12.

1946   *Problems of Men* (New York: Philosophical Library).

1948   "William James' Morals and Julien Benda's," *Commentary* 5 (January): 46–50.

1949   "Philosophy's Future in Our Scientific Age," *Commentary* 8 (October) : 388–94.

"The Field of Value," in Ray Lepley, *Value: A Cooperative Inquiry* (New York: Columbia University Press), pp. 64–77.

With Arthur F. Bentley. *Knowing and the Known* (Boston: Beacon Press) .

N.B. The most complete listing of Dewey titles is to be found in "Bibliography of the Writings of John Dewey (1882–1950) ," in *The Philosophy of John Dewey*, pp. 609–87. Volume 1 of the *Library of Living Philosophers*, ed. Paul A. Schilpp (Evanston, Illinois: Northwestern University Press, 1939).

SELECT REFERENCES

Archambault, R. D., ed. *John Dewey on Education*. New York: Modern Library, 1964.

Baker, Melvin C. *Foundations of John Dewey's Educational Theory*. New York: Atherton, 1965.

Bayles, Ernest E. *Pragmatism in Education*. New York: Harper & Row, 1966.

Bernstein, Richard J. *John Dewey*. New York: Square Press, 1966.

Black, Hugh C., Kenneth V. Lottich, and Donald S. Seckinger, eds. *The Great Educators*. Chicago: Nelson Hall Co., 1972.

Durkheim, Emile. *Education and Society*. Free Press, 1956.

Dykhuizen, George. *The Life and Mind of John Dewey*. Carbondale, Ill.: Southern Illinois University Press, 1973.

Ehrlich, Robert S. *Twentieth Century Philosophers*. New York: Monarch Press, 1965.

Fox, June T. "Epistemology, Psychology and their Relevance for 'Education in Bruner and Dewey. '" *Educational Theory* (Winter, 1969).

Geiger, George. *John Dewey in Perspective*. New York: McGraw-Hill, 1958.

Gouinlock, James. *John Dewey's Philosophy of Value*. New York: Humanities Press, 1972.

Graham, Patricia A. *Progressive Education: From Arcady to Academe*. New York: Teachers College Press, 1967.

Gross, Carl H., Stanley P. Wronski, and John W. Hanson, eds. *School and Society*. New York: Heath, 1962.

Horne, Herman H. *The Democratic Philosophy of Education*. New York: Macmillan, 1932.

Hutchins, Robert M. *The Learning Society*. New York: Praeger, 1968.

James, William. *Pragmatism*. New York: Longmans, Green, 1907.

———. *The Principles of Psychology*. New York: Holt, 1890.

———. *Talks to Teachers on Psychology*. New York: Holt, 1900.

Kilpatrick, William H., ed. *The Educational Frontier*. New York: Appleton, 1933.

———. *Philosophy of Education*. New York: Macmillan, 1951.

———. *Selfhood and Civilization*. New York: Macmillan, 1941.

Lawson, Douglas E., and Lean, Arthur E., eds. *John Dewey and the World View*. Carbondale, Ill.: Southern Illinois University Press, 1964.

Mayhew, K. C., and A. C. Edwards. *The Dewey School*. New York: Appleton, 1936.

McCluskey, Neal Gerard. *Public Schools and Moral Education*. New York: Columbia University Press, 1958.

Mead, George H. "The Philosophies of Royce, James and Dewey in their American Settings." *International Journal of Ethics* (Jan. 1930).

Nissen, Lowell. *John Dewey's Theory of Inquiry and Truth.* The Hague: Mouton & Co., 1966.

Pasch, Alan. "Dewey and the Analytic Philosophers," *Journal of Philosophy* (October 8, 1959).

Passmore, John. *A Hundred Years of Philosophy.* Gretna, La.: Pelican, 1970.

Peirce, Charles. *Chance, Love, and Logic.* New York: Harcourt, Brace, 1923.

Perkinson, Henry J. *The Imperfect Panacea: American Faith in Education 1865–1965.* New York: Random House, 1968.

Ratner, Joseph, ed. *Intelligence in the Modern World: John Dewey's Philosophy.* New York: Modern Library, 1939.

Schiller, F. S. C. *Humanistic Pragmatism.* New York: Free Press, 1966.

Schilpp, Paul A., ed. *The Philosophy of John Dewey.* Chicago: Northwestern University Press, 1939.

Stephens, W. Richard and William Van Till. *Education in American Life.* New York: Houghton Mifflin, 1972.

Stoops, John A. *Religious Values in Education.* Danville, Ill.: The Interstate Printers & Publishers, Inc., 1967.

Thayer, H. S. *Meaning and Action: A Critical History of Pragmatism.* New York: Bobbs-Merrill, 1968.

Thayer, V. T. *Formative Ideas in American Education.* New York: Dodd, Mead, 1965.

Troutner, Leroy F. "The Confrontation between Experimentalism and Existentialism: From Dewey through Heidegger and Beyond." *Harvard Educational Review* (Winter 1969).

Ulich, Robert. *Fundamentals of Democratic Education.* New York: American Book, 1940.

White, Morton G. *The Origin of Dewey's Instrumentalism.* New York: Octagon Books, Inc., 1964.

Wirth, Arthur G. *John Dewey as Educator.* New York: Wiley, 1966.

6

AFTER DEWEY, WHAT?

one is immediately seized by a genuine alarm at the dispro-
portion that still subsists today [in education], undiminished
since 1935, between the immensity of the efforts that have been
made and the absence of any fundamental renewal in our
methods, in our progress, in our programs, in the very position
of our problems, or indeed, in pedagogy as a whole considered
as a guiding discipline.

—Jean Piaget, *Science of Education and the
Psychology of the Child*, p. 3.

Success neither proves a cause to be good, nor indicates it to
be bad; and we demand that our cause should not be judged
by the event, but the event by the cause.[1]

The cause, as Jean Piaget points out in his masterpiece, *Science
of Education and the Psychology of the Child* (p. 3), is the
appalling ignorance, after the passage of so many years, in which
the profession of education still remains with regard to the results
achieved by educational techniques. The truth is that the profession of educator has not yet attained in society the status to
which it has a right in the scale of intellectual values. Piaget
continues:

Lucian Febvre . . . explained this lag, or rather this lack of
coordination, as resulting from the infinite complexity of our
social life, of which education is at once the reflection and the
instrument. This is no doubt true, but we are still left with
the problem—one that becomes daily more worrying.[2]

The relevance of this cause is shared progressively by the
triumvirate: Horace Mann in his nonsectarianism, William T.

Harris in his secularization, and John Dewey in his democracy for education. Together they lend their support to the causal or creative values[3] of:

	H	
common consent		
	U	
		moral responsibility
	M	
devotion to truth		
	A	
		moral equality
	N	
brotherhood		
		pursuit of happiness
	P	
spiritual enrichment		
	E	
		respect for excellence
	R	
	S	
institutions as the		
servants of men	O	
	N	
	A	
	L	
	I	
	T	
	Y	

Post-Dewey Enigma

A clash, however, exists within the harmony of the triumvirate. There is a post-Dewey enigma! The fruits of Dewey's experimentalism within value process-and-response education are being reaped on only a very limited basis. The estimated overall effects of John Dewey's thoughts and beliefs are still pending. They are not yet encountered, applied, and responded to by millions of students and teachers:

> It does not seem probable that a valid assessment of Dewey's influence can be made during the present century. It will remain for historians, favored by the greater perspective afforded by time and distance, to estimate that influence from the vantage point of a later era. For the present, the many disagreements will persist. But among those who dispute, there nevertheless is general agreement on some points; for no one doubts Professor Dewey's rightful place among those who believe in the ameliorative powers of human intelligence applied to the solution of man's problems.[4]

Jonas F. Soltis, however, warns in his recent assessment of the contemporary world scene:

> I . . . expect philosophers of education who become impatient with the . . . [post-Dewey enigma] to try to find some more acceptable answers or different ways to ask the questions by turning to the general area of philosophy of mind, or in the style of Piaget, to the pursuit of a philosophical-empirical study of "genetic epistemology" (cf. n32 below).

It appears that what is emerging in the triumvirate from Dewey's philosophy is mainly preparatory. Perhaps the long-awaited millennium, characterized by what is termed the real humanistic age of process, lies on the horizons. Dewey himself never intended his contributions to be an end or a final stage of educational growth and development of man within the process. Rather, he presented it as a necessary stage to further continual growth and greater scientific living.[5] He embraced an ever-widening social milieu discoverable here and now through the educational process itself. His creative perspectives of the relation of man to the world within a process are always related to that which is and still must come to be.

It is difficult to imagine a more challenging epoch for process education than when the old order of values in science and human affairs is merging with the new. As Michael Polanyi declares,[6] now there are no restrictions; nothing that ever existed seems to be able to bind man any more within the social process of growth toward self-fulfillment:

> I can't imagine a more exciting time in history. . . . There are no rules; nothing that ever existed binds us any more. The old order in science and human affairs is gone.[7]

Today the person is being oriented away from the past by assuming more responsibility for creating the future he desires. He is reaching for the beginning of what John Dewey terms the socialization of mankind, itself a stage of growth in the interpersonal.

Man is increasingly urged by events to seek an identity within the newly dawning age, to develop his especial commitment as fully as possible by sharing it with the community.[8] A growing response to existential needs of the times is particularly strong in the Dewey-inspired process of communitarianism today. This evolving process is one of new growth in the interpersonal, extending itself by the pursuit of still greater personalization in the future. "In a changing society," Dewey said, "to prepare [the child] for future life means to give him command of himself, it means so to train him that he will have the full and ready use of all his capacities."[9]

Dewey's thrust toward a higher and more complex form of creativity, reconstructing the old, called forth a personal response demanding the use of all man's powers of inventiveness; it challenged, as never before, all the possibilities in traditional education. Consequently, for Dewey, education is not a preparation for life. It is life or growth. . . . Each phase of a growing life has its own distinctive needs, qualities, and powers. The organization of study and methods of teaching must for each phase be such that the process of learning will satisfy the needs, enrich the qualities and mature the powers of the individual. . . . The qualities [values] of the good life should be inherent qualities of the educational process.[10]

As is consistent with the process of his instrumentalism, John Dewey no longer viewed learning and teaching as the great transmitters of past traditions. He conceived them to be developers of those distinctive qualities within each person which are requisite for achieving the fuller socialization demanded by the new humanism.[11] Although his influence is not in evidence today, he presented American education with the means necessary for growth toward ultimate communitarianism; building anew the future world of mankind:

More thoroughly than any other leader of American thought, he has explored the problems of democracy and has, with tireless persistency, revealed the obstacles that must be continually overcome if our democratic society is not to be just a promise but a living and flourishing reality.[12]

In the rather long wake of the post-Dewey enigma there emerged several outstanding men whose works are interwining themselves within Dewey's humanistic education for values and the future. They are Alfred North Whitehead (1861–1947), Jean Piaget (1896–   ), Jerome S. Bruner (1915–   ), and Jacques Maritain (1882–1973).

Whitehead challenged Dewey's pragmatism;[13] Piaget offers developmental enlightenment to both; Bruner's cognitive theory is at odds with Piaget's stance; and Maritain's new humanism exposed in their theories the dangerous exclusivism of the naturalistic values held in common. A brief synthesis of each man's contribution, integrated with Piaget's findings today, therefore becomes paramount. Their achievements toward a humanistic approach to the value-process of educational psychology and to philosophy are indispensable for forming the basis for a solution of the post-Dewey enigma.

The Challenge of Whitehead

Disturbing the scene of the post-Dewey enigma was Alfred North Whitehead, who challenged the triumvirate of Mann, Harris, and Dewey by conceiving values as an evolving process:

> There can be no successful democratic society [as proposed by John Dewey] till general education conveys a philosophic outlook, for the defect common to all such modern philosophies [of values] is the fallacy of misplaced concreteness, i.e., the mistaking an abstraction for concrete reality, or more generally the part for the whole.[14]

He saw these values as attaining ever-greater pragmatic relevance. In contrast to the static world view of previous centuries, he declared that "only by trying all possibilities" would there be hope of arriving at the better, or even the suitable. Whitehead thereby established that what is past is ground for the present and future.[15] He wrote that "the occasion arises as an *effect* facing the past and ends as a cause facing the future." The present, including in itself the essentials to which the future must conform, influences all succeeding events.[16]

In his own philosophy of organisms, Jean Piaget supports this Whiteheadian perspective, in which, according to Edith Hamilton, all that has gone before is now merging as one process with what is—our times, our issues, our hopes, our discussions, our discoveries, our ideals, our despairs—in a word, the existential contemporary scene of the "ever-present past."[17]

Whitehead's process philosophy of values also includes Dewey's unceasingly increasing continuum: "Development is a continuous process, and continuity signifies consecutiveness of action. . . . Here lies, perhaps, the greatest problem of the newer efforts in education."[18]

According to these insights, any effective future democracy would have to have a community of culture and values, a new humanism. Exactly what "the new" is, is difficult to discern. Out of a science of technology, this humanism is dawning within the industrialized age of rapid change and advances. Educationally gearing itself for scientific living within a socialized democracy, the emerging humanism forms a common core of values, as Charles A. Beard points out:

> While education constantly touches the practical affairs of the hour and day, and responds to political and economic exigencies, it has its own treasures heavy with the thought and sacrifice of the centuries. It possesses a heritage of knowledge and heroic examples—accepted values stamped with the seal of permanence.[19]

These values are sealed and perpetuated in the Declaration of Independence and the Bill of Rights, for, as Whitehead insists:

> We can be content with no less than the old summary of educational ideals (or values) which has been current at any time from the dawn of our civilization. The essence of education is that it be religious.[20]

When the contemporary scene is viewed as an integral part of a continual progression, the quest for values, in current educational arguments, constantly encounters new elements. This makes for a challenge, which Dewey earmarked as possibly "the greatest problem of the newer efforts in education." In it human survival hangs in the balance; making values relevant within education increasingly becomes, according to the late H. G. Wells, "a race between civilization and catastrophe."[21] Therefore,

> whatever answers we agree upon, whatever action we can bring to bear, must be terribly relevant to our lives today and to this crucial question of our making it. Ours is an urgent, seemingly overwhelming challenge.[22]

Whitehead significantly influenced the great historical eras that used the values of process-and-response in education and that now can be understood as being in living continuity with one another. Up to the present, civilization had reached for the future by mounting the scaffolding of the past. Until now, the educational forefathers maintained that education sustained—as part of itself—a corporate memory that redeemed death and time, and thus lifted all to the dignity of the teleological.[23]

Mass Man

Today man seems to have no place in the universe.[24] If education really did partake of the inherited civilization of its ancestors, it is now in danger of dropping this historical continuity as a ship drops its pilot at Land's End. By the phenomenon of displacement, this exclusionary apprehension severs the new humanism from the modern world. It is not only in the theoretical but also in the practical sense that: (1) hierarchical orders are disappearing into a collectivist society of mass men; (2) the relativity of man's universe is abolishing the concept and the reality of *place* itself; and (3) man is continuing to exist in the new world of tomorrow without being anywhere. Man's existence therefore seems to be rootless, a simple state of being or becoming.[25]

The rapid usurpation of civilization by scientific technology is encouraging radically different attitudes of value relevance. The new Mass man is finding antipathetic the ideal of the self-made man and the creative personality. To the point of being his own enemy, he refuses to grant that the person, the autonomous subject, is the measure of human values. In mass humanity he seems to be losing even his desire for independence or originality.

The management of his life is approaching anonymity and even nihilism. No longer does Mass man seek to create an environment belonging only to mankind, and gadgets and techniques are forcing upon him the patterned perspectives of machine production. The materialistic planning of the masses he is accepting as normal. It is becoming a way of life for him.[26]

To a greater or lesser degree, Mass man is gradually espousing the conviction that such conformity is both reasonable and tight. As a result, the new personality among the masses seems to have no real ambition, no desire to live a life in accord with principles uniquely his own, conformable to his human nature. Freedom of judgment seems for him today to have no special value—understandably, for he seems never to be experiencing it.[27]

The individual, in the Deweyan-Whiteheadian scheme of things, is so absorbed by society in some sort of universal culture, within process, that his personality is transformed. Dewey rallies his associates in support of absorbing the individual in the milieu:

> The ideal of perfecting any "inner" personality is a sure sign of social division. What is called inner is simply that which does not connect with others—which is not capable of free and full communication. What is termed spiritual culture has usually been futile, with something rotten about it, just because it has been conceived as a thing which a man might have internally—and therefore exclusively. What one is as a person is what one is as associated with others [mass man], in a free give and take of intercourse.[28]

As a matter of simple expediency, man in process is uniting himself with any "organization" modeled after the masses themselves; there he seems to obey whatever program is evolving before him. In this fashion, "the man without personality" finds himself on the one road that he thinks will assuredly carry him through life.

Of more significance is the regimentation of this new human type, Mass man, which forbids man to appear distinctive and compels him to appear anonymous. At times, he acts almost as if he felt that to be one's very self is both a source of injustice and a sign of peril.[29]

Out of the past comes a ray of hope from Francis Bacon's *The Advancement of Learning* (1605): "They are ill discoverers," he writes, ". . . [who] think there is no land when they see nothing but sea."[30]

Toward the close of his life, Dewey attempted to clarify his value perspectives in the humanism to which he devoted his efforts:

> Fidelity to the nature to which we belong, as parts however weak, demands that we cherish our desires and ideals till we have concerted them into intelligence, revised them in terms of the ways and means which nature makes possible. When we have used our thought to its utmost and have thrown into the moving unbalanced balance of things our puny strength, we know that though the universe slay us, still we may trust, for our lot is one with whatever is good in existence. We know that such thought and effort is one condition of the coming into existence of the better.[31]

Supporting Dewey's perspectives is Soltis in his "Analysis and Anomalies":

> my contention that one of the major anomalies in the current analytic approach to [Dewey's] philosophy of education is to be found in analytic treatments of the concept of learning. This is to suggest that within the continual stream of projected normal inquiry *via* analysis, there may arise a significant challenge to the paradigm because of the inadequacy of its treatment of that most central educational concept, *learning*.[32]

Existentialism in education, cautions Soltis, must be constantly analyzed in terms of the great objective, learning. He warns against stagnation.

To find more acceptable answers and new ways to ask the pertinent questions, he insists on turning to a new psychological area of the mind. This is precisely the style of Jean Piaget's new discipline. It is his philosophical-empirical study in genetic epistemology. Soltis continues:

> Will a crisis occur and will a new paradigm emerge [from Piaget's work] or will the analytic paradigm be sufficient to

the task? I have no way of knowing, but if a crisis and paradigm shift were to come in analysis, I would expect that the anomalies in analytic treatments of learning could prove to be one of the most fertile spawning grounds for revolution.[33]

Piaget's Developmental Approach[34]

Through his paradigm of the new discipline, Piaget begins with infancy and continues through adolescence in dealing with the discoverable. In all stages of learning he utilizes the psychological process structures underlying the fundamental concepts in learning. With these he formulated a gradual, developmental approach to science, the science that John Dewey incessantly stressed for the new age. Piaget's whole perspective of process-and-response is an approach to reality by seeing through the eyes of the other person, characterized by his own words: "In the beginning was the response. . . ."[35]

His is an up-dating of the old Aristotelian-Thomistic perspective, which began with the "operatio sequitur esse" (operation is according to essence) principle. It is:

> The clinical method . . . the art of questioning; it does not confine itself to superficial observation, but aims at capturing what is hidden behind the immediate appearance of things. It analyses down to its ultimate constituents the least littie remark made by the child. It does not give up the struggle when the child gives incomprehensible answers but only follows closer in chase of the ever-receding thought, drives it from cover, pursues and tracks it down, till it can seize it, dissect it and lay bare the secrets of its composition.[36]

From this observational-introspective approach, an ever-increasing number of psychologists, philosophers, and educators today are discovering a more meaningful involvement within the process of human understanding and learning. They are gradually applying findings from Piaget's many writings and research projects to current problems, especially, as Elizabeth Hall declares, in the field of child psychology:

Piaget's studies of mental processes in both children and adults were accomplished through observation and inquiry rather than from experimentation; nevertheless, his writings have greatly influenced the field of child development . . . [particularly] from his observations on the development of intelligence in children.[37]

Practically all of Piaget's writings since the 1920s reflect this process or developmental aspect—an approach that shows the direct influence of his doctrinal studies at the University of Neuchâtel and his work with Alfred Binet in Paris. In recalling his work at Binet's laboratory school in Paris, Piaget affirms that

it was Binet's school, but I was not working on Binet's test. My task was to standardize Cyril Burt's tests on the children of Paris. I never actually did it. Standardization was not at all interesting; I preferred to study the errors on the test. I became interested in the reasoning process behind the children's wrong answers.[38]

His process perspective continues to grow. Over the last half-century it has become so increasingly effective that today Jean Piaget is receiving universal acclaim as a "developmentalist." This is particularly true for his epistemological insights regarding the human organism's process of adaptation to the environment by means of intelligence.[39] His is a successful pioneering in studies of children from the first weeks of life through adolescence.

The technique that Piaget employs in his experiments is unique in its projectional approaches, and seems to penetrate the child's consciousness, so that Piaget actually sees the world of process through the eyes of the child.[40] As a result of these personalized projections, he describes psychological development that is initiated in terms of organic growth at birth and terminates with adulthood. As is true of growth in all organisms, Piaget discerns the child's activity as directed toward equilibration, that is, as progressing constantly in the direction of ever-expanding and permanent levels of organization.[41] In this perspective, Piaget declares:

> All operational subject structures, on the one hand, and all causal structures in the domain of physical experience, on the other hand, suppose a combination of production and conservation. There is always some production, that is, some kind of transformation taking place. Similarly there is always some conservation, something that remains unchanged throughout the transformation. These two are absolutely inseparable.[42]

Without this transformation there is only static identity. The world becomes rigid and unchanging in the sense that Parmenides (ca. 539 B.C.) conceived it. Without conservation there is only constant transformation, total change. The world is always new and it becomes unintelligible. It becomes like the world of Heracleitus (ca. early part of the fifth century B.C.), with its river in which one is never able to bathe twice. In reality, Piaget concludes, there are always both conservation and production:[43]

> Conservation demands compensation, and consequently *equilibration*. If something is changed, something else must change to compensate for it, in order to result in a conservation. Even in physics all the transformations that take place involve compensations in order to lead to a conservation. Those compensations are organized in group structures in the mathematical sense of the term. Furthermore, there is no conservation without production, and production with conservation results in a constant demand for new conservation. . . . So, simply stated, there is a continual search for a better equilibrium. In other words, equilibration is the search for a better and better equilibrium in the sense of an extended field, in the sense of an increase in the number of possible compositions, in the sense of a growth in coherence.[44]

In this sense, the development of the child from birth to adulthood can be likened to an inverted triangle balanced by a directed, progressive, mental-maturing interaction and a directed, progressive, organic-maturing interaction.

Major Stages[45]

Piaget's theory states that the body of an infant at birth evolves in a process toward a relatively stable level of development. He adds that the balanced perfection of the growth processes in organic maturity has evolved with the physical toward a balanced mental maturity. It has passed through at least four major (and many minor) stages before eventually attaining to the adult mind. Each of the major stages of the child's growth and development may be likened to a triangle, each building upon the one below it in inverted order. In the Piagetian outlook, then, development is a progressive equilibration from a lesser to a higher stage.[46] Physically and psychologically it interacts as a single process-and-response development, but all four stages are divided, for practical demonstration, into categories of action rather than into ideological classifications:

SCHEMA OF COGNITIVE DEVELOPMENT IN PIAGET'S DEVELOPMENTAL MODEL*

(from birth to about 15 years of age and beyond)

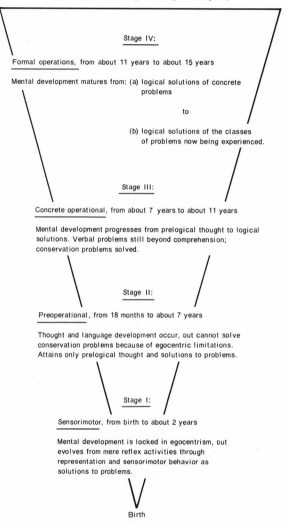

Stage IV:

Formal operations, from about 11 years to about 15 years

Mental development matures from: (a) logical solutions of concrete problems

to

(b) logical solutions of the classes of problems now being experienced.

Stage III:

Concrete operational, from about 7 years to about 11 years

Mental development progresses from prelogical thought to logical solutions. Verbal problems still beyond comprehension; conservation problems solved.

Stage II:

Preoperational, from 18 months to about 7 years

Thought and language development occur, but cannot solve conservation problems because of egocentric limitations. Attains only prelogical thought and solutions to problems.

Stage I:

Sensorimotor, from birth to about 2 years

Mental development is locked in egocentrism, but evolves from mere reflex activities through representation and sensorimotor behavior as solutions to problems.

Birth

Here developmental means "realizing ever more fully one's potential through equilibration."

Beginning Stage

The first of the Piagetian stages is termed the sensorimotor stage. It approximates the chronological ages from birth to two years. At eighteen months, however, this "sensorimotor assimilation" of the external world effects a miniature Copernican revolution.[47] Here Piaget's principle, "In the beginning was the response. . . ," is particularly apropos of the neonate. This period extends from the response in birth (and even the prenatal period) to the acquisition of language, indicating an extraordinary development of the mental. Interacting in and with the organic, this early mental development is of extreme importance. It determines the entire course of the child's psychological evolution because:

> There are no static stages as such. Each is the fulfillment of something begun in the preceding one and the beginning of something that will lead on to the next.[48]

In this perspective, mental development is that process begun with the response the day the infant is born. This does not imply that the child is born thinking, that is, internally representing objects in his mind, but it does mean that the sensorimotor behavior that occurs from birth is necessary for and even instrumental in later cognitive development. The roots of all intellectual development are found in early sensorimotor behavior.

Actually Piaget finds that four fundamental processes of the sensimotor stage compose the revolution that the child accomplishes during the first two years of his life. They consist in constructing the categories of objects, of space, of causality, and of time. With these he fills his first years of living through the sensorimotor stage, which evidences that children utilize logic in their actions rather than in their words:[49]

I. SENSORI MOTOR STAGE

(From birth to about 2 years)

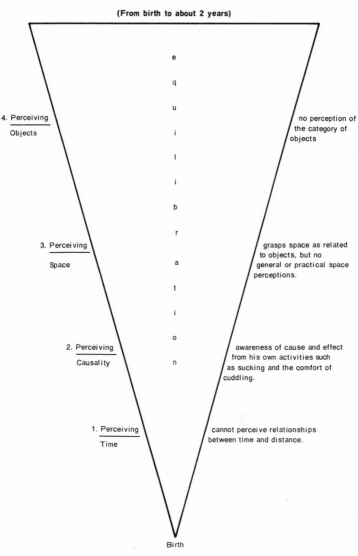

e
q
u
i
l
i
b
r
a
t
i
o
n

4. Perceiving
Objects

no perception of
the category of
objects

3. Perceiving
Space

grasps space as related
to objects, but no
general or practical space
perceptions.

2. Perceiving
Causality

awareness of cause and effect
from his own activities such
as sucking and the comfort of
cuddling.

1. Perceiving
Time

cannot perceive relationships
between time and distance.

Birth

The acts of behavior described here for the sensorimotor stage are typical
for ONLY this age group.

The Second Stage[50]

Preoperational or representational is the second major stage, extending from about eighteen months to about seven years. It necessarily overlaps the sensorimotor stage, engrafting itself as an outgrowth of the first stage. During this period of early childhood, behavior is profoundly modified affectively and intellectually with the appearance of languages. At about the age of two, the child begins to use words as symbols in place of objects. Beginning with one-word sentences, his language facility expands quickly. By the age of about four he has mastered the use of language.

This rapid development of language is instrumental in furthering a rapid conceptual development taking place during this period. Piaget declares that this acquisition of language has three important consequences affecting mental development: verbal exchange with others, heralding the onset of socialization of action; internalization of words, heralding the appearance of thought and supported by internal language with a system of signs; internalization of action, rather than a purely perceptual and motor reaction as in the previous stage, making possible an intuitive representation by means of images and mental activities. Even interpersonal feelings, such as sympathy, antipathy, respect, and love develop, becoming internally more organized as indicated in the illustration that follows, the Preoperational or Representational Stage:[51]

II. PREOPERATIONAL OR REPRESENTATIONAL STAGE

(From about 2 years to about 7 years)

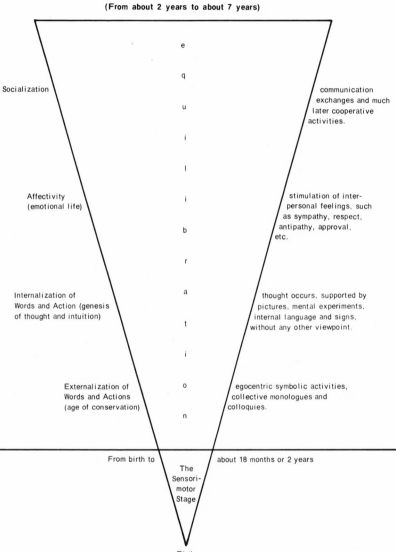

Socialization — communication exchanges and much later cooperative activities.

Affectivity (emotional life) — stimulation of interpersonal feelings, such as sympathy, respect, antipathy, approval, etc.

Internalization of Words and Action (genesis of thought and intuition) — thought occurs, supported by pictures, mental experiments, internal language and signs, without any other viewpoint.

Externalization of Words and Actions (age of conservation) — egocentric symbolic activities, collective monologues and colloquies.

equilibration

From birth to — The Sensori-motor Stage — about 18 months or 2 years

Birth

The Third Stage[52]

The next stage usually coincides with the beginning of formal education. It marks a decisive turning point so far as mental development is concerned. In the former stage the child with his needs and purposes formed the reason for the existence of the universe; the absence of notions of conversation was evident; this, along with animism, artificialism, and realism, locked him in an egocentrism that kept him in a distorted world of childhood magic, still unadapted in his thought life to reality.

In each stage new forms of psychological life and organization emerge. They make certain the completion of the equilibration already attained in the previous preoperational and sensorimotor stages. At the same time they inaugurate an uninterrupted, gradual series of new constructions in a continuing process-and-response development characteristic of the concrete operational stage.

The four groupings in this stage of concrete operations, Piaget maintains, are intellectual schemas that possess particular characteristics, such as closure, associativity, reversibility, and identity. Such schemata are are both sensorimotor equivalents of concepts, permitting the child to deal with different conditions of the same object or class, and sense schemata, consisting of the structure of mental development at any level.

In a child who has attained concrete operations (so-called because now the child puts into a particular act what he formerly achieved only intuitively), the substance of sensorimotor intelligence, then of intuition, is now applied to many diverse realities. These include arithmetic operation (multiplication, addition, division, subtraction, and even their inverses); time operations (series of events in history, etc.); and mechanical and physical functions. All of these operations are rooted in the intuitive before they become perfected in the stage of concrete operations:

In a child who has actually attained concrete operations, Each transformation can be compensated by its inverse, so that

III. STAGE OF CONCRETE OPERATIONS
(from about 7 to 12 years of childhood)

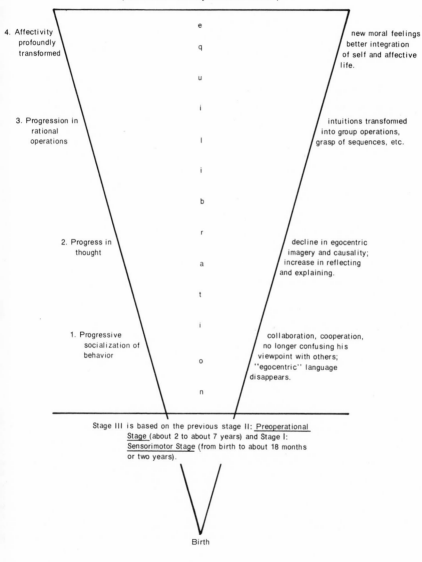

4. Affectivity
profoundly
transformed

new moral feelings
better integration
of self and affective
life.

3. Progression in
rational
operations

intuitions transformed
into group operations,
grasp of sequences, etc.

2. Progress in
thought

decline in egocentric
imagery and causality;
increase in reflecting
and explaining.

1. Progressive
socialization of
behavior

collaboration, cooperation,
no longer confusing his
viewpoint with others;
"egocentric" language
disappears.

equilibration

Stage III is based on the previous stage II: Preoperational
Stage (about 2 to about 7 years) and Stage I:
Sensorimotor Stage (from birth to about 18 months
or two years).

Birth

any arrangement may give rise to another, and conversely. Instead of relying on an all-important figure, the child proceeds exclusively by reference to the one-one correspondence, and thereby succeeds for the first time in decomposing the wholes and coordinating the relationships. From now on, therefore, his actions constitute a reversible system involving constancy of the set.[53]

Cognitive operations, therefore, become interiorized thought operations; this achievement may occur as early as age seven.

The final stage in the developmental approach of the child Piaget terms *formal operations*. Actually, the preceding three stages might lead to the conclusion that mental development is already completed at the age of eleven or twelve; that adolescence is simply a temporary condition resulting from puberty; that this stage of formal operations merely separates temporarily the child from the adult. In the research of Piaget, this assumption is far from what he actually uncovers. To avoid such misconceptions about the concrete and formal operational phases of the child's development, the third stage is termed the *Operational Stage,* with the concrete phase and the formal phase as subdivisions:[54]

THIRD STAGE:

OPERATIONAL

1. CONCRETE
2. FORMAL

Piaget found that children without formal operations are unable to solve adequately the following problem derived from one of Cyril Burt's tests, which he worked on early in his career when he attended Binet's laboratory school in Paris: Edith is fairer than Susan; Edith is darker than Lilly; who is the darkest of the three?[55]

Formal operations evolve out of concrete operations. The

period of formal operations, therefore, is the culmination of the development of mental structures and frequently reaches maximum qualitative maturity by about fifteen. During this stage children gradually learn how to attack problems from all possible combinations. Functionally, formal thought and concrete thought, Piaget declares, are the same; both employ logical operations. He finds that formal thought arises out of concrete operations in the same way that each new level of thought incorporates and modifies prior thinking.

The major difference between the concrete and the formal phases of operations is the much larger range of application. Children in the concrete operational stage are limited to solving tangible problems that are presented; hypothetical problems, complex verbal ones, and those involving the future are beyond their comprehension. Operations are not coordinated, so that the concrete-operational child must deal with each problem separately, that is, as distinct entities. He cannot integrate his separate solutions but must deal with them individually. General theories are too difficult for him to apply. For example, if a logical argument is prefixed to the statement, "Suppose that gold is black. . . ," the concrete-operational child declares that gold is not black and therefore he cannot answer the question. He cannot deal with an argument independently of content. Gold is not black and the problem is unsolvable. He can organize, classify, and separate only what is real.

The Final Stage[56]

The formal-operational child, however, is aware that logically derived conclusions have a validity independent of factual truth or mere appearance. Several assumptions and opinions can be brought to bear on a single problem. He can deal with many classes of problems—hypothetical, verbal, present, past, and future. He is finally free from the content of problems, as indicated in the stage of formal operations:

IV. STAGE OF FORMAL OPERATIONS

(from about 11 to about 15 years of age and beyond)

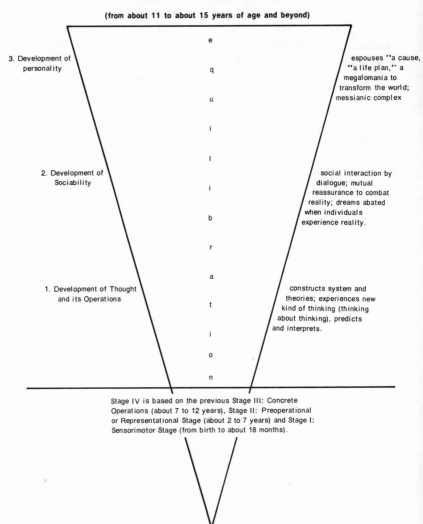

3. Development of
   personality

espouses "a cause,"
"a life plan," a
megalomania to
transform the world;
messianic complex

2. Development of
   Sociability

social interaction by
dialogue; mutual
reassurance to combat
reality; dreams abated
when individuals
experience reality.

1. Development of Thought
   and its Operations

constructs system and
theories; experiences new
kind of thinking (thinking
about thinking), predicts
and interprets.

Stage IV is based on the previous Stage III: Concrete
Operations (about 7 to 12 years), Stage II: Preoperational
or Representational Stage (about 2 to 7 years) and Stage I:
Sensorimotor Stage (from birth to about 18 months).

Birth

Jean Piaget acknowledges that as an adolescent he constructed such a "life plan."
Later he published it as a novel entitled Recherches (Researches).

In developing the period of formal operations in the child, Piaget, in addition to making use of the well-known facts of puberty (today made almost banal by such psychologists as Freud and Hall), prefers to describe *the structures* of the final forms of thought and the affective life of the adolescent. This is not to deny that the maturing sexual instinct marks a crisis in the affectivity of the child's life, but Piaget believes that the phenomenon of mental development gives the true significance of the child's psychological evolution. The marked crisis of disequilibrium caused by his sexual life far from exhausts the analysis of this period of formal operations:

> pubertal changes would play only a very secondary role if the thinking and emotions characteristic of adolescents were accorded their true significance.[57]

Rather than merely describing the problems of adolescence as a sexual revolution, Piaget chooses to avoid this form of exclusivism in his descriptions of formal operation. He thereby supplements, and often succeeds in putting into a more wholesome perspective, the mental-developmental stage preceding adulthood. Not to do so would be to distort the real significance of this final stage of cognitive growth.

Adolescence[58]

Piaget finds that the typical adolescent has the mental equipment to solve problems as logically as the adult person can. He has entered the period of formal operations. He is developing or has already developed his cognitive skills of the formal period. Yet he often seems to "think differently" from the adult. Why is this so?

The answer, Piaget believes, is to be found in what makes the characteristics of adolescent thinking unique: his level of cognitive development and his accompanying egocentrism of thought.

Although Piaget finds that egocentrism is the constant companion of cognitive development, each new stage of mental growth has its inability to differentiate. It assumes a particular form and is expressed in a unique set of actions. It is like a negative by-product, distorting the initial use of newly acquired cognitive structures in mental development. As each new plane of cognitive functioning is characterized by a type of egocentrism, so too is adolescence.

The adolescent becomes possessed with his new-found powers of logical thought, so that the criteria for making judgments becomes what is logical to him, not what is necessarily realistic. His form of egocentrism is the inability to differentiate between his own idealistic thoughts and the world of reality. He cannot seem to understand that the world is not always rationally ordered as he thinks it should be. He is enmeshed in egocentric belief in the omnipotence of logical thought.

This egocentrism is one of the most enduring features of adolescence. The adolescent can think logically about the future and about hypothetical people and events, but he feels that the world should submit to his idealistic, that is, logical ideals rather than to reality. He tries not only to adapt his ego to the social environment, but also to adjust the environment to his ego.

The result of this perspective is a relative failure to distinguish between his own point of view and the viewpoint of the group or world that he expects to reform. Piaget finds on the part of the adolescent more than a simple desire to deviate. It is rather a phase of his life during which he is absorbed in the attributes of the unlimited powers of his thoughts, in which he dreams of a magnificent future of transforming the times and people of his generation through his ideas and ideals.

Such a phase of his life seems to be much more than mere fantasy. It is an effective action-oriented period during which he modifies the empirical world in itself. He becomes involved in an all-absorbing idealistic crisis in which he is unable to distinguish between his own new powers of formal operations and the social order to which he is applying his theories. This egocentrism is so enslaving that it seems he is doomed forever to be an idealistic social critic.

According to Piaget, this egocentrism of adolescence gradually diminishes, like the egocentrism of other periods of growth and development, when the adolescent learns how to utilize his logic effectively in relation to the realities of life.[59] Since the principal intellectual characteristics of adolescents flow from the development of their formal structures directly, their maturing and applications are considered as the important events in the thinking found in this period.

Affects[60]

The adolescent must learn to embrace realistic roles in the world of reality. This involves cognitive development along with a parallel affective development. *Affects* is the term Piaget uses; he declares that

> the focal point of the decentering process . . . is the entrance into the occupational world or the beginning of serious professional training. The adolescent becomes an adult when he undertakes a real job. It is then that he is transformed from an idealistic reformer into an achiever. In other words, the job leads thinking away from the dangers of formalism back into reality. . . . True adaptation to society comes automatically when the adolescent reformer attempts to put his ideas to work.[61]

In comparison with most modern theories of personality, Piaget says much more about the cognitive and perceptual functionings than he does about the child's emotional life. He does not, however, overlook or deny the place of feeling while focusing his interest primarily on the growth of intelligence.

He develops affects and intelligence as integral to each other. Affects are essentially the other side of the same coin—the emotional aspects of behavior that include feelings, motivation, interest, and values in his developmental model. He insists that every intelligent act is accompanied by feelings of interest, pleasure, effort, and the like. These, he admits, provide the energy that sparks intellectual growth in all stages of maturation and development:

STAGES OF EMOTIONAL (AFFECTS) DEVELOPMENT

Stage IV:

Adolescence includes the major emotional achievements of the development of ideals; the individual begins to take up adult roles; tends to have nothing but contempt for the society that produced him, often espousing radical causes.

Stage III:

Middle years of childhood include: cooperation; mutual respect; if one lies to his peers or tattles becoming a social outcast; replacement of morality of submission to authority by morality of cooperation; appearance of will power as regulator of energy.

Stage II:

Preoperational period includes: emerging sense of self-in-relation-to-others; acquiring new interests and values; emerging moral sentiments; developing interpersonal emotions reflecting one's attitudes and self-image; respecting adults as the source of earliest moral feelings.

Stage I:

Sensorimotor period includes: primary emotional reflexes of love, rage, and fear; instinctive strivings for food and comfort; motivation dawns in pleasing mother, reflecting her moods and affection.

Birth

As designed by Piaget, these four stages compose the full process of mental development. In them he portrays how, beginning with infantile sensorimotor intelligence along with affects, the child gradually reconstructs his world of values. Each structural change, he points out, incorporates and improves upon previous structures and affects. The whole process of mental development begins at birth and culminates in adolescence. The deductive thinking of the adolescent, hypothetical in reality, rests on experience of the concrete world but is still based on the system of operation in early and middle childhood. His successive construction coordinates the terminal groupings (stages) by a succession of schemata involving a dispelling of unreality and egocentrism. This ever-widening reality results through a trial-and-error progression.

With all stages of process, however, new elements are constantly upsetting equilibrium. The previous structures are being altered according to the conditions of reality being experienced at the time equilibrium is restored.[62] Accordingly,

> intelligence is said to originate within a biological substrate, a substrate beyond which it soon extends. At its core are the invariant attributes of organization and adaptation, the latter including the two interacting functions, assimilation and accommodation. Through the continued operation of these last[,] structural units called *schemata* are born, develop, and eventually form inter-locking systems or networks. . . . Changes in the assimilation-accommodation relationship occur both within and between stages of development.[63]

All resulting equilibrium, however, is constantly being upset with new elements (demonstrated by smear at lower right of triangle). These in turn become the (new) beginning equilibrium and so on in an unending adaptation of process and response:

PERSPECTIVES OF PROCESS-AND-RESPONSE WITHIN EACH STAGE OF DEVELOPMENTAL MODEL

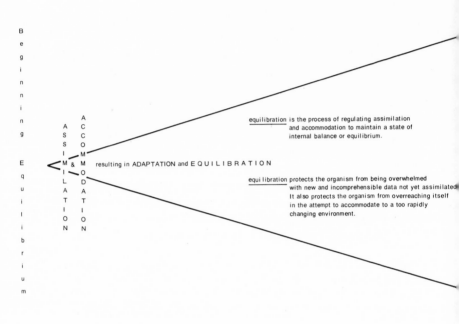

equilibration is the process of regulating assimilation and accommodation to maintain a state of internal balance or equilibrium.

resulting in ADAPTATION and E QU I L I B R A T I O N

equilibration protects the organism from being overwhelmed with new and incomprehensible data not yet assimilated. It also protects the organism from overreaching itself in the attempt to accommodate to a too rapidly changing environment.

In connection with these operations, Piaget believes that as-similation and accommodation, although complementary in the human process, occur simultaneously; also that a balance between the two is necessary for adaptation to reality:[64]

THE

PROCESS

OF

ADAPTATION

ASSIMILATION is an incorporating process of an operative action. By this, environmental data are constantly absorbed as a function into mental structures. As an activity, it involves the organizing, structuring, and functioning of the cognitive powers.

ACCOMMODATION is an outgoing process of an operative action. By it, application of the general structure to some particular reality is achieved. As an activity, it involves modifications of thought patterns to the new reality.

Parallelling this intellectual trial-and-error activity, there is an affectivity (emotionalism) disengaging itself from self. This affectivity, however, still remains the incentive for the actions that ensue. It is the way persons assign value and energy to activities. As an important aspect of all behavior, affectivity has to do with: (1) interest, (2) motivation, (3) emotion, (4) dynamics, and (5) energy in the Piagetian schemata indissolubly linked to the structural aspects of knowing.

Affectivity means very little in mental development without intelligence, for it is intelligence, Piaget insists, that furnishes affectivity with its means and clarifies its ends. It would be erroneous, he contends, to attribute the causes of mental growth to great ancestral tendencies. The essence of the mental process is the faculty of reasoning, acquired through the four stages and not of hereditary origin.

Activities and biological growth, however, as in the Deweyan concepts, are in no way foreign to reason. *The profound tendency of human activity,* Piaget finds, *is progression toward equilibrium.* Reason expresses the highest form of equilibrium, as he indicates in Stage Four of formal operations. It reunites intelligence and emotions (affectivity). In summary, therefore:

During the stage of formal operations, the adolescent acquires the adult capacity for abstract thought, no longer exclusively preoccupied with trying to stabilize and organize just what comes directly to the senses. He has a new orientation, the potentiality of imagining all that might be there—both the very obvious and the very subtle—and thereby exercises a much better assurance of discovering all that is there.[65]

This reasoning is one of the deepest value perspectives in the Piagetian discipline of genetic epistemology. In contrast, Dewey considered the imagination as man's highest form of mental activity. Piaget, in his four stages of growth and development, challenges this climax of the Dewey enigma and shatters it through his highly controlled experiments that demonstrate its inadequacy.

Genetic Epistemology

Piaget's emergence as the leader in genetic epistemology is due to his developmental and dynamic-process approaches to intelligence.[66] He finds that reflexes and other automatic patterns of behavior have a minor role in the development of human intelligence. It is not until the growing child reaches the two formal stages of process in his development that he begins to acquire the various concepts of conservation (the idea that the mass of an object remains constant no matter how much the form changes).

As proof, he gives a four- or five-year-old two containers. Each is only partly full of pink lemonade. When the child agrees that each has the same amount of liquid, he pours the contents of one of the containers into another that is taller, yet not so wide. It is then that the child declares there is more pink lemonade in the new container than in the original one. Neither did Piaget find that the child at this age has any idea of the conservation of length. When put to the test, he insists that a string of beads laid out in a straight line is longer than one that is in the form of a circle, although their length is identical.

Later Piaget discovered how the average child corrected these concepts of conservation by the time he was eight years of age.[67] Hess reports that

> at the larger session [at the City University of New York on October 17, 1972], Mr. Piaget alluded again to his revolutionary experiments. He demonstrated how children learn "conservation"—for example, that things can change their shape without changing their volume. . . . the Piagetians lay down two rows of 10 checkers each, but with one row spaced out longer than the other. To age 5 and 6 children insist that there are more checkers in the longer row, even after they have counted them.

> A questioner observed that recent tests among primitive tribes in Africa and in some slums of America showed an inability to grasp the concept of conservation even among adults. He asked whether this did not call for a change in the Piagetian thesis.

> "Absolutely not at all," Mr. Piaget retorted. "The development of children's intelligence implies a constant exchange with the social environment. Obviously, progress is slow or fast, according to the environment."[68]

In his institute at Geneva, Piaget explains, the most precocious children are those of atomic physicists: "Now I don't think these parents taught their children the notion of conservation, in fact, they don't understand it. The proof is that when I explained it to Einstein in Princeton, he was enchanted."[69] Piaget maintains that no adult up to his time ever actually seems to think of the idea of asking children about conservation, that is, the recognition of permanence in the face of apparent change. Perhaps it is so obvious, when the shape of an object, such as, for example, a tumbler's, is changed that the quantity of liquid it contains will not be affected but conserved, why even ask the child? The novelty for Piaget, however, lay in asking this very question:

> I first discovered the problem of conservation when I worked with young epileptics from 10 to 15. I wanted to find some

empirical way of distinguishing them from normal children. I went around with four coins and four beads, and I would put the coins and beads in one-to-one correspondence and then hide one of the coins. If the three remaining coins were then stretched out into a longer line, the epileptic children said they had more coins than beads. No conservation at all. I thought I had discovered a method to distinguish normal from abnormal children. Then I went on to work with normal children and discovered that all children lack conservation.[70]

When asked just what he means when he says that the young child is egocentric, Piaget answers that this term is subject to the worst interpretations of any word he has ever used. When he uses the term *egocentric,* he insists that it is in an epistemological sense and not in an affective or a moral one, which is the reason it is so often misinterpreted:

> The egocentric child—and all children are egocentric—considers his own point of view as the only possible one. He is incapable of putting himself in someone's place because he is unaware that the other person has a point of view.[71]

Piaget sees egocentrism as a natural tendency of the intelligence that becomes corrected very slowly as the child matures. Many children, he finds, believe that the sun and the moon follow them as they walk. A more prosaic example is the way a young child makes up a word such as *Tom-prop,* and assumes that everyone knows exactly what he means by it.

Piaget's extensive work includes the way children develop a sense of right and wrong. More than forty years ago he discovered that morality does not enter the child's world until he is aware of other viewpoints, and then he is likely to disregard them. Today his position is still the same. In this perspective, however, Piaget distinguishes between two periods in the development of moral judgment; in the first period, a child accepts his rules from authority and the ideas of adults are important to him; in the second period, he strives to become independent of adults.

As solidarity grows between children, Piaget maintains that a morality develops based on cooperation. If the adults are ready to discuss matters with the children, he finds that the latter will form a system of cooperation with the adults. Unfortunately, children often have to discover the idea of justice not from, but at the expense of, their parents. It is especially important to realize that, from the age of about seven or eight, justice tends to prevail over obedience. Here, Piaget finds the beginning of conflict between generations.[72]

With regard to his major stages of mental growth and development, Piaget is often quizzed on what he labels *the American question*: Is it possible to speed up the learning (of conservation) concepts? Usually he replies with a counterquestion: Is it a good thing to accelerate the learning of these concepts? Then he adds:

> We know the average speed of the children we have studied in our Swiss culture but there is nothing that says that the average speed is the optimum. But blindly to accelerate the learning of conservation concepts could be even worse than doing nothing.[73]

Piaget is of the opinion that it is very difficult to decide just how to shorten studies. If one year is spent studying something verbally that requires two years of active study, then one year seems lost. If, however, a little more time is given to permitting the children to be active, letting them use trial-and-error techniques on different things in the Deweyan sense, he thinks that the time the child seems to lose may actually be gained. It is precisely in this manner that children develop a general method that they can use on other subjects:

> Now if you examine the way a child develops his idea of space, you will see that he first develops topological intuitions, so that the child's ideas are closer to mathematical theory than to history.[74]

When Piaget is asked if anyone is trying to compose an intelligence test based on his research, he answers in the affirmative:

That kind of research is going on in two places right now. Here at the University of Geneva, Vinh Bang—a Vietnamese psychologist—is working on a test. And Monique Laurendeau and Adrien Pinard, two psychologists at the University of Montreal, have been using my experimental methods and giving all the various tests to a single child. Just now they are back-checking to see if their experiments and mine produce similar results, and they are publishing volumes on different aspects of the experiments.[75]

This experimenting, Piaget explained, will eventually produce a battery of tests that can be given to a group of children. However, there is a risk that they may get distorted answers. But the difference in this experiment is that the clinical method will already have been utilized in the studying of reasoning in each stage of development. This assures a background to help interpret the answers. The advantages of this experiment are to be found in that the method of reasoning is already known and in that a reliance on the answers is no longer necessary.[76]

Piaget and Dewey

Jean Piaget's notable accomplishments in studying the human process over the last half century of his professional life make it almost impossible to compare him to any other process scholar except John Dewey. This educator, at 90, did not cease to write and publish about his instrumentalistic approach to learning and teaching. In an interview with Mary Harrington Hall, Piaget was asked if his theory that the child must discover for himself the method of learning through his own activity is not similar to John Dewey's concept of 'earning by doing. With this he fully concurred: "Indeed it does; John Dewey was a great man."[77] Then he added that the schools have been paying lip service to "learning by doing" since the days of Dewey—but most of the time it is merely a cliché.[78] Unlike Dewey's, only during this last decade or so have Piaget's writings created a great surge of interest among Europeans and Americans. Many are now succeeding in translating his findings on the functioning of the mind and their application to values in the educational process.[79]

A salient feature of both Piaget and Dewey is evident in the former's recently translated book entitled *Insights and Illusions of Philosophy*. The literal translation of the original French edition published in Paris in 1965 reads: "Wisdom and the Illusion of Philosophy."[80] Although written specifically as his answer to whether he is an empirical scientist or a psychologizing philosopher, the book created more stir in European intellectual circles than any of his many books published previously. Its popularity is so strong that it commanded a second French edition within a short time. The reasons seem to lie in the theme of the book, which touches a sensitive philosophical nerve, especially in the life of French intellectuals. In it, Jean Piaget, not unlike John Dewey in America before him, tells the public and his academic colleagues that he is enamored of the goals and promises of philosophy. Gradually he came to realize that a seeker of knowledge like himself was unable to find ultimate satisfaction in the philosophical enterprise.[81] There is also a close analogy between Piaget's potential impact on European philosophy and J. B. Watson's impact on mentalistic psychology in his behaviorism, as espoused more than fifty years ago in the United States, concerning which Piaget states:

> Give me a dozen healthy infants, well formed and my own specified world to bring them up in, and I'll guarantee to take any one at random and train him to become any type of specialist I might select—doctor, lawyer, artist, merchant, chief, and, yes, even beggarman and thief—regardless of his talents, penchants, tendencies, abilities, vocations, and race of ancestors.[82]

This behavioristic impact becomes more evident when Piaget is interrogated as to whether man learns about man only by studying man. Perhaps he could go into the laboratory and study rats and primates as well? He admits that comparative studies are necessary, but that one must not make the mistake of believing that studying a rat is sufficient. "Many theories of some schools that I will not name," he says, "are based on the rat. It is not enough for me."[83]

When specifically taking up the topic of behaviorist empiricism, however, Piaget criticizes the famous stimulus-response schema and how behavioral psychologists today are retaining a strictly Lamarckian outlook.[84] In this challenge he exposes the parallelism existing between the biological changes of man and the development of his mental, moral, emotional, and social traits. He is also critical of how empiricism implies that reality can be reduced to observable features. He claims that biologists have shown conclusively how the organism constantly interacts with its environment. The view that it submits passively to the environment is becoming more and more untenable. Piaget asks: "How then can man be simply a recorder of outside events? When he transforms his environment by acting upon it he gains a deeper knowledge of the world than any copy of reality ever could provide. What is more[,] empiricism cannot explain the existence of mathematics[,] which deals with unobservable features and with cognitive constructions."[85]

Piaget, a professor of biology, sees the Lamarckian theory of variation and evolution as a long-abandoned doctrine. He maintains that to get a tenable stimulus-response theory (Lamarckian perspective), it is essential to modify and complete its classical meaning. As he sees it:

> Before a stimulus can set off a response the organism must be capable of providing it. If this concept [of competence in embryology] applies to learning—and my research indicates that it does—then learning will be different at different development levels. It would depend upon the evolution of competences. The classical concept of learning suddenly becomes inadequate.[86]

Nature-Nurture

Piaget hastens to state that individual development is not all innate. If each man is the product of interaction between heredity and environment, to draw a clear line between innate and acquired behavior patterns become virtually impossible. The dangerous pitfalls to psychologists, as he sees them, lie in practical applications. All too often psychologists make such applications before they know what they are applying. Piaget cautions that in all learning there must be provision for fundamental research; one must also be cautious of the practical if the foundations of theories are doubtful.[87]

When Piaget is questioned whether language determines a child's view of the world, he defines a close relationship between language and thought, but language does not govern thought or operation; operations do not influence language but do influence thought. He appeals to the experiments of Dr. Hermina Sinclair, who has made some interesting studies along this line:

> She had two groups of children; one group had conservation, the other group did not. She took the group of children that did not understand conservation and taught them the language used by the children who understood the concept. They learned to use "long" and "short" and "wide" and "narrow" in a consistent way. She wanted to see if the concepts would come once the language was learned. They did not. If a ball of clay was pulled into a sausage, the children could describe it as "long" and "thin". But they did not understand that the clay was longer but thinner than the ball and therefore the same quantity.[88]

What changes with different languages, Piaget says, is the way man partitions reality, the way he dissects the world into its component parts. He hastens to add that translation of concepts into their parts is not essential in thought.[89]

Philosophy Challenged

It seems strange that philosophers on the Continent should respond to Piaget's work by classifying him as a "positivist" in a pejorative sense.[90] Many tend to regard Piaget as a scholar who has turned from philosophical values, to the neglect of the truly human aspects of the human person, an attitude similar to their earlier one toward John Dewey.[91] Professor Wolfe Mays, however, explicates Piaget's belief vis-à-vis philosophy in the introduction to *Insights and Illusions of Philosophy*, where he writes:[92]

> Piaget believes that philosophy still has an important part to play in our culture as a "wisdom"—namely, in helping us to coordinate our values, ethical, aesthetic, and social. He makes the interesting point that if Western philosophy had not in its origin been so closely tied up with the development of science, which was not the case with Oriental thought, it would like the latter have followed the path of "wisdom".[93]

Piaget states emphatically that there is a place for philosophical activities; he even calls them indispensable for the rational human life, but he proposes that the product of philosophizing should not be called knowledge. At best, he sees it as a wisdom, a sort of mixture of knowledge and personal values and norms, which differs from knowledge by having two additional factors: the one, of decision or commitment, gives vital meaning to one's life and gives a system of provisionally accepted opinions or hypotheses that allow one to live in cognitive harmony with his personal decisions; the other restricts the scope of knowledge to objective meaning. By asserting that knowledge at all levels entails built-in controls or criteria for truth, it does this implicitly, as in spontaneous manifestations of rational thinking, or explicitly, as in scientific methodology of controlled observations of facts or formalized systems of deductive reasoning.[94]

Piaget sees philosophy as the easy way out. It encourages trying to solve problems by sitting around in the office, as an armchair philosopher, reasoning them out. "But," he asserts, "because I am a biologist, I knew that deductions must be made from facts. Only after the facts do you go back into your office to work out the problem." Then, he maintains, not to cultivate a philosophical outlook is to be a poor scientist, for abstract reflection is fundamental to seeing problems clearly. "But," he says, "the error of philosophy—its demon—is to believe that you can go ahead and solve the problem you formulated in the office without going into the field and establishing the facts."[95] In his respect Piaget is re-presenting Dewey's views when he argued for the necessity of establishing an experimental school in connection with pedagogy.

To appreciate better the modern message of his book, one must realize that what Piaget sees as the decline of philosophy has deep epistemological roots; it is also a sociological and psychological problem institutionalized in the settings of universities and scholastic circles. It is not dissimilar to what John Dewey rebelled against in the late nineteenth and early twentieth centuries. Like Piaget, Dewey had the philosophical courage to speak out against abuses of philosophy in an environment where it had become an almost sacrosanct profession, the sacred cow of the untouchables, the prerequisite, if not the substitute, for religion itself. Since Piaget frankly admits that he is not exempt from self-motivated assumptions, he defends the publication of his book on the basis that he thinks it best to describe how it happened that "a future philosopher eventually became an epistemologist of the development of thinking."[96]

Piaget's book turns out to be an indictment of philosophy as it is being practiced today in his own environment. In this perspective, his publication has a close affinity with John Dewey's instrumentalism or experimentalism, which philosophy has sometimes been called *humanism* because of its emphasis on the continuity of values in the stream of human experience. Thus, to those formed in one of the traditional schools of philosophy or psychology, Piaget, like Dewey, appears to be philosophizing with a hammer in his hand.[97]

Bruner's Discovery Approach[98]

One of the finest contributions of Jerome S. Bruner is the introduction of Jean Piaget to Americans. Piaget, on being requested to explain the difference between his theoretical approach to the child and that of Bruner's replied: "It is very difficult to explain the difference between Bruner and me." Then he added:

> Bruner is a mobile and active man and has held a sequence of different points of view. (Essentially he does not believe in mental operation while I do.) Bruner replaces operations with factors that have varied through his different stages—Bruner's stages, not the child's. Bruner uses things like language, like image. When Bruner was at the stage of strategies he used to say that his strategies were more or less Piaget's operations. At that time our theories were closest. Since then he has changed his point of view.[99]

Arthur W. Foshay states how "cognitive style" and the idea regarding structure, or logic, or each of the scholarly disciplines as a way of learning any discipline were "in the air" during the latter part of the fifties. Jerome Bruner developed this new relationship vividly in his work *The Process of Education,* which became the most influential educational writing of its time.[100] Since Jean Piaget's new discipline borders on Bruner's contributions to the learning-teaching process, he was pressed further and asked if one day Bruner might not reach the operational stage that he was proposing. Piaget commented only: "Bruner is an unpredictable man—this is what makes his charm."[101]

Referring to his American critics, Bruner and Skinner, for example, in a lecture at the City University of New York on October 17, 1972, Piaget did not hesitate to admit candidly: "I hope I'm not the No. 1 Piagetian revisionist, because there are great gaps to be filled."[102] There he also acknowledged his disagreement with Noan Chomsky, a fellow structuralist, who held that language capacity is an inborn structure.

"How can you explain biologically the relation between the subject and the predicate?" Piaget demanded when provoked by another question, one on "cognitive style," a concept associated with Jerome Bruner. Here, by implication, Piaget struck still another blow in a debate that has been titillating the profession for quite some time: "I never understood Jerome Bruner," he confessed, "and I don't think he ever understood me."[103]

In constructing a theory of cognitive growth, as Bruner has done today, psychologists work in the long shadow of Jean Piaget. But in developing his theory, Bruner presented an alternative to the work of the Swiss giant and designed some of his research problems in responding to Piaget's findings.[104] Consequently, in his process-discovery approaches to psychology as they apply to relevance of values in the educative process, Bruner, professor of psychology and director of the Center for Cognitive Studies, Harvard University, is probably creating more excitement on the American scene than any other professor or educator since the time of John Dewey. In producing so many writings dealing with the cognitive man and applying them to the school through different curriculum projects sponsored by the former Educational Services Incorporated, now termed Education Development Services, he is influencing the educative process in a unique way. By his popularly termed *discovery approach* to learning, he is greatly increasing the effectiveness of John Dewey's problematic approaches within the American school system. His long-range objective of improving scientific knowledge, especially in achieving a greater sense of the substance of, and method for, science, is engendering new progress in the developmental techniques of its rationale.[105]

Two of his best books are *The Process of Education,* which he wrote as a result of the ten-day conference called by the National Academy of Sciences, of which he is chairman, and *Toward a Theory of Instruction,* a series of his own essays that he produced while engaged in what he terms the practical tasks of public education.[106] In retrospect, Bruner declares that each of his essays in his publications is still going through its own metamorphosis, and that the pragmatism therein he hopes some day to convert into a more systematic way of proceeding. That day he sees as being hastened by the schools taking seriously the task of building a theory of instruction.[107]

Ten years later, in discussing the most widely quoted principle from his *The Process of Education*—that the foundations of any subject may be taught to anybody at any age in some form—

Bruner still insisted that it was an honest statement, even though he received a lot of scars in controversies over such a recommendation, and he still maintains that there is still not one single shred of evidence that goes counter to it. He does admit that there is a tremendous amount of misunderstanding regarding it, and that his great friend, Jean Piaget, probably has misunderstood it more than most, ". . . although his misunderstanding is very natural and consistent with the set of filters through which he sees development. His misunderstanding is itself instructive."[108]

As Bruner views it, Piaget's genius is to study those aspects of mental functioning that show as little possible difference as the child goes from one school or class or culture or curriculum to another. For example, if the description of the typical formal-operational thought process is taken, there is no way whatever to distinguish between the average 14-year-old boy and Einstein. Basically, the "missing part" in Piaget, as Bruner perceives it, is how the human being learns to use, to deploy, his operations and rules—how he learns to bring them into conscious, verbalized awareness. Thus, he finds many things he cannot fit into *Le Patron's* system. Focusing on training in attention, for example, he mobilizes a long sequence of problem-solving skills or strategies that he believes begin to be learned in the early months of life.[109]

In Bruner's system, the child moves through three stages, very different in their perspectives from those of the Piagetian stages of growth and development. In the first stage, Bruner represents ideas through action. Adults use this *enactive* representation primarily to represent motor skills; with the very young child it is an important means of representing objectives. In the *ikonic* or second stage, information is represented in visual images. The third stage is that of *symbolic* representations using arbitrary and abstract methods to represent ideas, with language as an obvious example. Thus Bruner maintains that from the first "the baby's behavior is intelligent, adaptive, and flexible."

BRUNER'S MAJOR STAGES OF COGNITIVE
D E V E L O P M E N T

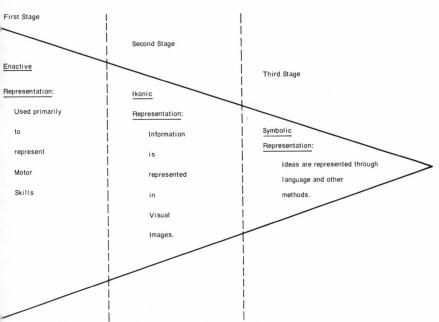

According to Bruner, the foundations of any subject in some representation may be taught to anybody at any stage. In contrast with this position, review Piaget's stages.

He is convinced that a psychologist cannot, by himself, construct a theory of cognitive development or learn how to enrich and amplify the growing mind. He feels that it must be a cooperative project, that the entire intellectual community, artist as well as scientist, must share in the task. "People have enormous confidence in scientists and will do what they ask them to do," Bruner maintains; ". . . this is also potentially dangerous."[110]

Beyond a doubt, numerous Piagetian insights do confirm and expand many of Bruner's contributions to the educative process of previous years. It is still an arduous task to translate Piaget's original French into its English equivalent. Against this difficulty, Bruner has contributed much to making Piaget's works less likely to be misunderstood. When he was composing his tentative manuscript of *The Process of Education* in 1959, Bruner was criticized as giving too much prominence to the theory of Jean Piaget in his developmental approach to the child, especially in the stage from preoperational to operational thought.[111]

Even at present Bruner shows more and more evidence of adopting the developmental or process approach of educational literature. He refers to Piaget's conclusions and interpretations relative to human behavior and to the human-being-in-process aspects of the complete person that are involved in process learning. Until recently, many of these insights have been truncated, only partially understood, and very poorly applied, even by so-called experts in the field.[112]

Jerome Bruner sees the ideal curriculum as the one that builds itself around the great issues, principles, and values that a society deems worthy of the continuing concern of its members. "For," he declares, "these often permit the greatest yield." In one study after another he indicates that ". . . if you don't teach the child problem-solving, you haven't done much, no matter what the subject." He sees traditional nursery programs as too often like "undifferentiated, uncommitted love," a supporting, loving atmosphere with nothing to do and failing to encourage the kinds of activity that children grow on:

> I think that the crucial problem is an opportunity to set goals for oneself, to learn to mobilize means for reaching them and to withstand the frustrations of detours and indirect means—all this in an atmosphere of support and affection. That's far from the idea of "enriched stimulation."[113]

In his *The Relevance of Education* (1971), Bruner presents a collection of some nine additional essays, taking up the difficulties he alludes to in his previous works by reflecting his response to the societal problems of the last decade. In it he stresses more the responsibility of people, in their intellectual development, during the present decade, for meeting the great task of reconstruction of social values amid the pernicious effects of poverty, prejudice, and neglect of the past.[114] He states emphatically that today education is in a state of crisis and is failing to respond to changing social needs, that it is lagging behind rather than leading:

> My last six months' work on early education and social class, for example, convinces me that the educational system is in effect our way of maintaining a class system—a group at the bottom. It cripples the capacity of children in the lowest socio-economic quarter of the population to participate effectively in society, and does so early and effectively.[115]

Bruner maintains that conditions are getting so bad that he is "ready to call a moratorium on the development of problem-solving curricula for the intelligent kids." He sees the warping of the children at the bottom of the educational ladder as a much more urgent problem. At this point in his life he declares that he is looking more for the social invention, however radical, that will make it possible for people to work together on the massive problems of poverty, urban life, and, especially, learning to use technology effectively.

Without an all-out, cooperative effort today, Bruner sees no alternative to a crisis-facing education that will climax in the old, familiar "We can no longer fool around with this mess. You are all under arrest." What needs to be done right now, he cautions, is to recapture the sense that action is possible. He admits that he delights in his colleague, Fred Skinner, "because he is so candidly a political man. I seldom agree with his image of utopia but I admire his willingness to commit himself. I wish more of us would at least cut bait."[116]

When Bruner is asked if he can sum up his approach to his work in just a few words, he complies by stating that "for many ordinary kids school does not symbolize the place where the heart and head are fully engaged." His style of inquiry, he adds, probably fits into the pragmatic tradition of Charles Sanders Peirce and William James, for he is "trying to find out how human beings cope, what they require for it by way of information processing, anticipation, and intention."

Functionalist that Bruner is, he wonders whether psychologists are coping with the problems of the time. After all, he says, he was born blind and it was his curiosity and wonder about how people know anything that made him decide to become a psychologist. The marvelous thing about it all, he maintains, is that he has been concerned with dispelling the darkness that has prevented children from getting a square deal in the school system as he ponders the tremendous task of righting this wrong.[117]

He confesses that he is troubled because he feels that he should devote all of his energy to making the schools responsive to the needs of children from lower socioeconomic backgrounds: "You don't get immune from these crises in your career just because you are reaching the mid-fifties, [but] in some ways they get more severe." In this perspective, he thinks that all schools of education should be abolished, for education ought to be the responsibility of the entire faculty:

> If we can give degrees in theoretical physics and experimental physics and applied physics, then we can surely give a degree in *pedagogical* physics. Let physicists train physics teachers and mathematicians train math teachers and let me and my colleagues in psychology become educational psychologists as well.[118]

Bruner foresees a great difficulty in his proposal, because today so many professional educators would think twice about losing their autonomy. He says, however, that losing autonomy and gaining effectiveness may be just what the new social invention of relevance of values is all about.

As a corollary to John Dewey's views, for example, Bruner sees as paramount today the problem of determining the right balance between individuals and society in the light of exactly what this new humanistic education should be. His is a philosophical-psychological-process approach to the future. In these dimensions he supplements and integrates into a more meaningful whole most of the facets of the ideal humanism inaugurated by Dewey. Presently engaged in writing what has been earmarked as "the great synthesis," Bruner promises with this work to be of inestimable benefit to those struggling to meet the ever-greater demands for change and relevance in their educational undertakings.[119]

Maritain's New Humanism

> Maritain, Maritain—We are beginning to be beset by his name. At first it approached us from footnotes, then from quotations of him by others, then from title pages of his own works which have been translated into English. Beset we are, and glad we are beset.[120]

Daniel Sargent's message reveals what any serious student of educational philosophy already comprehends, namely, that Maritain's voice is still a prominent one today; that he dares to philosophize about the relevance of values in education during a time of flux, crisis, and ambivalence, even using the imperative when recommending a practical course of action; that he dares, as a philosopher of process, to descend to the level of the practical at a time when such a descent is perhaps most discouraging.

Although the present indictments of ultra-humanism seem to be imposing upon the schools an almost unbelievable commitment to change, actually the essence of education in process, according to Jacques Maritain (1882–1973), remains relatively stable.

As in the life and work of John Dewey, present social and ethical problems of the greatest magnitude prove to be the transforming factor that makes Maritain's philosophy more "humanizingly" in tune with those useful and encouraging educators who urge entering "into the thick of human affairs," and who thereby proclaim the necessity of wrestling with the problems of the times.[121] Thus Maritain, with his sensitivity and readiness to grasp the importance of practical matters, persistently claimed that, without the principle of permanence in life, all the innovations in the world have little if any meaning for the fulfillment of man. He sees them as mere burdens, possibly retarding and at times even precluding progress in the new age, which, above everything else, must be genuine in its provisions for assisting man in perfecting himself.[122]

Is it not, then, to Maritain, as one of the great educational philosophers during this post-Dewey period of personalized relevance and sensitivity, that the schools can turn? Does he not help to alert all to the possible pitfalls, which are inherent in an anthropocentric humanism, if incomplete understanding of the human person and his destiny in the world becomes too prevalent? As Brameld points out:

> Man is integrally both material and spiritual, but he becomes fully himself in the degree that he rises to the heights always latent within him. . . . Nevertheless, it is not to be denied that Maritain, in contrast to some perennialists, has earnestly sought to reconcile his philosophy with the revolutionary events of our century and to apply it in behalf of humane values accepted by the most ardent advocates of a radically socialized order . . . [and] to tolerate many differences in religious individuals who swear to none.[123]

Maritain maintains that whenever there is any serious distortion of the significance of man's nature or of the world itself in the humanism being espoused, there is likewise a corresponding, grave danger of dehumanization and destructive pollution of the world.[124] In the name of personalization within the process of self-fulfillment, self-integration, and self-determination, he sees as part of the identity crisis an exaggerated emphasis resulting in a spurious self-reliance. This can reduce man to the level of a creature having merely sensory knowledge. The malady then becomes greater through overemphasis of the all-engrossing affective aspects of man's being.

He explains why persons are now, as never before in modern history, in danger of being reduced to such a mere pragmatic level. So marginal in its nature is man's malaise that it leaves him barely able to suspect his real dignity and genuine worth.[125] Here John Milton's description of success is apropos in capturing the discerning spirit of Maritain's humanism: "Success neither proves a cause to be good, nor indicates it to be bad. Demand, therefore, that the cause be not judged by the event, but the event by the cause; for the vulgar judge of it according to the event, and the learned, according to the purpose of them that do it."[126]

To Maritain the crucial problems of personhood are operative within the ultrahumanism of the day.[127] He sees them of prime importance for better comprehending the new crisis of process and how they merge in civilization with the culture that any education for relevance of values must of necessity face and challenge. This challenge is often referred to by Vatican II as: "the new humanism dealing with a balance between the spiritual and the secular."[128] Thus, the great dichotomy of sacred and profane, which tends to expand itself from ages past, is resulting in an ever more meaningful confrontation process. It challenges both the cause and the success of the "old" humanism as no longer adequate.

In the culture that is coming of age, now struggling for survival within the new, Maritain sees an uncontrolled virus. He calls it an "ultrahumanism," which gradually expresses itself by an evolution in which there is a sort of materialistic reversal of man's values. He sees it as coercing human nature to achieve its maximal material output but failing in the process of appreciating man's total dimension.[129] As a result, man is likely to tend toward his own destruction and even to universal ruin.[130] Maritain envisions reciprocal interaction of the spiritual and the secular as the key issue for mankind in progress today, pregnant with life or death.[131]

Maritain has gone so far as to term mere materialism "the twilight of civilization," a humanism that is in danger of betraying itself just as twilight ushers in the night. Night, however, precedes the day and, in this sense, it can help prepare man for the new dawn. In his intelligence man must see clearly how to pierce, with the early rays of light in process, the all-encompassing darkness that precedes the dawn.

In the "death struggle" of man and the world in process, Maritain discerns the preparation for new life. The complete renewal of civilization he presents as the aim of the developmental, enlightening process of education.[132] To this future renewal education is being called through a completely new, and newly oriented, humanistic personalization of self-development within society. As envisioned by John W. Gardner in his *Self-Renewal*:

> society can do much to encourage such self-development. The most important thing it can do is to remove the obstacles to individual fulfillment. This means doing away with the gross inequalities of opportunity imposed on some of our citizens by race prejudice and economic hardship. And it means a continuous and effective operation of "talent salvage" to assist young people to achieve the promise that is in them. The benefits are not only to the individual but to the society. The renewing society must be continuously refreshed by a stream of new talent from all segments or strata of society. Nothing is more decisive for social renewal than the mobility of talent.[133]

Developmental—in Retrospect

Clearly, the key word for describing Piaget and Maritain is similar to the one for describing Bruner, Dewey, Harris, and Mann—*developmental*. As a unique concept, it is gradually coming into its own under the new humanism. When properly appreciated, *developmental* extends to the term *process* its most comprehensive meaning. It identifies how values are integral to all human experience and become so dynamic as to demand constant redefining and reapplying in everyday living.

In his "vitalization" of activity, John Dewey strongly linked all values with educational growth, in both the interpersonal and social realms, as the nucleus of life:

the process of growth, of improvement and progress rather than the static outcome and result, becomes the significant thing. Not health as an end fixed once and for all, but the needed improvement in health—a continual process—is the end and good. The end is no longer a terminus or limit to be reached. It is the active process of transforming the existing situation. Not perfection as a final goal, but the ever-enduring process of perfecting, maturing, refining is the aim of living. Honesty, industry, temperance, justice, like health, wealth, and learning, are not goods to be possessed as they would be if they expressed fixed ends to be attained. They are directions of change in the quality of experience.[134]

Thus growth is desirable as its own sufficient criterion of basic value and is even necessary at times as an intrinsic good. It is also valuable instrumentally and, therefore, beneficial extrinsically. Jean Piaget observes that nature amply demonstrates how an organism matures by adding steadily to its life, broadening its connections with cross sections of the present cultural and natural environment. At the same time the organism appears to explore the limitless opportunities for potential change that time so abundantly provides.

Is it not in this Deweyan-Piagetian dimension of growth that all levels of development apply to man in process? As pointed out by Maritain and Bruner, are they not esstential to the fuller realization of his human excellence both as an individual and as a social being? Awareness of process is uniquely a twentieth-century fruition, providing for its own continual renewal by the only stability possible in a world buffeted by change: the stability of motion or innovation.[135] For man and the world evolving together, is there not emerging today, in social perspective, the opportunity for teleological fulfillment of personalization?

Although none of the theorists described here ever claimed to have perfected a process philosophy or a process-and response education for values as such, all of them have influenced American education in that direction. One of the purposes of this work is to credit these men—especially Horace Mann, William T. Harris, and John Dewey—in a historical dimension of relevance of values, and thus give them the recognition they deserve. Did they not lay the foundations for those perspectives whereby we realize better that process is the key to solving the practical problem of values in education within the ever-changing needs of the times? In the words of Friedrich Wilhelm Nietzsche (1844–1900), calling for a reevaluation of values in his day: "That which is ahead is just as much a condition of what is present as that which is past."[136]

In comparing the following statements on the perspectives of education as they evolved over the centuries from Socrates to Piaget, this interrelationship of past, present, and future of which Nietzsche wrote is evident:[137]

VALUE PERSPECTIVES OF
EDUCATION THROUGH THE CENTURIES

(470–399 B.C.)—SOCRATES   The true aim in the process of education is to dispel error and to discover truth.

(ca. 427–347 B.C.)—PLATO   Education consists of giving to the body and soul all the perfection for their development of which they are susceptible and capable.

(ca. 384–322 B.C.)—ARISTOTLE   The true aim in the process of education is the attainment of happiness through developing perfect virtue.

(ca. 436–338 B.C.)—ISOCRATES   The object of education is to attain development of perfectibility through morality and truth and critical thinking.

(A.D. ca. 35–95)—QUINTILIAN   Education is more a process of understanding than of hardship and punishment.

(A.D. 354–430)—AUGUSTINE   The purpose of education is to bring to fruition the whole man who is only potentially present in the child.

(A.D. ca. 1225–1274)—AQUINAS   Education is to help the learner to realize his potential through self-development.

(A.D. 1466–1536)—ERASMUS   Education consists in a cooperative process of assisting the students rather than in the teacher displaying his own learning.[138]

(A.D. 1483–1546)—LUTHER   The objects of education is the development of the individual as a preparation for effective service in state and church.

(A.D. 1533–1592)—MONTAIGNE   Education is the art of forming men, not specialists.

(A.D. 1561–1626)—BACON   Education consists in making human powers and human science coincide so man can grow in dominance over all things.

(A.D. 1592–1670)—COMENIUS   Education consists in teaching all things to all men thereby developing the whole man.

(A.D. 1608–1674)—MILTON   A complete . . . education is one which develops a man to perform justly, skillfully and magnanimously all the offices, both private and public of peace and war.

(A.D. 1706–1790)—FRANKLIN   Education should include in the developmental process all that is ornamental and all that is useful.

(A.D. 1712–1778)—ROUSSEAU   Education is nothing but the formation of habits.

(A.D. 1746–1827)—PESTALOZZI   Education means a natural, progressive, and systematic development of all man's powers.

(A.D. 1770–1831)—HEGEL   Education is that process through which the individual becomes ethical.

(A.D. 1776–1841)—HERBART   The aim of education is to produce a well-balanced many sidedness of interest with morality as the highest aim of humanity and consequently of the educative process.

(A.D. 1782–1852)—FROEBEL   Self-activity is of the highest educative value and education consists in its fullest development and utilization.

(A.D. 1796–1859)—MANN   Education consists in *embracing* the proper care and training of the body, that its health and longevity may be secured; in *cultivating* the faculties by which is compared, analyzed, combined, remembered, reasoned, and perceived the natural fitness and beauty of things so as to know more of the world and of the glorious attributes of its Maker thereby more faithfully harmonizing with its laws and better enjoying its exquisite adaptations to human welfare; in *fashioning* moral nature into some resemblance of its divine original—*subordinating* propensities to the law of duty, *expanding* benevolence into a sentiment of universal brotherhood, and *lifting* hearts to the grateful and devout contemplation of God.

(A.D. 1803–1882)—EMERSON   The end of education is to train away all impediment, and to leave only pure powers.

(A.D. 1820–1903)—SPENCER   The function which education has to discharge is to prepare man for complete living.

(A.D. 1835–1909)—HARRIS   Education is that process through which the individual becomes ethical.

(A.D. 1842–1900)—JAMES   Education is the organization of acquired habits of action such as will fit the individual, to his physical and social environment.

(A.D. 1859–1952)—DEWEY   Education is life.

(A.D. 1861–1947)—WHITEHEAD   Education is discipline for the adventure of life.

(A.D. 1862–1947)—BUTLER   Education consists in a gradual adjustment to the spiritual possessions of the race: the scientific, literary, aesthetic, institutional, and religious inheritances.

(A.D. 1866–1946)—WELLS   Education is a race between civilization and catastrophe.

(A.D. 1874–1949)—THORNDIKE   The work of education is to make changes in human minds and bodies.

(A.D. 1879–1946)—BAGLEY   Education is the process by means of which the individual acquires experience that will function in rendering more efficient his future action.

(A.D. 1882–1973)—MARITAIN   Education consists in entering into "the thick of human affairs by wrestling with the problems of the times in assisting man to perfect himself and others."[139]

(1896–   )—PIAGET   Education consists in adapting the individual to his surrounding social environment, in creating men who are capable of doing new things . . . men who are creative, inventive, and discoverers . . . and in forming minds which can be critical, can verify, and not accept everything they are offered.

(1904–   )—SKINNER   The basic processes of education are learning and teaching based on a scientific analysis of behavior as a true technology.

(1915–   )—BRUNER   Education should build itself around the great issues, principles, and values that a society deems worthy of the continuing concern of its members.

To become more sensitive, therefore, to the process perspectives of these pioneers, a deliberate attempt is made above to draw out the rich implications of their legacy by applying the concept *process* wherever it appears. This provides greater insight into their already highly recognized contributions. Is it any exaggeration to say that Piaget and Maritain, along with Bruner, Dewey, Harris, and Mann, have immortalized themselves through their record of unstinting service to what they believed to be the greatest need of their day? Did they not see in education for values how, through process-and-response, mankind would constantly renew itself as a wellspring for all generations to come?

In accordance with their clarion call, should not the countless opportunities inherent in the evolution of educational values today be a practical route toward helping shape the tomorrow that is now in process? In the words of Whitehead:

> Philosophy—and we may add, education—never reverts to its old position after the shock of a great philosopher.[140]

Whitehead's evaluation of these idea men of modern times is especially apropos of Jean Piaget, for his genetic epistemology today is revolutionizing the world of knowledge. Its relevance to the human personality has never before been so significantly experienced in the historic process.

SELECT REFERENCES

Allen, Edgar Leonard. *Christian Humanism: A Guide to the Thought of Jacques Maritain.* New York: Philosophical Library, 1951.

Bailey, Alice A. *Education in the New Age.* New York: Lucis Press, 1954.

Black, Hugh C., Lottich, Kenneth V., and Seckinger, Donald S., eds. *The Great Educators.* Chicago: Nelson-Hall Co., 1972.

Brameld, Theodore. *Patterns of Educational Philosophy.* New York: Holt, Rinehart and Winston, Inc., 1971.

———. *The Use of Explosive Ideas in Education.* Pittsburgh, Pa.: University of Pittsburgh Press, 1965.

———. *Toward a Reconstructed Philosophy of Education.* New York: Holt, Rinehart and Winston, Inc., 1956.

Bruner, Jerome S. *On Knowing: Essays For the Left Hand.* Cambridge, Mass.: Belknap Press of Harvard University, 1962.

———. *The Process of Education.* Cambridge, Mass.: Harvard University Press, 1963.

———. *The Relevance of Education.* New York: W. W. Norton & Co., Inc., 1971.

———. *Toward a Theory of Instruction.* New York: W. W. Norton & Co., Inc., 1968.

———, ed. *Learning About Learning: A Conference Report.* Washington, D.C.: U.S. Office of Education, 1966.

———, Smith, M. Brewster, and White, Robert W. in collaboration with David Aberle. *Opinions and Personality.* New York: Wiley, 1956.

———, Goodnow, Jacqueline J., and Austin, George. *A Study of Thinking.* New York: John Wiley & Sons, Inc., 1956.

———, Olver, Rose R., Greenfield, Patricia M., et al. *Studies in Cognitive Development.* New York: John Wiley & Sons, Inc., 1966.

Cole, Henry P. *Process Education.* Englewood, Cliffs, N.J.: Educational Technology, 1974.

Dewey, John. *Democracy and Education: An Introduction to the Philosophy of Education.* New York: Macmillan, 1916.

———. *Education Today.* Edited and with a foreword by Joseph Ratner. New York: Putnam's Sons, 1940.

———. *Freedom and Culture.* New York: G. P. Putnam, 1939.

———. *Individualism, Old and New.* New York: Minton, Balch and Co., 1930.

———. *Reconstruction in Philosophy.* New York: Henry Holt and Co., 1920.

Flavell, John H. *The Development Psychology of Jean Piaget.* Princeton, N.J.: D. Van Nostrand Co., Inc., 1963.

Furth, Hans G. *Piaget and Knowledge.* Englewood Cliffs, N.J.: Prentice-Hall, 1969.

———. *Piaget for Teachers.* Englewood Cliffs, N.J.: Prentice-Hall, 1970.

Gallagher, Donald and Gallagher, Idella, eds. *The Education of Man: The Educational Philosophy of Jacques Maritain.* New York: Doubleday, 1962.

Gardner, Howard. *The Quest for Mind.* New York: Knopf, 1973.

Gardner, John. *Excellence.* New York: Harper & Row, 1961.

———. *Self-Renewal.* New York: Harper & Row, 1964.

Ginsburg, Herbert and Opper, Sylvia. *Piaget's Theory of Intellectual Development: an Introduction.* Englewood Cliffs, N.J.: Prentice-Hall, 1969.

Glenn, Paul J. *History of Philosophy.* St. Louis: B. Herder Book Co., 1929.

Guardini, Romano. *The End of the Modern World.* Translated by Joseph Theman and Herbert Burke. Edited with an introduction by Frederick D. Wilhelmsen. New York: Sheed & Ward, 1956.

Handy, Rollo. *Value Theory and the Behavioral Sciences.* St. Kaukauma, Wis.: Thomas Publishing, 1969.

Hook, Sidney, ed. *Philosopher of Science and Freedom: Symposium.* New York: Dial Press, 1950.

———. *Education for Modern Man.* New York: Dial Press, 1945.

Inhelder, Bärbel, and Chipman, Harold, eds. *Piaget and His School.* New York: Springer-Verlag New York Inc., 1976.

Joseph, Ellis A. *Jacques Maritain on Humanism and Education.* Fresno, Calif.: Academy Guild Press, 1966.

Lawson, Douglas E. and Lean, Arthur E., eds. *John Dewey and the World View.* Carbondale, Ill.: Southern Illinois Press, 1964.

Maritain, Jacques. *A Preface to Metaphysics.* New York: Sheed and Ward, 1948.

———. *Christianity and Democracy.* Translated by Doris C. Anson. New York: Charles Scribner's Sons, 1944.

———. *Education at the Crossroads.* New Haven, Conn.: Yale University Press, 1943.

———. *Reflections on America.* New York: Charles Scribner's Sons, 1958.

———. *The Responsibility of the Artist.* New York: Charles Scribner's Sons, 1958.

———. *Theonas Conversations with a Sage.* Translated by Frank J. Sheed. New York: Sheed and Ward, 1933.

———. *The Range of Reason.* New York: Charles Scribner's Sons, 1952.

———. *The Twilight of Civilization.* Translated by Lionel Landry. New York: Sheed and Ward, 1943.

————. *On the Grace and Humanity of Jesus.* New York: Herder & Herder, 1969.

Maritain, Raissa. *Adventures in Grace.* Translated by Julia Kernan. New York: Longmans Green and Company, 1945.

May, Rollo, ed. *Existential Psychology.* New York: Random House, 1961.

————, Angel, Ernest, and Ellenberger, Henri F., eds. *Existence.* New York: Basic Books, 1958.

Mellert, Robert B. *What is Process Theology?* New York: Paulist Press, 1975.

Pegis, Anton C., in the preface to Norah W. Michener, *Maritain on the Nature of Man in a Christian Democracy.* Hull, Can., Editions "L'Eclair," 1955.

Phelan, Gerald B. *Jacques Maritain.* New York: Sheed and Ward, 1937.

Piaget, Jean. *Insights and Illusions of Philosophy.* Translated from the French by Wolfe Mays. New York: The World Publishing Company, 1971.

————. *Six Psychological Studies.* Translated from the French by Anita Tenzer with an Introduction, Notes and Glossary by David Elkind, who also edited the translation. New York: Random House, Inc., 1967.

————. *The Place of the Sciences of Man in the System of Sciences.* New York: Harper Torchbooks, 1974.

Polanyi, Michael. *Personal Knowledge: Towards a Post-Critical Philosophy.* New York: Harper Torchbooks, 1958.

————. *The Study of Man.* Chicago: The University of Chicago Press, 1959.

————. *The Tacit Dimension.* New York: Doubleday and Co., 1967.

Rousseau, Jean-Jacques. *The Social Contract.* New York: Putnam, 1906.

Rozak, Theodore. *The Making of a Counter-Culture.* New York: Doubleday, 1969.

Skinner, B. F. *Beyond Freedom and Dignity.* New York: Knopf, 1971.

Smith, Vincent Edward. *Idea Men of Today.* Milwaukee, Wis.: Bruce, 1950.

Wadsworth, Harry J. *Piaget's Theory of Cognitive Development.* New York: David McKay Co., 1971.

Whitehead, Alfred North. *Adventures of Ideas.* New York: Pelican Books, 1948.

——. *Interpretation of Science.* New York: Bobbs-Merrill Co., Inc., 1961.

——. *Science and the Modern World.* New York: Macmillan, 1925.

——. *The Aims of Education.* New York: The Macmillan Co., 1929.

7

FURTHER SIGNIFICANT
PIAGETIAN INSIGHTS

Childhood has its own ways of seeing, thinking and feeling
(Rousseau). . . . [for] Each stage . . . [of life] has a perfection
of its own. (Piaget)

Could the sun have been called "moon" and the moon
"sun"?—No.—Why not?—Because the sun shines brighter than
the moon. . . . But if everyone had called the sun "moon"
and the moon "sun" would we have known it was wrong?—
Yes, because the sun is always bigger, it always stays like it
is and so does the moon.—Yes, but the sun isn't changed, only
its name. Could it have been called . . . No . . . Because the
moon rises in the evening, and the sun in the day.

—J. Piaget, *The Child's Conception
of the World*

In this dialogue with the child, Jean Piaget illustrates exactly
what his response-process method means when he says, "In the
beginning was the response. . . ." Here he indicates the ontogenetic[1] interacting of language and cognitive responses. In this
perspective is hidden the process at the very heart of his activities. As a genetic epistemologist, he is still contributing new

insights to developmental psychology after more than half a century of experimentation. His

> theory, in the most general sense, is that of subject-object equilibration, the view that mental growth is governed by a continual activity [process] aimed at balancing the intrusions of the social and physical environment with the organism's need to conserve its structural system.[2]

Since his publications deal mainly with an experimental approach based on the natural sciences, they are largely descriptions. These include applications of systematic growth and development of the intellectual structure. They also reveal an evolving of knowledge through the natural biological maturational processes.

The Response

It is now more than forty years ago that Elton Mayo (1930), in presenting his appraisal of Jean Piaget's earliest publications (notably *The Child's Conception of Physical Causality*, *The Child's Conception of the World*, *The Language and Thought of the Child*, and *Judgment and Reasoning in the Child*) to the tenth annual session of the Ohio State Educational Conference,[3] apologized that

> he [Piaget] is still a young man; he is studying, in these days, his own infant children. We may hope for further enlightenment as his research proceeds.[4]

The hope expressed by Mayo is being realized and the present decade is witnessing a tremendous upsurge of interest in the work of Jean Piaget. This is due partly to America's increasing concern over the values crisis in education. The present interest is centering on his research into the psychology of intelligence[5] and logical thinking. Piaget's early work on language, judgment, reasoning, and moral aspects of the child serves as the background to this recent development. Piaget's studies are now encouraging a variety of investigations, many of which deal with the relations among perception, intelligence, and the role of mental images in the evolution of cognitive structures as a process.

Piaget is now recognized as one of the greatest European psychological authorities of the century, casting new light on the epistemological and maturational processes of man. For explaining man's nature, especially with regard to the acquisition of knowledge:

> Piaget seems to be the child psychologist in the eyes of the American public. His name crops up in countless publications and his ideas are discussed in many different circles—psychological, educational, philosophical, psychiatric. In spite of his popularity, however, he remains a difficult author, especially for an English-speaking reader.[6]

His chief inquiry into these problems ranges from the moment of birth through adolescence. As he observes:

> An infant comes in contact for the first time with a ring suspended from a string. He makes a series of exploratory accommodations: He looks at it, touches it, causes it to swing back and forth, grasps it, and so on . . . [whereby] the ring is assimilated to concepts of touching, moving, seeing, etc., concepts which [become] part of the child's cognitive organization.[7]

Piaget compares infant consciousness at the dawn of life to "a slate on which nothing is yet recorded", but the child gradually becomes more and more knowledgeable through maturational and environmental influences. Piaget's specialization, as a discipline, is resulting in a relatively new frontier designated as "genetic epistemological psychology." In it he is discovering and clarifying the psychological structures within the various stages of growth and development that underlie the formation of concepts basic to science.[8]

The Mystery of Piaget

Now the discoveries of Jean Piaget are becoming applicable to practically every phase of the learning-teaching process. This is being realized in the United States today by an ever-increasing number of psychologists, philosophers, and educators. They are finding more meaningful approaches to human intelligence and cognition as ontogenetic responses. When Piaget's long-time associate, Eleanor Duckworth, of the Atlantic Institute of Education, Halifax, Nova Scotia, asked why educators are getting so enthusiastic about his work, he replied frankly:[9] "It's a mystery. I don't know what happened. In Geneva no one pays any attention."

Piaget's works are attaining so cosmopolitan an outlook in experimental psychology that he is being termed the "gracious giant" who is literally upsetting the world of behavioral psychology. In this way he is doing more to shake the faith of psychologists in the stimulus-response approaches to child psychology than all the humanistic psychologists of the Third Force combined,[10] that is, all those psychologists outside of the established profession. Although Sigmund Freud (1856–1939) is given credit for discovering the unconscious, it is Jean Piaget who is discovering the conscious. As he himself declares: "I have always preferred the workings of the intellect to the tricks of the unconscious." Recently John L. Hess wrote:

Piaget, the Einstein of child psychology, flew in from Geneva Tuesday [October 17, 1972] and gently shook up an admiring throng of specialists at the City University of New York.

He predicted that psychoanalytical theory—the whole school of training and therapy deriving from Freud—would be exposed as "mythical" by studies on hormones and the way the brain functions.[11]

The 76-year-old genetic psychologist appeared before this seminar of 50 students of clinical psychology in the university's graduate center on 43rd Street.[12] When asked by a student of abnormal behavioral psychology, "Is there a place for emotion in your study?" Dr. Piaget replied good-naturedly:[13]

> I always find this question amusing because one would really be out of one's mind to work without emotion. Emotion is the motive factor of any behavior whatever. . . . The question is whether the emotional factor will modify the structure. For my part, I doubt it.[14]

As he continued, he made a specific reference to schizophrenia:

> I think schizophrenia attacks both the emotion and the structure. As for the normal subject, I don't think the motive force modifies the structure.[15]

He told his audience that a child who is at ease with arithmetic, for example, would learn it faster than one who is inhibited about it, but that they would arrive at the same structure—2 and 2 make 4.[16]

As to the spate of tests showing that children in Western societies advance faster and further in learning than do children in primitive societies or urban slums, Piaget holds that this is merely environmental, that it does not affect the structure of the learning process.[17] He implies in this that values in education must go through about the same phases for all. Then he draws this interesting observation about current theories of learning:

> Now I think that psychological research on emotion, especially psychoanalytical research, is quite provisional. . . . When the endocrinologists find certain answers, much psychoanalytical theory will be found entirely mythical.
>
> Studies of the brain will find the mechanisms [of learning] but will change nothing of the structure.[18]

In passing from the seminar to the auditorium where Piaget

was to address more than 500 specialists from the metropolitan area and New England, a group of clinical psychology students confided that they were dismayed.[19] "Sure they're upset," said Professor Harry Beilin, Piaget's host and a leading interpreter of his work. "It implies that their house is resting on quicksand. I think so, too."[20]

Time-Lag

It is difficult to understand the time-lag that has prevented Piaget's achievements from attaining their full stature here in the United States. One thing is clear—their impact is still being retarded because of the delimiting effects inherent in the prevailing behavioristic traditions. Such men as Thorndike (1874–1949), Hull (1884–1952), Watson (1878–1958), Tolman (1886–1959), Spence (1907–1967), and especially B. F. Skinner (1904–   ) of Harvard, still dominate the American scene.

When considering the background and works of the latest exponent of scientific behavior, B. F. Skinner, and his influence upon Jean Piaget's contributions, it must be noted that, in contrast to Piaget who is not educationally oriented, much of what he is writing bears directly on classroom learning and practice. As the foremost behavioral psychologists today, Skinner is the great pioneer in work on teaching machines.[21] His emphasis on reinforcement is particularly intriguing:

> Human behavior is remarkably influenced by small results. Describing something with the right word is often reinforcing. Other simple reinforcers are to be found in the clarification of a puzzlement or simply in moving forward after completing one stage of activity.[22]

Skinner maintains that the most widely publicized efforts to improve education show an extraordinary neglect of method. He feels that learning and teaching are not sufficiently analyzed and that almost no effort is being made to improve teaching as such. The aid that education receives, he says, usually means money. He analyzes the proposals for spending as following a few familiar lines:

> High-school and grade-school teaching is taught primarily through apprenticeships, in which students receive the advice and counsel of experienced teachers. . . . Any special knowledge of pedagogy as a basic science of teaching is felt to be unnecessary.[23]

This situation he sees as regrettable. He is convinced that education as an enterprise cannot improve itself to the fullest without examining its basic processes. Insisting that a really effective educational system can not be set up until there is a much better understanding of the processes of learning and teaching, he declares that human behavior is far too complex to be left to casual experience. Organized experience in the restricted environment of the classroom is essential. Therefore,

> Teachers need help. In particular they need the kind of help offered by a scientific analysis of behavior. . . . a true technology of teaching is imminent. It is beginning to suggest effective alternatives to the average practices that have caused us so much trouble.[24]

Many of the behavioral influences that dominate American psychology, quite alien to the Piagetian school, are attributed to Skinner. This effect does not trouble him the way it does others today. He considers the environment so important in the lives of man that to substantiate his thesis he placed his own baby daughter in a box and literally raised her under glass.[25] Thus,

> Years ago, after he designed a controlled-temperature box for infants, the aircrib, his second daughter, Deborah, slept in it for two and one half years. He chuckles at the persistent rumor that she became a hopeless neurotic, and wants me to tell you about her: "She's an artist working in London, doing very well."

His proposal is to redesign all of culture—government, education, and economics—invoking a vision of the world as a Skinner box.[26]

He is consistently publishing. His first book, which appeared in 1938, discusses the topic *The Behavior of Organisms: An Experimental Analysis.* In his *Walden Two,* coming just a decade later, he used the guise of fiction to express his views. After becoming expansive on the subject of the goal to be assigned in the behavior he proposes, namely, "let man be happy, informed, skillful, well-behaved, and productive,"[27] his hero says:

> Well, what do you say to the design of personalities? Would that interest you? The control of temperament? Give me the specifications, and I'll give you the man! What do you say to the control of motivation, building the interests which will make men most productive and most successful? Does that seem to you fantastic? Yet more of the techniques are available, and more can be worked out experimentally. Think of the possibilities. . . . Let us control the lives of our children and see what we can make of them.[28]

What Skinner is essentially saying in *Walden Two* is that the current knowledge in the behavioral sciences, plus that which the future will bring, will enable man to specify, to a degree that today would seem incredible, the kind of behavioral and personality results that he wants to achieve.[29]

Walden Two was followed by *Science and Human Behavior* in 1953, which treated such topics as mind and behavior, "operant' behavior and "operant" conditioning. Positive reinforcement appeared at great length in chapters 5, 6, and 11. In 1957 his works *Verbal Behavior* and *Schedules of Reinforcement* were published. They were followed by three more books in the sixties—*Cumulative Record Revised Edition* (1961), *The Technology of Teaching* (1968), and *Contingencies of Reinforcement: A Theoretical Analysis* (1969). This latter work treats such important topics as mind and behavior, "possession," feelings, contingencies of reinforcement, utopias as experimental cultures, leisure, and internal copies of the environment. All this was presented along with the significance of reinforcers in the evolution of the species in the framework of chapter 1, which deals with the overall role of environment.

The year 1971 bore witness to the most controversial work of his career: *Beyond Freedom and Dignity*. This book flowed through six printings in less than three months. In it he approached the crisis of the 1970s in this provocative fashion:

> In trying to solve the terrifying problems that face us in the world today, we naturally turn to the things we do best. We play from strength and our strength is science and technology. . . . As Darlington has said, "Every source from which man has increased his power on the earth has been used to diminish the prospects of his successors. All his progress has been made at the expense of damage to his environment which he cannot repair and could not foresee" (cf. G. Hardin, "Genetics and History," *Science*, 168 [12 June 1970]: 1332–33 Copyright 1970 by the American Association for the Advancement of Science).
>
> Whether or not he could have foreseen the damage, man must repair it or all is lost. And he can do so if he will recognize the nature of the difficulty. . . .
>
> What we need is a technology of behavior. . . . But a behavioral technology comparable in power and precision to physical and biological technology is lacking, and those who do not find the very possibility ridiculous are more likely to be frightened by it than reassured. That is how far we are from "understanding human issues" in the sense in which physics and biology understand their fields, and how far we are from preventing the catastrophe toward which the world seems to be inexorably moving.[30]

Other Reasons

The contributions of B. F. Skinner have so captivated behavioristic traditionalists in this century that they have retarded for decades the impact of Jean Piaget on American education in process. There are other reasons, however, for this retardation. Many of these center around the problems confronting those who translate his writings. Most of his original ideas are expressed in English in words coined from the French because for these psychological and epistemological phenomena, practically speaking, most American scholars can find no meaningful equivalents in English. Consequently the key words, so necessary for getting the full significance of the translations, could be only approximately expressed. Even experts today often take so long to translate his works that they are published in this country years after their original appearance.

Two of the most common pitfalls for translators of Piaget's publications have been the unfortunate tendency to oversimplify and at the same time to adapt the difficult Piagetian terminology without adequate explanations.[31] Thus, up to recently, many of Piaget's concepts, such as egocentrism, conservation, assimilation, accommodation, equilibrium, and stages of development are too technical and not clearly developed.

After decades of either ignoring such intellectual processes entirely or reducing them to sensory and even behavioral responses, American psychology in the second half of this century is taking a renewed interest in the subject. Psychological investigation of intellectual cognition and how reality is known has proliferated of late, much of it from a developmental standpoint. Representative are the writings of T. V. Moore, Charles E. Osgood, Jerome S. Bruner, and especially Jean Piaget.[32]

But it is within the last decade, as more translations are gradually making their appearance in the United States, that these questions are now being asked by an ever-increasing number: Who is Jean Piaget? How does he compare with B. F. Skinner? Is he an empirical scientist or a psychologizing philosopher?[33] Or what? As Jerome Bruner well writes:

Let me dispose of one matter, a central one in the theory of development. Unquestionably, the most impressive figure in the field of cognitive development today is Jean Piaget. We and the generations that follow us will be grateful for his pioneering work. Piaget, however, is often interpreted in the wrong way by those who think that his principal mission is psychological. It is not. It is epistemological. He is deeply concerned with the nature of knowledge per se, knowledge as it exists at different points in the development of the child.[34]

Considering the growing spirit of inquiry about himself and his works pressing, Jean Piaget, in 1965 at Paris, published his own partial answers in a book entitled *Insights and Illusions of Philosophy*. This book is a typical example of the obstacles and undue delay following the French publication. (The original tentative title—*Uses and Abuses of Philosophy*—is barely a literal translation of the original one: *Wisdom and the Illusions of Philosophy*). In spite of the title, however, it created a greater stir in French intellectual circles than any of his previous books. A second edition became necessary within a very short time. The English edition, however, was not released to the public until 1971, six years after its original publication. In spite of this delay, the volume is very provocative, since Piaget describes vividly how it happens that he, as "a former would-be philosopher . . . [became] a psychologist and an epistemologist of the development of thought."[35]

Evolution of a New Discipline

Much of "the mystery of Piaget" is traceable to his youth. Jean Piaget was born in Neuchâtel, Switzerland. An intellectually precocious child, he began his scholastic career early as a zoology assistant in his native town. He narrates how this happened in *Insights and Illusions of Philosophy*:

Like many children I was fascinated by natural history, and at the age of eleven I had the good fortune to become *famulus,* as he called me, of an old zoologist, Paul Godot, who directed the Museum at Neuchâtel solely on his own resources. In exchange for my small services, he introduced me to malacology and gave me a number of shells of land and freshwater mollusks with which I made my own collection at home. When he died in 1911, I published at the age of fifteen several notes by way of a supplement to his *Catalogue of Neuchâtel Mollusks* as well as on alpine mollusks, which much interested me in their variability of adaptation to altitude.[36]

In telling how he spent the earliest period of his scholastic career working with mollusks, he indicated that much of his free time was devoted to studying their development in and around the many lakes at Neuchâtel. Already, at the age of ten, he had presaged his literary career by publishing his first "scientific" paper, a one-page note on a partly albino sparrow that he had observed in the park. During his tenure as laboratory assistant he published no fewer than twenty-five papers on mollusks, of which twenty were in print before he reached his majority. In his autobiography he refers to the humorous, but very complimentary, incident of having been offered the position of curator of the mollusk collection in the Geneva museum while he was studying in the secondary school.[37]

At the age of fifteen, the youthful Piaget decided to direct his interests toward a biological explanation of knowledge, a goal that he still reflects in his present works. Within this context he discovered philosophy and decided to devote himself to it as soon as he was introduced to the subject by his godfather:

> my godfather, a man of letters without children who took an interest in me, was alarmed by this exclusive specialization [biological knowledge] and one summer invited me to stay at his house on the shores of Lake Annecy, his intention being to have me read and to explain to me *Bergson's Evolution Creatrice*. This was a tremendous experience, and for two equally strong reasons, both of which merged with those basic interests that impel adolescents toward philosophy.[38]

In Bergson he hoped to find the answer to the great problems he confronted during his intellectual development, for it was a philosophy answering exactly to his then intellectual interests.

On the other hand, since he was a Protestant by dint of having a believing mother, whereas his father was a nonbeliever, he sought to resolve the conflict of science and religion:

> Reading Bergson was again a revelation from this second point of view: in a moment of enthusiasm close to ecstatic joy, I was struck by the certainty that God is Life, under the form of the *élan vital,* and my biological interests provided me at the same time with a small sector of study. Internal unity was thus achieved in the direction of an immanentism which has long satisfied me.[39]

Henri Bergson, the philosopher of change, was practically a contemporary of Piaget, having died only in 1941. His theory, based on a change as a constant process, appealed to Piaget and enabled him to formulate a philosophical basis on which to establish his research in zoology and biology:

> I had been struck by a remark of Bergson that appeared to give me a guilding thread for the start of my philosophico-biological studies. This was his surprise at the disappearance of the problem of "kinds" in modern philosophy in favor of the problem of laws.[40]

In essence Bergson's theory maintains that all creation is in a state of dynamic stability. By *dynamic stability* he means that any apparent nonvariations, any apparently stable conditions, can arise only from variations within process. A concrete example of this is what is understood as the state of equilibrium. It is the result of a chaotic state where all variables are equal and changes inside are going on continually. But the whole is not a mere combination of various parts. Essentially, it is a complete intertwining or integration of change. The fact is that any change occurring is doing so gradually and constantly.

Bergson maintains, however, that whatever changes do occur are only accidental, but *that* they occur is predictable and non-accidental. In scientific mutations, he asserts, scientists admit that the period of change is a mystery—it is unfolding constantly and

not just happening at random. Bergson describes this continuity
of change in its relation to material qualities when he writes that

> each of these qualities (color, sound, touch) taken separately
> is a state which seems as such immovable until another releases
> it. Yet each of these qualities resolves itself, on analysis into
> an enormous nmber of elementary movements. Whether we
> see in it vibration or rather [sic] we represent it in any other
> way, one fact is certain, it is that every quality is change.[41]

Jean Piaget found a practical application of Bergson's philosophy of change when he applied it to human perception. The
function of perception as Bergson sees it is to grasp a series of
elementary changes under one basic form. For him, any permanence in the quality of an object consists in a repetitious
presentation of a characteristic. Thus a man with a keener
perception can perceive a greater number of changes in a given
period and can better understand how change is continuous.
Consequently, the more changes there are observed, the easier
it is to comprehend the constancy of change.

Besides change within qualities, objects undergo other changes.
Relations are constantly evolving. In this evolution, Bergson
teaches, there are brought into existence many differences that
result in many more changes. But one should see them as parts
of a whole. "He who perceives successive events one by one,"
says Bergson, "will allow himself to be led by them. He who
grasps them as a whole will dominate them." Hence the vital
importance of realizing that the principle of continual change
is a continual process-response, because: "To exist is to change,
to change is to mature, to mature is to go on creating oneself
endlessly."[42]

The Bergsonian principle of change so powerfully attracted
Piaget that in his initial enthusiasm he decided to devote his
career to philosophy. Subsequently, however, the problem appeared to him in a different light. He discerned that most of
the knowledge in philosophy consisted in reality of problems
of knowledge and many of them were problems of biology in

a subject-object relationship. Then, in consequence, he decided to dedicate his life to the biological explanation of knowledge.[43]

It was his intensive work in biology that led Piaget to conclude that biological development was due not only to maturation and heredity but also to many variables in the environment of man. For, having observed in successive stages how mollusks' structures change in keeping with their movements from large lakes with much wave action to small ponds with hardly any at all, he deduced that biological development, although mainly a process of adaptation to the environment, might possibly be explained only in part by maturation. Piaget became so fascinated with cognitive development that even his biological experiments and philosophical convictions were gradually assimilated into his view of mental development within the human process. In this way he discovered that mental life was contingent upon adaptation and accommodation to environment and was therefore an extension of the biological in man:

> I had arrived at two ideas central for my point of view and which, moreover, I have never given up. The first is that . . . every organism has a permanent structure which can be modified under the influence of the environment but is always *assimilation* of a datum external to the subject's structure. . . . The second is that the normative factors of thought correspond biologically to a necessity of *equilibrium* by self-regulation: thus logic would in the subject correspond to a process of equilibrium.[44]

Piaget, after completing graduate studies at the University of Neuchâtel, directed his ambition to the study of psychology. For several years he had been reading widely in this subject and attending classes in it. At first he spent some time in Zurich. There he studied and worked in psychological clinics, practically immersing himself in their experimentations. Then, Piaget writes:

> I left for Paris, determined to combine researches in psychology with the teaching of Brunschvicg and Lalande. I had the

extraordinary luck to work almost alone in Binet's laboratory, in a school where I was given a free hand, and to be entrusted with a study aiming in principle to restandardize intelligence tests, but which in fact allowed me to analyze the different levels of the logic of classes and relations in child thought. Lalande was willing to read and approve these results before publication, and I finally had the feeling of having found a way of reconciling epistemological research with respect for the facts, and a field of studies intermediary between the domain of psychological development and problems of normative structures.[45]

When Piaget was offered a post at the Institute J. J. Rousseau, he was happy to develop his research there. Here it fully dawned on him that genuinely successful testing of intelligence must begin with the experimental approaches of the brilliant Frenchman Alfred Binet. He recalls that in the late 1890s the school authorities of Paris asked Binet whether he could differentiate between pupils capable of doing regular school work and those who were mentally retarded. Until that time, attempts at measuring intelligence had centered around compiling a composite score of physical attributes and reactions. For example, a final score might be derived from height, weight, size of head, visual acuity, and reaction time. When such scores were compared with teacher estimates of ability and success in school, however, little relationship was found to exist.

Piaget also remembers that Binet decided that an entirely different approach was necessary. He reasoned that the basis for intelligent behavior was more likely to be discoverable through examination of the higher thought processes, such as reasoning, the capacity to grasp concepts, and the ability to deal with the abstract. Accordingly, he began to write test questions that would measure these qualities. Immediately Binet found himself faced with a vexing problem: How could he get some uncomplicated and easy-to-obtain evidence as to whether his question did indeed measure intelligence? Finally, was his brilliant and simple solution to be found within the maturational process itself?

Piaget also recalls that Binet decided to operate on the assumption that the average older child was more intelligent than the average younger one. At first he tried his questions on children of different ages, and if older children were able to answer them more consistently than younger ones, he assumed that the questions were measures of intelligence. Then when he found the age at which certain questions were more readily grasped than at other age levels, he was provided with a convenient basis for organizing the test items, grouping his questions by age levels. Binet's age-level scale succeeded in differentiating between bright and dull pupils and eventually became the first intelligence test scale to work.[46]

Upon invitation, Jean Piaget spent two years at the Sorbonne, and was greatly influenced by this work of Alfred Binet in his laboratory for standardizing intelligence testing in elementary education. Admittedly bored at first, he became particularly concerned with the incorrect answers that children gave in response to questions on the standardized tests. Soon he was examining the cognitive processes underlying the children's incorrect responses. In Paris he was to discover his life-long research interest in testing children to discern the process of cognitive development and to initiate his unique experimental approach to psychology.

Unfortunately, Binet died in the prime of life, before he could perfect his brainchild. Piaget, however, benefited immensely from his imagination, creativity, and drive, and incorporated many of Binet's ideas on intelligence into his own clinical method at the Institute J. J. Rousseau. From this experience he evolved a clinical-descriptive process technique that eventually came to serve as a trademark for his work. Most of his research, however, has not been strictly experimental, and it is seldom that he employs elaborate statistics and test hypotheses for his experimental investigations. His method essentially involves asking individual children carefully selected questions and noting their responses. As a result, data often consist in nothing more than the observation of behavior invariably systematic and exceedingly detailed in analysis, designed to detect developmental changes in cognitive functioning.

Only four years after his first appointment to the faculty of philosophy at the University of Neuchâtel, Piaget joined the faculty of science at the University of Geneva. There he realized that his epistemological activity must be much more than a peripheral philosophical question. For here he taught

> at first the history of scientific thought, then experimental psychology . . . in order to find a more extensive field of experience.[47]

From this time on, he espoused as his specialty the formation of a scientific epistemology that was independent of philosophical opinions. It became his chief and lasting contribution.[48]

Knowledge

To Piaget intuition as a form of knowledge is not acceptable. He sees that

> adult intellectual activities are conditioned by earlier forms of behavior. He argues that the Achilles heel of philosophers like Bergson and Husserl, who believe in intuition as an immediate source of knowledge, lies precisely in their neglect of the historical and genetic viewpoints.[49]

Knowledge in the Piagetian sense of the word is not a mere copy of objectively given reality. Neither is it the uncritical projection of a subjective mentality endowed with supernatural powers or arbitrary intuitions. What Piaget was looking for in his new discipline was a dynamic theory of human knowing entailing more subjectivity that is not personal. He sought an introspective subjectivity within a broad, impersonal, human capacity of cognition—a specific subjectivity through empirical methods that would enable him to discern gradually how the general developmental process evolved in constructing both subjectivity and objectivity. For him, therefore, knowledge is living, not static;

it is demanding of response, and is not satisfied with mere recognition. In his vocabulary,

> to know an object, to know an event, is not simply to look at it and make a mental copy, or image of it. To know is to modify, to transform the object, and to understand the process of this transformation, and as a consequence to understand the way the object is constructed. An operation is thus the essence of knowledge; it is an interiorized action which modifies the object of knowledge.[50]

To Piaget knowledge is the structuring of behavior through an interchange between organism and environment. Behavior at every level and in every stage of the child's growth and development implies a certain amount of knowledge on the part of the organism concerning the environment—a personalized interaction. In this sense, general, objective knowledge becomes identical with intelligence as "the totality of possible coordinations that structure the behavior of an organism." According to Hans G. Furth,

> the conclusion . . . appears to be this: human adult intelligence is the terminal stage of an evolutionary and developmental process that is inherent in the self-regulation of an equilibrated organism.[51]

Although Piaget applies commonly accepted propositions of contemporary biology, on the level of logic and the theory of knowledge he finds himself in critical disagreement with most other theoreticians (Bruner, for example) and frequently also with the thinking of the educated man in today's culture.[52]

The concept of two kinds of knowledge, however, as proposed by Bergson and Husserl, is a different, but not an indifferent, matter for Piaget. He rejects the vital or existential grasp of an intuition, which they claim leads to knowledge in a way different from the usual methods of knowing employed in obtaining scientific facts. He insists again and again that his rejection is not because the problems are invalid or because the introspective method is inherently false. Conscience, existence, intuition, and all the other problems of existential phenonomenology in process are real problems and he says he has no objections to these in themselves.

What is unacceptable is the claim that beyond observation and deduction there is another method of obtaining knowledge—by intuition that is reflective wisdom. This claim he continues to reject, especially in his *Insights and Illusions of Philosophy,* because it implies a radical difference in types of knowing or truth. He denies that this implies his being a disembodied rationalist. In actual life, however, he readily admits that reflection is part and parcel of knowledge without being an autonomous source of truth.[53] As he states frankly,

> I have nearly every day been faced with the conflicts that slow down the development of disciplines trying to become scientific. And I have arrived at the conviction that, under the extremely complex set of individual or group factors, university or ideological, epistemological or moral, historical or actual, etc., which enter into each of these conflicts, one always discovers the same problem and under forms that have seemed to me to involve a question of simple intellectual honesty: under what conditions can one speak of knowledge, and how can one guard against the internal and external dangers that continually threaten it? . . . the boundary that separates verification from speculation.[54]

Insights and Illusions

Piaget's intellectual Odyssey, the theme of his *Insights and Illusions of Philosophy,* grew out of his many developmental changes over the last sixty or more years. It climaxes in the way by which he finally arrived at his personal "epistemologie genetique." This frank account touches many a sensitive nerve in the life of European intellectuals and is continuing to do the same here in the United States today. He explains to the public and his academic colleagues how it happened that, attracted by Henri Bergson's philosophy of change, he early became enamored of the goals and promises of philosophy but gradually realized that an aspiring genetic epistemologist could scarcely find ultimate satisfaction in the philosophical enterprise.[55]

To appreciate the message of his work, it is essential to realize that what Piaget sees as the decline of philosophy has very deep epistemological roots; that this decline constitutes also a vital sociological and psychological problem institutionalized in the settings of most universities and scholastic circles; that it is "philosophical courage" that prompts Piaget to speak against abuses of philosophy today in an environment where philosophy is an almost sacred profession, a prerequisite of, if not a substitute for, religion.[56] In exposing the sacrosanct by substituting wholeheartedly the scientific in place of the philosophical in his newly created discipline, he confesses:

> In short, two very deepening convictions were forced on me at the beginning of my teaching career. One is that there is a kind of intellectual dishonesty in making assertions in a domain concerned with facts, without a publicly vertifiable method of testing, and in formal domains without a logistic one. The other is that the sharpest possible distinction should at all times be made between personal improvisation, the dogma of a school, or whatever is centered in the self or on a restricted group, and, on the other hand, the domains in which mutual agreement is possible, independently of metaphysical beliefs or of ideologies.[57]

His position on the relation of the sciences to philosophy is developmental. He sees that all great philosophical systems are reflections within the framework of scientific discoveries and that the characteristic epistemological stance of each system mirrors philosophy's dependence on the progress of scientific knowledge. He further states that philosophy assumes a rational position toward the whole of reality. In some philosophies the thing in itself exists but is considered unknowable. Yet a philosophical position always involves a general conception of knowledge, among other things. The most important reason why philosophy is always considered as a form of knowledge in

Western civilization, Piaget declares, is that it has long been related to science. Even from the time of the earliest Greek thinkers, he points out, no distinction between science and philosophy has existed.

Piaget sees no fundamental difference in nature between philosophical and scientific cognitive problems except in their delimitations or specializations and in their methods. These are either purely reflective, or based upon systematic or experimental observation in the case of facts and rigorous algorithms in the case of deduction.[58] For, he says:

> Philosophy is a "wisdom," indispensable to rational creatures to coordinate the various activities of man; but it does not attain a knowing properly speaking since knowledge characteristically involves some guarantees or means of control; these controls are not provided by philosophy.[59]

According to Piaget, the modern viewpoint regarding philosophy, among other scholastic disciplines, as a kind of knowledge different from, or superior to, scientific knowledge, is a relatively recent phenomenon. In the pre-Kantian period the great philosophers were also great scientists. Even during the pre-Cartesian times, the difference between philosophical opinions and scientific facts was implicitly acceptable, and the two were explicitly considered complementary. The notion of a double truth or knowledge—one for science, another for philosophy—was unthinkable.[60]

Piaget delights in recalling that Descartes counseled limiting philosophical speculations to one day a month and using all the other days for calculus and dissection. He notes, too, how this ratio in favor of science is now completely forgotten in the training and practice of philosophers. He recalls, too, that Descartes's and Leibnitz's discovery of the human person, active in knowing, became the "epistemic" subject, and that these philosophers made eminent discoveries in logical and mathematical operations and were the first to demonstrate how mathematics fits the movements of the changing universe. He observes that both were impressed by the active operational character of knowing, although they posited ideas as innate.[61]

> Leibnitz's system, like that of Descartes, was, as is well known, directly influenced by his own scientific discoveries. He has derived the principles of continuity and indiscernibles from the infinitesimal calculus, and its applications have led him to the philosophical use which he made of the principle of sufficient reason. Proceeding from the algebra of the finite to that of the infinite, which is his new calculus, he has grasped better than anyone else the dynamic operational character of intelligence and has been able to answer Locke that the latter's empiricism could not explain the *ipse intellectus.*[62]

By way of contrast, Piaget points to the empirical epistemology of Locke and Hume, with its initial tendency from psychological considerations not found in Descartes and Leibnitz, and shows how philosophically this psychology is pursued. To Piaget the psychology of these English empiricists is almost totally derived from a personal, egocentric commitment of its authors to certain values. While Locke and Hume criticize justifiably the inadequacy of innate ideas, they fall, according to Piaget, into the serious error of projecting their own philosophical perspectives into psychological facts.[63]

In retrospect, Jean Piaget sees questions about the meaning of life and the general coordination of values as dominant factors at work today in the history of philosophy. These he terms the constant factors. Consequently, Plato's perspective he considers as relevant, or more relevant than, philosophical endeavors.[64] For in Plato's transcendental, idealistic realism, reality is conceived as residing in externally stable ideas, whose reflection the human being passively receives. This epistemology, Piaget declares, is the counterpart of a statically conceived mathematical science unable to describe the changing movements of the physical world in process.

The problem of knowledge has a variable development, since epistemology reflects the actual state of scientific knowledge in any given period. In the immanent realism of Aristotle there is presented a system, based in part on empirical biological facts and in part on the deductive reasoning of logic. Here reality is conceived within the appearances of things, while knowledge is a conformity of the immanent reality of the physical world in process to the "informed" mind in process. Piaget, therefore, stresses in his unique perspective that the mainspring of this development is in the sciences themselves. He sees reflected in today's common separation of the sciences from philosophy a mentality that erroneously ascribes the motive of this movement to the scientific rather than to the philosophical.

Piaget views Kant's epistemology as a culminating synthesis of previous systems and as a reflection of Newton's physical science, for knowledge here is fully conceived as a construction of an epistemic subject with the limit only that the inherent necessity of logical constructs be given a priori. Finally, in summarizing his position on the relation of the sciences to philosophy, he suggests that Hegel's dialectic system can be seen as based on sociological considerations and foreshadowing the emergence of sociolgy as an independent science.[65]

In concluding *Insights and Illusions of Philosophy,* Piaget surveys the philosophical problems of metaphysics, morals, logic, psychology, and epistemology, and considers it characteristic of all scientific knowledge to bring about consensus. It seems to him that, with the exception of metaphysics, all philosophical research on problems that can be limited tends to become different from philosophy and takes on increasingly the form of scientific research, thus tending toward a potential consensus. He cautions that the difference between science and philosophy is not in the problems but in the limited scope and in the increasing technicality of the methods of verification:

> We need to remember that the boundary between philosophy and science is always changing because it does not depend on the problems themselves, none of which can ever be said to be definitely scientific or metaphysical, but only on their possible delimitation and on the selection of methods enabling us to deal with these circumscribed questions in relying on experimentation on logic-mathematical formalization or both.[66]

In spite of this Piagetian insight, European philosophy seems to flourish without bothering much about the nature of facts. It even appears at times to lack a basic reverence for what is implied by the word *knowledge*. As Piaget observes: "It costs much less to reflect and deduce than to experiment." He notes that a specialist of limited talent can still perform some useful tasks in a limited area in the scientific profession, whereas a mediocre philosopher is somewhat like a novelist or an artist with little talent.

His intellectual critique, *Insights and Illusions of Philosophy*, is also the personal testimony of one who has throughout his long professional life come to understand how dangerous, delicate, and especially difficult it is to be a philosopher or a scientist in an exclusive sense. His is an anti-exclusivism based on his many experiences and predicated on bold convictions. By formulating the new discipline of genetic epistemology, he presents a unifying perspective from the past, one almost entirely distorted today: Philosophy without science is incomplete and science without philosophy is at its best directionless.

Piaget's Paradox

Piaget's paradox is that in his scientific work he stresses antipositivistic conclusions on the acquisition of knowledge; in his own theoretical approach, however, he continues to ask questions that, until now, only philosophers ask. He therefore appears to scientists as a philosopher, but to philosophers as a scientist. To his audience of American psychologists, his image as an iconoclast either does or does not ring true. This erroneous antithesis aroused the suspicions of Piaget's colleagues and resulted in a distorted view of his scientific methodology.[67]

For those who admire Piaget's empirical work, even his interpretations and theoretical elaborations appear all too close to philosophy. His critics say that J. B. Watson, and American psychology with him, continue to turn away from these varied speculations and resolutely study human behavior as something external within the framework of a mechanistic-physical causality. Piaget's work, in their view, classifies him in a pejorative sense as a "positivist," or as a scholar who has turned from philosophical values and, therefore, neglects the truly human aspects of the human person.[68]

In spite of such criticisms, Piaget claims that one of the factors responsible for the emergence of philosophical psychology in its various forms is a reaction against the newly evolving discipline of scientific psychology. He writes that

> the seriousness of this misunderstanding not only depends on the question of method, . . . [but also on that] there is nothing in the hypotheses of the philosophical psychologies . . . that is in itself *a priori* contrary to a scientific position, because science is only valid if it is open.[69]

This new science he views as conceived within a mechanistic and associationist framework of thinking. Continuing to be guided by implicit or explicit assumptions closely related to a positivist, or, better, an empiricist epistemology, he sees the determinants of knowledge as chiefly environmental contingencies. Outside the organism and mental constructs, behaviorism becomes primarily an internalized copy of the given real world in process. Any notions of mental capacities that transcend the physical world are mere rejects, unnecessary entities devoid of scientific value.

Face to face with these opposing views, empiricism and mentalism, Piaget rejects them both with equal vigor. In his experiments on children's thinking, he actually, by his empirical study, refuted empiricism, making the bold claim that "his way" satisfies the positive values of both approaches to knowledge without falling into the negative aspects of the two extremes. He thereby nullifies the strictures of positivism, for which questions about the knower and the known are practically meaningless and often harmful in the scientific enterprise.[70]

By what right, asks Piaget, can positivism limit truth as a copy of physical reality? By what right, again, can logical positivism limit knowledge to mere physical phenomena, together with a language with which to describe the phenomena? Yet he maintains that

> first, what is meaningless in terms of a scientific proposition can still be valid as personal or collective wisdom. Secondly, phenomena that in the past could not be approached by scientific methods and therefore were meaningless in the strict sense of science have become subject to scientific scrutiny, thanks to progress in general scientific thinking and methodology.[71]

Finally, Piaget demands: by what scientific criteria can anyone divide problems into those called scientific and those called metaphysical? By way of an example, he recalls how the concept of finality, once anathema to positivist scientists in the past, is beginning to have scientific respectability today; how feedback and self-regulatory systems are becoming scientifically meaningful process concepts in cybernetics and embryology.

Dr. Piaget separates himself from an exclusively philosophical approach to the investgation of knowledge. At the same time he accepts the subject-object relation as most central in the nature of knowledge. Although he does not use the experimental method, he does base his theory of knowledge on empirical observations and not, like Bergson or Sartre, on introspection or relative personalism. He sees in these extremes the illusions of a super-scientific knowledge on the one hand and the excesses of dogmatic empiricism on the other.

The model of an empty organism and a ready-made environment may be a more or lass adequate theory; but when science exalts this into a world view, Piaget sees science as going beyond its limits and becoming a distorting philosophical dogma. Thus, in the emergence of scientists posing as philosophers he sees the counterpart to the emergence of philosophers proposing para-scientific or super-scientific knowledge. At the base of both extremes he points out in his new discipline a common misunderstanding concerning human knowledge:[72]

THE PIAGETIAN PERSPECTIVE OF KNOWLEDGE

KNOWLEDGE
from
SCIENCE   or   PHILOSOPHY
is one and the same

k
n
o
w
l
e
d
g
e

The difference is not two kinds of knowledge: reflective wisdom from philosophy called *intuitive knowledge* and from science, through observation and deduction and verification, *objective knowledge*. All knowledge to be true knowledge must be verified; all knowledge to be knowledge implies both objectivity and subjectivity. IN ALL KNOWLEDGE THERE MUST BE A CONSENSUS.

The New Discipline

In his epistemological perspective, Jean Piaget maintains that any philosophy, when used exclusively as a language to describe the concepts of knowledge, limits the methods of acquisitions and interpretations thereof. In his view, philosophy, hand in hand with science, enables him to give a fuller and more exact account of his genetic epistemological findings. But, he adds,

I had, therefore, dreamed of a "genetic epistemology," which would delimit the problems of knowledge in dealing with the question "how does knowledge grow?" which concerns both its formation and historical development. But the criterion of the success of a scientific discipline is intellectual cooperation, and since my disenchantment with philosophy, I have been increasingly of the opinion that any individual piece of work was vitiated by a latent defect, and that to the extent to which one would be able to speak of "Piaget's system," this would be a conclusive proof of my failure. . . . If genetic epistemology is possible, it ought also to be necessarily interdisciplinary.[73]

Holding to his conviction that "if genetic epistemology is possible, it ought to be necessarily interdisciplinary," Piaget tried to prove it by sending his program of research to the Rockefeller Foundation. In this undertaking, he implied that different viewpoints laid bare different levels of reality in process. But he agrees that all critical observations are, at least in part, a function of the instruments or methods of observation. An object reveals properties under the microscope different from those that are visible; an electrical analysis demonstrates facts different from a chemical analysis, for it is not a question of one absolute, unchanging truth. What he insists on as essential in his new discipline is the implicit possibility that genetic epistemology can relate all the different aspects of knowledge so that there are no internal inconsistencies or contradictions.[74] He states that this is the usual manner of enlarging knowledge. Even when no readily available way of combining two partial forms of knowledge is at hand, for example, a not-yet-discovered interpretation may reconcile the given facts in the future:

The concept of two kinds of knowledge as illustrated in the philosophies of Bergson and Husserl is, however, a different matter. Here it is proposed that the left hand should know nothing of what the right hand is doing. The vital or existential grasp of an intuition is claimed to lead to a knowledge of different from, and need not obey, the usual methods of knowing employed in obtaining some scientific fact.[75]

J. Marshall, who is friendly toward Piaget, at first replied that his colleagues in consultation were unable to find anything in the report to the Rockefeller Foundation differing from on-going research in the U.S.A. Piaget answered Marshall by pro-posing that an Anglo-Saxon epistemologist spend three months at Geneva, then make a report to the Foundation as to whether his results agreed with, or differed from, American and English studies. The Foundation accepted his proposal. W. Mays of Man-chester went to Geneva, where he wrote a favorable report that enabled the project to go forward. In good humor, Piaget wrote:

> my ambitious project interested all departments. I have been subjected to the customary tests, consisting in one or two excellent dinners on the top story of the Rockefeller Building in New York, in the company of the heads of these depart-ments who had prepared their examination questions. . . . In short, I tried to cope with them, and some months later ob-tained the necessary funds for establishing a "Centre interna-tional d'Epistémologie génétique" in the Faculty of Science of Geneva.[76]

Piaget recalls with obvious satisfaction how his founding of the International Center of Genetic Epistemology, in 1955, per-mitted three eminent scholars each year to visit and do research with the Geneva group that has grown up around him. There, relevant questions about the nature and attainment of knowledge are scientifically investigated through interdisciplinary efforts.

For Piaget, the difference between philosophical psychology and scientific psychology at the International Center lies not in the fact that the former concerns itself with "essences" according to Husserl, with "irrationality" according to Sartre, or with the Bergsonian use of introspection. He stresses the difference as being rather one of method, because philosophical psychology often neglects objective verification and grounds itself in sub-jectivity, although claiming to arrive at objective knowledge through intuition.

At the very time of the founding of Piaget's International Center of Genetic Epistemology, the faculty of philosophy at Geneva established a chair in philosophical psychology, in spite of, or perhaps to counteract, his defection from their philosophical fold. This expansion in philosophy, as opposed to a scientific, empirical psychology, at the University of Geneva provoked Piaget to reconstruct at his new Center a philosophical psychology that is more concerned with the process of discovery than with justification. Americans are participating in the program, and, to this extent, are spreading interest in his work abroad.

Piaget's Own Stages in Process[77]

Jean Piaget's new discipline did not emerge full-blown. Rather, it developed as an exclusive study among the many twentieth-century philosophical-scientific works. Following the emerging pattern of process-response so characteristic of all his writings, Piaget's contributions go through their metamorphoses, typical of all evolving reality. Comparable to the growth of a human organism, his research falls into three distinct phases: childhood, youth, and adulthood:

PIAGET'S OWN STAGES OF PROCESS IN GENETIC EPISTEMOLOGY

Childhood

The earliest period is marked by the publication of five books: *The Moral Judgment of The Child, Judgment and Reasoning in the Child, The Child's Conception of Physical Causality, The Child's Conception of the World, The Language and Thought of the Child.* During this stage of process, Piaget sought (at least in part) to find parallels between the thoughts of children and the philosophical systems created by thinkers of antiquity, demonstrating the partial consistency of cognitive structuring across long periods of time. He used social role-taking as the mediator of the cognitive development process. By these studies he indicated that mental growth is determined neither entirely

by innate structures nor entirely by the influence of environment. Rather, the determinant is the constant action and interaction of both factors in process.

Youth

This second phase is marked by the publication of three books:
*Play, Dreams and Imitation in Childhood; The Origins of Intel-
ligence in Childhood, The Construction of Reality in the Child.*
During this intermediate stage of process, Piaget traced in great
detail the origin of the structures of knowing to the sensorimotor
coordinations of infants—in this case his own three children. As
a result of these studies, he demonstrated the infantile fore-
runners of both the form and content of adult thought.

Adulthood

The third period is marked by all of Piaget's publications since
1940. In them he traces the development of logico-mathematical
thought from early childhood through adolescence, the four
major stages of cognitive development. As in the previous phases,
Piaget's emphasis continues to be epistemological. This resulted
in his establishing The International Center for Genetic Epistemology at Geneva. Equilibration is the dominant explanatory
process, for, as he stated on May 26, 1971, when addressing an
audience of 3,000 scholars at Temple University, "there is a
continual search for a better equilibrium."

During the first period he concerned himself with the parallels
between the comprehending activities of children and the phi-
losophical-system thinkers of antiquity. His aim was not like
the doctrine of G. Stanley Hall (1846–1924) to demonstrate
recapitulation, for example, which insists that the mind of the
child summarizes that of the race.

Instead, Piaget demonstrated that the partial constancy of

cognition, structuring itself across long periods of time, indicates the relatively stable nature of the human being. When the pre-Socratics created a philosophical system around ideas that are now implicit in the thinking of modern-day children, Piaget concluded that, as children, the pre-Socratics retained similar ideas which, as adults, they proceeded to elaborate into a comprehensive philosophy. Parallels between antiquity and the world views of today's children constitute in his discipline evidence of a constancy of modes. This process is a conceptualization which, at least in children, is relatively independent of historical cultural conditions.

During this earliest period of his professional career, Piaget frequently permitted himself to be led by his own "intuition" when interviewing children, particularly in his clinical approaches. He never asked any two children the same questions in the same setting. In effect, no two children ever received the same experimental treatment.

The Child's Conception of the World, published in 1929, is a good example of Piaget's skillful selection of questions. The book is without statistical tables and sample sizes are small. The main sources are his and his wife's observations of their own three children, born between 1925 and 1931. This meticulous study of children provides him with an exceptional and authentic awareness of the relationship between early sensorimotor actions and later cognitive development. From these exceedingly complete and carefully detailed descriptions of behavior he drew major conclusions regarding intellectual development within ontogenetic processes from birth to about age 2.

At first Piaget did not carry out his experimentations in protest to the extreme physiological, psychological, and philosophical perspectives that tended to dominate social scientific thinking during the early decades of the twentieth century. But his findings challenged the all-nurture views of child development, such as those of J. B. Watson, an extremist among the behaviorists.

In discovering that the child constructs ideas about the world that are very different from those of his parents and teachers, an absolute Watsonian environmentalism no longer seems defensible. The fact that the child spontaneously arrives at notions about the world that are contrary to the adult point of view indicates that the acquisition of knowledge is a much more complex process than previously assumed; it can no longer be considered a simple environmentalistic learning process. With this evidence Piaget demonstrated how knowledge is a surrendering of erroneous ideas for correct ones; that it consists in a transformation of ideas into higher levels with more adequate conceptions. In brief, his studies reveal that mental growth is not determined entirely by the unfolding of innate structures. It is not entirely determined by the influence of the environment, but rather by the constant interaction of the latter with the mental as co-factors within a continuing process.

The most recent phase of Piaget's work is marked by his publications since the 1940s. In them he records the development of logicomathematical thought from early childhood through adolescence. He completes his stages of process involved in growth and development not as specific behaviors, but with the following stages being dominant:

1. Sensorimotor stage (from birth to about 18 months or even 2 years).
2. Preoperational or representational stage (from about 18 months to about 7 years).
3. Concrete operations (from about 7 years to 11 or 12 years).
4. Formal operations (from abut 7 years to 15 years).

Piaget cautions, however, against a too-literal identification of stage and age. Insisting that his findings give only a rough estimate at best of the mean ages at which various stages are usually attained, he explains the stage-age relationship in this fashion:

The age of seven is a relative one in a double sense. In our research we say that a problem is solved by children of a certain age when three-quarters of the children of this age respond correctly. As a result, to say that a question is solved at seven years old means that already one-half of the six-year-olds can solve, and a third of the five-year-olds, etc. So, it's essentially relative to a statistical convention. Secondly, it's relative to the society in which one is working. We did our work in Geneva and the ages that I quote are the ages we found there. I know that in certain societies, for instance in Martinique, where our experiments have been done by Monique Laurendeau and Father Pinard, we have found a systematic delay of three or four years. Consequently the age at which those problems are solved is also relative to the society in question. What is important about these stages is the order of the succession. The mean chronological age is variable.[80]

Piaget admits that the old structures are altered, but not as in an interval scale. He finds that all manner of variables may affect the chronological age at which a given stage of functioning is dominant in a given child, such as intelligence, previous experience, and the culture in which the child lives. It is for this reason that he cautions against an over-literal identification of stage with age.

As for intelligence specifically, Piaget proposes that intellectual growth starts with an egocentric stage. Beginning in the sensori-motor state and basing itself on the inability to make a distinction between internal and external reality, probably the first type of acquired representation of the world the child achieves is in the form of an egocentrically oriented schema. It is a joint representation of action intended along with the consequences of that action. This is a matter to which Piaget (1954) devotes some of his most exquisite description.

This initial egocentric stage is followed by a more developed egocentrism. In it inner and outer realities are distinguished but confused in the preoperational or representational state. When inner psychological phenomena are attributed to inanimate features of the external environment, *animism* results; when psychological processes are given characteristics of the inanimate, external world, Piaget terms it *realism*. These two tendencies

in the Piagetian perspective are the complementary and universal forms of childish thought. For the child, their mutual presence indicates a preliminary distinction between inner and outer
reality. They are preparatory for more advanced stages of intellectual growth and development manifesting itself in the concrete and formal operational stages.[81]

Once the child reaches the age at which he dissociates his
thought from its object, then the stage is set for symbolic
processes to run ahead of concrete facts and for thought to be
in terms of possibility rather than actuality. In this destruction
of nominal or verbal realism as an outgrowth of maturation,
Piaget finds the wedge that ultimately fragments the unitary
solidarity of the child's "realistic" world view. At this point,
Bruner sees symbolic representation as being realizable, as going
beyond the capacities of an ikonic world and the way opened
for the Piagetian stage of formal operations. Here the real becomes but a "subset of the possible."[82]

During the intermediate or second phase, Piaget sought another direction: to trace further the origins and structures of
knowing to the sensorimotor coordinations of infants. These experiments are marked by the publication of three books—*The
Child's Conception of the World, The Origins of Intelligence in
Children*, and *The Construction of Reality in the Child*. They
all demonstrate his genius for careful observation.

In these studies he succeeds in transforming what might at
first appear to be mere ordinary behavior into significant evidence for the development of cognitive structures. As a result of
always being alert to theoretical considerations, he is able to
demonstrate better how the infantile behavior is the forerunner
of both the form and content of adult thought; how such intelligence grows from inside out; how it gains support from
the environment in the form of aliment appropriate to the
stage of individual development.[83]

From these complete and carefully controlled descriptions of
behavioral responses over a period of years, Piaget draws significant conclusions. His type of research, however, is often severely

criticized by experts who complain that his samples are too few and therefore not sufficiently experimental. These criticisms diminish in importance when the Piagetian assumptions are properly related to the development of intellectual structures, for they are basically the same in all persons. In this perspective, sample sizes become practically meaningless. That there is real merit in using the longitudinal approach of Piaget must not be minimized. While frequently studying small numbers of children, his observations of the same subjects range over years. The observations of Robert Oppenheimer seem apropos:

> I have been immensely impressed by the work of one man who visited us last year at the Institute, Jean Piaget. When you look at his work, his statistics really consist of one or two cases. It is just a start; and yet I think he has added greatly to our understanding. It is not that I am sure he is right, but he has given us something worthy of which to enquire whether it is right; and I make this plea not to treat too harshly those who tell you a story, having observed carefully without having established that they are sure that the story is the whole story and the general story. . . . It is of course in that light that I look at the immense discipline of practice, that with all its pitfalls, with all the danger that it leads to premature and incorrect solutions, does give an incredible amount of experience.[84]

The technique that Piaget employs to discover these operations in process is that of getting "inside the child's mind and see[ing] the world through the child's eyes." It is a projectional approach, almost unique in itself. As a result of this approach, he reduces the mental activities of the child to the barest essentials. These can be expressed simply, as *the child in process*.

Beginning Equilibrium—The preparatory stage or actual conditions in process in which the child finds himself at the time of the experiment (in any stage of growth and development).

ASSIMILATION—The developmental process-response or
and   reaction in which, during the experi-
ACCOMMODATION   ment, the outside stimuli are gradually
incorporated into the child's mental
capacities in process. This occurs
through his own activity, with the main
emphasis on his *adaptability* to his
functional system of organization and
mental structural patterns that reach
out and adjust to new and changing
conditions in the environment.

ADAPTATION—The dual processes of taking in (as-
similating) and reaching out and adjusting to (accommodating), which goes
on continuously.

Resulting   Equilibrium—If results or intelligible responses are
achieved at a higher level than the be-
ginning equilibrium, then the child
must be mentally active. Thus self-
activity becomes the single most important element in this adaptive process
(in any stage of growth and development).

When reduced to the barest essentials, these mental activities
can be summarized in this simplified manner:[85]

Beginning Equilibrium

assimilation

The process by which information is taken into mental structures; also the functioning of that system of which organization
is the structural aspect.

accommodation

The process of modifying and adapting thought to reality.

RESULTING EQUILIBRIUM

With reference to these operations, Piaget believes that the
functional invariants, known as organization and adaptation (as-

similation and accommodation), and the psychological structures are inextricably intertwined. Thus, assimilation and accommodation, although complementary, nevertheless occur simultaneously. A balance, though, between the two is necessary for adaptation. Adaptation, however, is not separate from organization. In this process the individual assimilates a novel event, such as the birth of Siamese kittens, into his preexisting structures. His concept of quadrupeds must meet the demands of the new situation. Furthermore, the functional invariants (organization and adaptation) are closely related to the structures of intelligence.[86] An excellent application of the Piagetian stages of growth and development to the process of thinking is to be found in Bruner's approach to the subject of mathematics:

> If you have an eventual pedagogical objective in mind, you can translate the way of thought [in the years from preschool through, say, high school] of a discipline into its Piagetian (or other) equivalent appropriate to a given level of development and take the child onward from there. The Cambridge Mathematics Project of the Education Development Center argues that if the child is to master the calculus early in his high school years, he should start work early with the idea of limits, the earliest work being manipulative, later going to images and diagrams, and finally moving on to the more abstract notation needed for delineating the more precise idea of limits.[87]

When studying Jean Piaget analytically, it is important to keep in mind that he is responsible for creating a new discipline that he terms genetic epistemology and in which, over the last half-century, many chang s of terminology, emphasis, and conceptualizations have evolved. The phase in which he accomplishes them is a significantly relevant variable.

In his early work, Piaget leaned heavily upon social role-taking as the mediator of cognitive development. In the recent phase of his experiments, he stresses the regulatory factor that unifies evolution and development as an explanatory process (equilibration). Consequently, in any scientific discipline, he sees both a history and a future for his genetic epistemology because his is an evolving system, with open, changing, process-approaches to the human reality.

His genetic epistemology is broad, rather than narrow, often leaping over established scientific boundaries. It looks at the child's behavior from many different points of view, encompassing diverse disciplines. It does not confine itself to a mere acquaintance with biology, physics, logic, and philosophy in its transdisciplinal approach.[88]

Moral Development[89]

Although Piaget's new discipline is essentially cognitive in its approach to the child, by no means does he neglect the moral. He considers it not merely complementary to, but integrally part of cognition. Like two sides of the same coin, these two aspects of human nature act and interact in his stages of process within the developmental. The foundation for this Piagetian dynamism is the fact that the child receives impressions from without and reacts to impressions from within.

The basis of Piaget's four basic stages of process stems from his thesis that the human child is not only different from animal children, but also different at each stage of his development. In this perspective, he finds a dominant stage of morality characteristic of each level of growth. By getting down on his hands and knees and playing a game of marbles with the children, he discovers that even here there is to be found such respect for rules, rituals, and conventional expressions as to enable him to study moral development at the early periods in life.

As a result of his extensive and intensive studies, Piaget published *The Moral Judgment of the Child,* wherein he describes his theory of moral development in great depth, identifying three major stages of moral growth:

STAGES OF MORAL DEVELOPMENT

Stage III:

Morality of cooperation takes into account the motives and degree of responsibility of the offender; punishment is not based just on the amount of damage done. This stage is characteristic of concrete operations.

Stage II:

Morality of constraint based on sense of moral realism; punishment is meted out according to the amount of damage, regardless of intention; the harshest punishment is the fairest. This stage of morality is characteristic of preoperational children.

Stage I:

Motor manipulation with no consciousness of rules, playing in an egocentric way.

The essence of morality, Piaget finds, is respect for rules.

Birth

That the essence of morality consists in respect for rules is the basis today for the definition of moral education given by Carter Good in his *Dictionary of Education*: "Moral education is formal or incidental instruction in morale or rules of conduct." As presented by Good, moral education cannot be separated from the essence in moral development, which is that

> *process of experience* and growth by which the capacity to distinguish between standards of right and wrong is gradually achieved and becomes progressively more influential in the individual's social behavior.

Piaget developed his theory of moral development within the framework of his four major stages through personalized interviews with children. Giving children problems to solve, he asks them which child is naughtier, for example, when Bill takes his father's fountain pen and then accidentally makes a little blot on the table cloth and when Jim, who notices that his father's pen is empty, decides to help his father by filling it with ink but while doing so makes a big blot on the table cloth. In comparing responses to paired stories such as these, he finds that children under the age of ten usually measure the seriousness of the deed in terms of the damage done. Thus the child who breaks nine glasses accidentally is naughtier than the one who breaks only two deliberately. Based upon data from such sources, Piaget is able to include with his long and detailed descriptions of moral development in *The Moral Judgment of the Child* that there are two major process-levels of formation in moral judgment: the level of morality of constraint and the level of cooperation:

A D O L E S C E N C E

The second major process of moral development, which gradually replaces that of the morality of constraint, is THE HIGHER PROCESS OF MORALITY OF COOPERATION. By the end of the primary grades and with the beginning of the intermediate grades (somewhere between about the ages eight to ten years), the child develops reciprocal respect and sympathy for peers. Losing much of his sense of objective responsibility, he begins to place greater emphasis on subjective intentions.

The first major process of moral development is THE MORALITY OF CONSTRAINT. During this period the child regards adults as all-powerful and re-gards the letter of the law as the terms of justice without the intention behind any violation entering into his judgments. Thus, the parents are the source of the child's moral realism.

Birth

In the child who is still in the process of the morality of constraint, any violation of the law is strictly viewed as a serious transgression. The question is often asked of Piaget: "Doesn't a three- or four-year-old child know about intention when deliberately violating rules?" The master's answer is yes, but in that stage of growth and development the child can justify the intention only by answering, "I didn't do it on purpose."

The salient feature of the process of the morality of constraint is that the same age child has difficulty in applying logical principles of intentions to the actions of others. This is due to what Piaget calls egocentrism. In problems of recognizing someone else's point of view, the child has great difficulties because he does not know that there is any other point of view but his own. Consequently, he judges another's actions by results, such as the ink blots or the number of glasses broken. These judgments are based more upon the letter of the law rather than upon the intentions behind the results.

In the second major process of moral development, the morality of cooperation, egocentrism diminishes. The child's concept of justice changes as the morality of cooperation gradually replaces the morality of constraint. Now the eight- to ten-year-old sees justice as a concern for inequalities and a concern for social injustices. The older child's notion of justice changes from a punitive view of justice to one of restitution. In the results that Piaget obtained by asking one hundred young children: "What do you consider to be unfair?" he demonstrates this change of position. Their responses fell into the following four types of examples:[90]

1. Unfair acts are when children do something that Dad and Mom have told them not to do. (Note the low level view of justice.)
2. Unfair acts are when children do something that goes against the rules of the game. (Here again is a low level view of justice.)
3. Unfair acts are inequalities in punishment or treatment. (Note the higher view of justice. Here is an example of the morality of cooperation.)

4. Unfair acts are injustices connected with the adult society. (Note this high level concept of justice.)

Refining these states of moral development so as to make them parallel within a specific concept, Piaget found that there are four broad stages that affect the moral development of the child so far as his readiness for conceptual theories of God is concerned:[91]

READINESS FOR THE THEORY OF GOD-CONCEPTS

Stage IV:

Period of immanent artificialism (from about 9 to 10 years of age and beyond) during which the child no longer regards nature as being made by men.

Stage III:

Period of technical artificialism (from about 7 to 10 years of age) during which the child continues to ascribe to men the general disposition of things, but limits this activity to operations which are technically realizable.

Stage II:

Mythological artificialism (approximately 5 or 6-7 years of age) during which the child ascribes coming-into-being in nature to the immediate action of men or of God.

Stage I:

Diffuse artificialism (present until 5 or 6 years of of age) during which the child believes that nature is under the control of men or at least that what happens in nature is always in some relation to the purposes of men. Piaget considers diffuse artificialism to be the direct result of the child's material dependence upon his parents. Initially the child regards his parents (and other adults) as all-powerful, all-knowing, and divine.

Artificialism is the child's belief that human beings created natural phenomena such as the sun, the moon, lakes, rivers, and mountains. It is integral to the two major processes of moral development as discovered in the child, gradually replacing the morality of constraint with the morality of cooperation. Like the early stage of moral realism, diffuse artificialism is a natural and spontaneous product of childish thought.

Birth

Kohlberg and Piaget[92]

It is particularly enlightening to compare Lawrence Kohlberg's studies of moral growth and development with those of Jean Piaget. Probably of all the developmentalists today, Kohlberg (1927–   ), through following Piaget's work, is producing the most extensive analysis of moral maturation. The following six major stages form his basic framework of moral growth in children:

KOHLBERG'S STAGES OF MORAL DEVELOPMENT

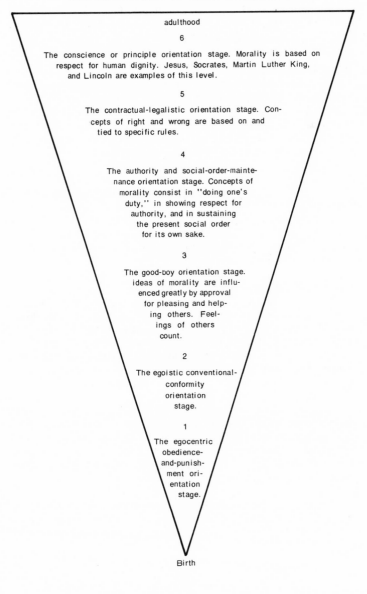

adulthood

6

The conscience or principle orientation stage. Morality is based on respect for human dignity. Jesus, Socrates, Martin Luther King, and Lincoln are examples of this level.

5

The contractual-legalistic orientation stage. Concepts of right and wrong are based on and tied to specific rules.

4

The authority and social-order-mainte-nance orientation stage. Concepts of morality consist in "doing one's duty," in showing respect for authority, and in sustaining the present social order for its own sake.

3

The good-boy orientation stage. ideas of morality are influenced greatly by approval for pleasing and help-ing others. Feel-ings of others count.

2

The egoistic conventional-conformity orientation stage.

1

The egocentric obedience-and-punish-ment ori-entation stage.

Birth

These six stages of orientation Kohlberg terms the framework basic to moral growth and development. He further subdivides the six, however, into twenty-five aspects of growth development, basing them on the premises that[93]

> the effort to force the child to agree that an act of cheating was very bad when he does not really believe it . . . will only be effective in encouraging morally immature tendencies toward expedient outward compliance. In contrast, a more difficult but more valid approach involves getting the child to examine the pros and cons of his conduct in his own terms (as well as introducing more *developmentally* advanced considerations).

> if one asks a child, "Is it very bad to cheat?" or "Would you ever cheat?", a child who cheats a lot in reality is somewhat more likely to give the conforming answer than is the child who does not cheat in reality. This is because the same desire to "look good" on a spelling test by cheating impels him to "look good" on the moral-attitude test by lying.

> the teacher is constantly and unavoidably moralizing to children about rules and values and about his students' behavior toward each other. Since such moralizing is unavoidable, it seems logical that it be done in terms of consciously formulated goals of moral development. As it stands, liberal teachers do not want to indoctrinate children with their own private moral values. Since the classroom social situation requires moralizing toward the necessities of classroom management, that is, upon the immediate and relatively trivial acts of behavior that are disrupting to him and to the other children. Exposure to the diversity of moral views of teachers is undoubtedly one of the enlightening experiences of growing up, but the present system of thoughtlessness as to which of the teacher's moral attitudes or views he communicates to children and which he does not leaves much to be desired.

> both conventional character-education classes or preaching and conventional moralizing by teachers about petty school routines are essentially "Mickey Mouse" stuff in relationship to the real

need for moral stimulation of the child. To be more than "Mickey Mouse," a teacher's moralizings must be cognitively novel and challenging to the child and they must be related to matters of obvious, real significance and seriousness.

Finally, by synthesizing his twenty-five aspects of growth development, Kohlberg succeeds in producing the following major categories or levels of moral development:

ADULTHOOD

Category III

The Level of Self-Accepted Moral Principles. This includes both
stages six (the conscience or principle orientation) and
five (the contractual-legalistic orientation).*

Category II

The Level of Conventional Role Conformity. This
includes both stages four (the authority and
social-order-maintenance orientation) and
three (the good-boy orientation).

Category I

The Premoral Level

This includes both stages two
(the egoistic conventional
orientation) and one
(The egocentric
obedience-and-
punishment
orientation).

BIRTH

*In his article ''Stages and Aging in Moral Development: Some
Speculations,'' Kohlberg proposes a new adult stage.

Like Piaget, Kohlberg conceptualizes how moral thinking occurs throughout the process of growth and development. Unlike Piaget, however, he analyzes moral growth by means of theoretical constructs, which he calls moral stages. His stage concept implies that a child must go through each moral stage, step by step. Kohlberg also says that children go through stages of moral development without skipping any steps or stages, and that children and adults do not progress at the same rate through the stages of moral development. His contention is that some adults remain in lower stages of moral development throughout their lives.

Using Piaget's theory of moral growth and development, Kohlberg defines six stages of moral development. His first group of developmental stages corresponds to Piaget's first major process of moral development: The Morality of Constraint.

The initial stage of moral development, Kohlberg designates as: OBEDIENCE-AND-PUNISHMENT ORIENTATION. In it he finds that children obey rules mainly to avoid punishments. To them, right means "obeying those in authority." There is only objective responsibility present along with an egocentrism that gives deference to superior power or prestige dominated by a trouble-avoiding perspective. A typical example is Johnny. He eats his potatoes and vegetables so that he can have his dessert, for he refused to do so yesterday and had no dessert.

His second stage Kohlberg calls the NAIVELY EGOISTIC ORIENTATION. In this stage he claims that the child feels that his behavior and his possessions should be for personal pleasure regardless of whether his behavior conflicts with any of the rights or privileges of others. Here, the child modifies his behavior mainly because of social praise or blame. He looks upon right action as instrumentally satisfying his self-needs and only occasionally those of others. He manifests an unsophisticated egalitarianism and orientation to exchange and reciprocity, as illustrated by the examples of Lisa and Jeff:[94]

1. Lisa lets Jeff go in front of her in line at school, knowing

that at a later time, when she asks it of him, he will let her go in front of him.

2. Jeff plays dolls with Lisa today because he is aware that Lisa enjoys playing dolls, but mainly because she previously agreed to play pitch-and-catch with him later.

In both of these examples the emphasis is on conventional role-conformity due to social rewards: "I do what you want and you do what I want." It is a mild indication of what Piaget terms in his processes of moral development the basic process of the morality of constraint beginning to be replaced by the higher process of the morality of cooperation.

Stage three manifests itself by seeking approval through pleasing and assisting others. Kohlberg therefore calls it the GOOD-BOY ORIENTATION stage. Generally, the child conforms mainly to avoid disapproval and dislike on the part of others. Conformity with the majority in a class is common, even with regard to the natural role of judging intentions as well as behavior. A frequent application showing the strong influence of approval and conformity in moral thinking is evident in Johnny again, who holds back his tears at being disappointed in school because "he does not want to be called a cry baby, for he has been told that 'big boys' don't cry." Here, too, are indications that the process of the morality of cooperation continues to supplant the basic process of the morality of constraint.

Kohlberg terms his stage four AUTHORITY- AND SOCIAL-ORDER-MAINTAINING ORIENTATION because in this stage the child moves toward an authority-maintaining morality. When disapproved by recognized adults, such as his parents, the child feels guilt or blame. Now he begins to recognize "a right as an earned privilege," hence the increasing perspectives on the process of the morality of cooperation and the lessening of the basic process of the morality of constraint. There develops in this stage a great regard for earned appreciation and respect of others. An example of this stage is the following incident:[95]

Millie has assumed the responsibility of caring for the plants in her classroom at the beginning of recess each day. On one occasion several of her friends invite her to play hopscotch with them—a favorite game of hers. She says she will join them only after she has watered the plants.

CONTRACTUAL AND LEGALISTIC ORIENTATION is Kohlberg's fifth stage of moral growth and development. This stage is based upon the recognition and acceptance of democratic laws with the recognition of an arbitrary starting point of agreement being important to the person. The approval or disapproval of actions by the greater community becomes important to the individual. One's duty is usually defined in terms of generally avoiding any violation of the will or rights of others or of their welfare, especially when reflected in the majority will.

The approval or disapproval of actions by the majority, with an especial emphasis on the recognition of the legality of group contracts, seems to predominate in this category of morality. The concept of rights becomes tied to a person's role or status in the group. There begins to emerge the concept of unearned rights granted to all human beings, so that now Piaget's second major process of moral development, the higher process of the morality of cooperation, generally dominates:

> By an example of the principle of people's earned and un-earned rights in a particular setting—a snowball fight—Kohlberg gives an anecdote about the legalistic tendencies of this stage. He observed a group of ten- and eleven-year-old boys who were getting ready to have a snowball fight. Before the fight, they spent a considerable amount of time splitting into teams, choosing officers inventing a set of rules to regulate the throwing of snowballs, and agreeing on a system of punishments for those who did not adhere to the rules. Before they had actually finished with the legalistic aspects of the game, it was time to go home and no snowball fight had taken place. Yet, to Kohlberg all the players seemed content with their afternoon.[96]

The last stage of moral development Kohlberg designates as the CONSCIENCE OR PRINCIPLE ORIENTATION. In stage six, he sees a morality emerge based upon individual principles. Feeling good about one's self becomes the motivation for moral action. Rights take on the broad meaning of a genuine concern for man and a respect for human dignity and personhood. The following three examples of moral development dealing with the principles of logical choice, consistency, mutual respect, and trust illustrate this orientation:[97]

1. Peter comes from a deeply religious family. His mother and father are having extreme marital difficulties. He is wrestling with the idea of his parents getting a divorce even though his church and general society do not condone that course of action.
2. Wally has always wanted a pocket knife. One day, while walking on the playground, he sees a knife like the one he has dreamed about. Even though he really wants to keep the knife, he gives it to the teacher for the lost and found.
3. Richard's parents are racist. He shares their beliefs and when faced with playing basketball with a black he becomes upset. After extended experience, Richard realizes that this boy is a human being just as he is. As an outcome of playing basketball, Richard discovers that they have many things in common.

Here the orientation is not only to actually ordained social rules, but also to principles of choice as they involve appealing to logical consistency, reasoning, and universality. The individual's orientation is to the conscience as a directing agent of the person, and to mutual respect and trust.

Kohlberg, like Bruner modeling his work on Piaget, suggests that mental and moral growth proceed in an orderly progression. "All movement is forward in sequence, and does not skip steps."[98] He concedes, as does Piaget, that children can move through these "true" stages at varying speeds and that an individual's growth may stop at any stage within his own developmental process.[99] The following chart contrasts the chief characteristics of Piaget's perspectives with those of Kohlberg:

CHARACTERISTICS OF PIAGET'S PROCESSES/LEVELS OF
MORAL DEVELOPMENT[100]

Processes/Levels

Concept	Morality of Constraint	Morality of Cooperation

1. Control-Authority	1. Duty is obeying authorities
	  a. Good defined by obedience to rules
	  b. Rules or laws not analyzed
		1. Mutual agreement
		  a. Lessening of adult constraint
		  b. Rules can be modified

2. Justice	2. Letter of the Law
	  a. Anxiety over forbidden behavior
	  b. Concern for violation of game rules
	  c. Punitive justice
	  d. Any transgression is serious
		2. Restitutive justice
		  a. Concern for inequalities
		  b. Concern for social injustices
		  c. Spirit of the law considered

3. Responsibility	3. Objective view
	  a. Intentions not considered
	  b. Egocentric position
	  c. Judgments in relation to conformity to the law
		3. Subjective view
		  a. Motives considered
		  b. Rights of others to their opinions
		  c. Judgments by situation

CHARACTERISTICS OF KOHLBERG'S STAGES OF MORAL DEVELOPMENT

State	Concept of Motivation	Concept of Right
1. Obedience-and-punishment orientation	1. Punishment by another	1. No real concept of right
2. Naively egoistic orientation	2. Rewards by another	2. Rights are factual ownership
3. Good-child orientation	3. Disapproval by others	3. No one has right to do evil
4. Authority- and social-order-maintaining orientation	4. Censure by legitimate authorities followed by guilt feelings	4. A right is an earned claim on the actions of others
5. Contractual-legalistic orientation	5. Community respect and disrespect	5. Concept of unearned, universal rights
6. Conscience or principle orientation	6. Self-condemnation	6. Respect for individual life and personality of others

Three major ideas sum up both Piaget's and Kohlberg's theories of moral development: First, all children go through the processes and stages of moral development in a step-by-step fashion; children and adults do not jump stages of moral development. Second, development is not merely learning verbal values, in rote fashion or paper rules required to be given back on examinations. Third, regardless of race, sex, creed, and culture, moral development is universal across all children and societies.

Practical Insights[101]

There are many applications of moral development based on the writings of Piaget and Kohlberg that can be and are being applied to values process-and-response education. Kohlberg, in particular, has made numerous applications of his research on moral development in the framework of Piagetian perspectives to learning and teaching, as indicated by the following chronology of his works:

Articles and Essays by Lawrence Kohlberg

"The Development of Modes of Moral Thinking and Choice in the Years Ten to Sixteen." Doctoral dissertation, University of Chicago, 1958.

"Moral Development and Identification." In H. A. Stevenson, ed., *Child Psychology 62nd Yearbook National Society for the Study of Education. Part I.* Chicago: University of Chicago Press, 1963.

"The Development of Children's Orientation towards a Moral Order. 1. Sequence in the Development of Moral Thought." *Vita Humana* 6 (1963) : 11-13.

"Stages in Conceptions of the Physical and Social World." Unpublished monograph, 1963.

"The Development of Moral Character and Ideology." In M. L. Hoffman, ed., *Review of Child Development Research*, vol. 1. New York: Russell Sage Foundation, 1964.

"Psychosexual Development, a Cognitive-Developmental Approach." Unpublished mimeographed manuscript, University of Chicago, 1965.

"Cognitive Stages and Preschool Education." *Human Development* 9 (1966) : 15–17.

"A Cognitive and Developmental Analysis of Children's Sex-Role Concepts and Attitudes." In E. Maccoby, ed., *The Development of Sex Differences*. Stanford, Calif.: Stanford University Press, 1966.

"Moral Education in the Schools." *School Review* 74, no. 1 (1966): 1–30.

"Moral and Religious Education and the Public Schools: A Developmental View." In T. Sizer, ed., *Religion and Public Education*. Boston: Houghton-Mifflin, 1967.

"Preschool Education: A Cognitive-Developmental Approach." *Child Development* 9 (1968) : 5–17.

"The CHILD as a Moral Philosopher." *Psychology Today* 7 (1968): 25–30.

"Moral Development." *International Encyclopedia of the Social Sciences*. Crowell, Collier and Macmillan, 1968. Pp. 483–94.

"Stage and Sequence: The Cognitive-Developmental Approach to Socialization." In D. Goslin, ed., *Handbook of Socialization: Theory and Research*. New York: Rand McNally and Co., 1969. Pp. 347–480.

"Stages in the Development of Moral Thought and Action." New York: Holt, Rinehart and Winston, 1969.

"The Moral Atmosphere of the School." Paper delivered at Association for Supervision and Curriculum Development, Conference on the "Unstudied Curriculum," Washington D.C., January 9, 1969 (printed in *AASC Yearbook 1970*).

"Education for Justice: A Modern Statement of the Platonic View." In T. Sizer, ed., *Moral Education*. Cambridge, Mass.: Harvard University Press, 1970.

"Stages of Moral Development as a Basis for Moral Education." In C. Beck and E. Sullivan, eds., *Moral Education*. Toronto: University of Toronto, 1970.

"From *is* to *ought*: How to Commit the Naturalistic Fallacy and Get Away with It in the Study of Moral Development." In T. Mischel, ed., *Cognitive Development and Epistemology*. New York: Academic Press, 1970.

"The Contributions of Developmental Psychology to Education—Examples for Moral Education." Invited address presented at the annual meeting of the American Psychological Association, Washington D.C., September 7, 1971.

"Cognitive-Developmental Theory and Practice of Collective Moral Education." In M. Wolins and M. Gottesman, eds., *Group Care: The Educational Path of Youth Aliyah*. New York: Gordon and Breach, 1971.

"A Developmental Approach to School Psychology." *School Psychology Digest* 1, no. 3 (1972): 3–7.

"Stages and Aging in Moral Development: Some Speculations." *Gerontologist* 13 (1973): 497–502.

Co-Authored Articles

Bar-Yam, M. and Kohlberg, L. "Development of Moral Judgment in the Kibbutz." In L. Kohlberg and E. Turiel, eds., *Recent Research in Moral Development*. New York: Holt, Rinehart and Winston, 1971.

Blatt, M. and Kohlberg, L. "The Effects of Classroom Discussion upon Children's Level of Moral Judgment." In L. Kohlberg and E. Turiel, eds. *Recent Research in Moral Development*. New York: Holt, Rinehart and Winston, 1971.

Freundlich, D. and Kohlberg, L. "Moral Judgment in Delinquents." In L. Kohlberg and E. Turiel, eds., *Recent Research in Moral Development*. New York: Holt, Rinehart and Winston, 1971.

Gilligan, C.; Kohlberg, L.; Lerner, J.; Belenky, M. "Moral Reasoning about Sexual Dilemmas: The Development of an Interview and Scoring System." Washington, D. C., President's Commission on Pornography and Obscenity, 1970.

Grim, P., Kohlberg, L., and White, S. "Some Relationships between Conscience and Attentional Processes." *Journal of Personality and Social Psychology* 8 (1968): 239–52.

Kohlberg, L. and De Vries, R. "Relations between Piaget and Psychometric Assessments of Intelligence." In C. Lavatelli, ed., *The Natural Curriculum*. Urbana, Ill.: University of Illinois Press, 1971.

———— and Kramer, R. "Continuities and Discontinuties in Children and Adult Moral Development." *Human Development* 12 (1969): 93–120.

————, La Crosse, J., and Ricks, D. "The Predictability of Adult Mental Health from Childhood Behavior." In B. Wolman, ed., *Handbook of Child Psychology*. New York: McGraw-Hill, 1970.

———— and Lockwood, A. "Cognitive-Developmental Psychology and Political Education-Process in the Sixties." Speech for Social Studies Consortium Convention, Boulder, Colorado, 1970.

———— and Mayer, R. "Preschool Research and Preschool Educational Objectives: A Critique and a Proposal." Washington, D.C.: Office of Economic Opportunity, Government Printing Office, 1971.

———— and Selman, R. "Preparing School Personnel Relative to Values: A Look at Moral Education in the Schools." ERIC Clearing House on Teacher Education, Washington, D.C. Contract OEC–0–8–080490–3706 (010)

———— and Turiel, E., eds., *Recent Research in Moral Education.* New York: Holt, Rinehart and Winston, 1972.

———— and Turiel, E. "Moral Development and Moral Education." In G. Lesser, ed., *Psychology and Educational Process.* Chicago: Scott, Foresman, 1971.

————, with Whitten, P. "Understanding the Hidden Curriculum." *Learning* 1, no. 2 (1972) : 10–14.

————, Yaeger, J., and Hjertholm, E. "The Development of Private Speech: Four Studies and a Review of Theory." *Child Development* 39 (1968) : 691–736.

———— and Zigler, E. "The Impact of Cognitive Maturity upon the Development of Sex-Role Attitudes in the Years Four to Eight." *Genetic Psychology Monographs* 75 (1967): 89–165.

———— et al. "Moral Judgment Instruction Guide for Learning to Issue Score." Unpublished mimeographed manuscript, Harvard University, 1971.

Rest J., Turiel, E., and Kohlberg, L. "Level of Moral Development as a Determinant of Preference and Comprehension of Moral Judgments Made by Others." *Journal of Personality* 37 (June 1969) : 225–52.

In this research, Kohlberg suggests something that he calls "the match" and "the match plus one." He contends that a proper match exists between a child's stage of moral thinking and his responses to moral problems and dilemmas. In particular "the match plus one," he says, can be used to advance the level of moral thinking. Using the six stages of moral development, Kohlberg asks teachers and administrators to diagnose the child's level of moral development. This is done by observing the child and his answers to the questions asked about moral problems, not dissimilar to Piaget's techniques of observation, termed the clinical method.

After diagnosing the level of moral development in which the child is currently functioning, Kohlberg tells teachers to develop moral problems whose solution requires moral reasoning at the next higher stage to solve but that are in "tip-toe reach" of the child. This is Kohlberg's idea of "the match plus one." The most important notion here is the idea of using "the match" and "the match plus one" in helping children to progress from one level of moral development to another. An example of "the match" and "the match plus one" is the following:

> Sue was playing in the sandbox and Sarah, even though Sue did not want her to play in the sand, stepped into the sandbox. The teacher observed that Sue threw sand at Sarah. These actions and similar ones showed evidence of stage one in moral development. One solution that could be used by a teacher might be to group Sue with two or three children who are at the next higher level of moral development. These children either directly or indirectly will suggest that sharing is fun not only with the sandbox but with other toys. Using this type of interaction based upon "the match plus one," Sue will realize over a period of time that sharing can be fun. Sharing here is a form of reward. Sue's actions will move from actions motivated by fear of punishment to actions motivated by promise of reward. Sue would then be moving from stage one to stage two in moral development.[102]

Such moral dilemmas, when given to children to solve, produce and induce tension in their moral reasoning. This tension Kohlberg calls *dissonance* or, simply put, *conflict*. Piaget, however, prefers to designate this dissonance as *disequilibrium,* which results from the tension produced. The tension encourages the child to wrestle with the current difficulty, requiring him, for a solution, to seek one step higher than the stage he is currently operating at. Kohlberg believes that this conflict over a period of continuous interaction, requiring the next higher stage for its solution, eventually encourages, and even causes, the child to progress to the next higher level of moral development. In sum, the most important notion here is the idea of using "the match" and "the match plus one" in moving children from one level of moral development to the next.

Just as Lawrence Kohlberg specializes in the moral thinking and developmental moral levels of the growing child, so Jean Piaget primarily concerns himself with using the study of the child to answer questions aboue the nature and origin of knowledge. There are numerous equally important cognitive-moral insights that Piaget has formulated in his life's work that directly affect the nature of the learner and have specific implications for teacher. The following ones are especially apropos:

Mental growth is an extension of biological growth. As such, it is governed by the same laws and principles. The four major stages of mental development, as previously outlined, indicate how mental growth parallels that of physical growth in the learner. In each stage the environment serves as nourishment for the growth of mental structures or abilities, the developmental pattern of which follows a course that is laid down in the genes. In this relationship, Piaget has found through controlled experimentation that children can utilize whatever stimuli are in their environment to foster mental growth, provided they are in keeping with the child's maturation level. He observes that

> too many people take the theory of stages to be simply a series of limitations. That is a disastrous view. The positive aspect is that as soon as each stage is reached it offers new possibilities to the child. . . . It is just as disastrous, moreover, to assume that a child has or has not reached a certain stage just because he is a certain age. The ages I have mentioned are only averages. Any child may be a year or so beyond or behind the average capabilities reached by most children his age.[103]

Normative aspects of children's behavior and development determine capacity for learning. Piaget believes that an understanding of normal development is the necessary starting point for a fuller comprehension of differences between individuals. He claims that a child merely lacks experience, but his capacity to learn is no different in kind from that of an adult. Through careful experimentation he demonstrates conclusively how capacity determines learning, and not the reverse:

> I have a horror of teaching methods that are predetermined.
> . . . I think children learn from trying to work out their own
> ways of doing things—even if it does not end up as we might
> expect. But children's errors are also instructive for teachers.
> Above all, teachers should be able to see the reasons behind
> errors. Very often a child's errors are valuable clues to his
> thinking. As Seymour Papert says, a child always answers his
> own question correctly; the cause of an apparent error is that
> he did not ask himself the same question that you have asked
> him.[104]

This, of course, is the antithesis of what earlier educators understood when they advocated the acceleration of mental growth. For, although this is still full of mystery, as Piaget expresses it, "It seems probable that assimilation that is done too rapidly does not result in a structure that can be generalized as readily to apply to other situations" (cf. ibid., p. 272 n120).

Empathy is essential to valid observation of children. Only then do the observations have the solid ring of truth. Through this type of observation, Piaget says, adequate provisions can be made for the physical development that sets limits as to exactly what can be learned at any particular point in the child's life. He emphasizes the necessity of providing the child with the settings and stimuli that will free him to realize his capacities at his own time and place as an individual:

> In a great many cases it's just that the language we use is bad.
> We simply do not make ourselves understood. I have often
> questioned children who have been identified as being poor
> in mathematics. If I gave them problems and made sure they
> knew what I was talking about, they solved them very well.
> Then afterwards I told them that was arithmetic, and they were
> amazed. It could be another world. I do not believe in aptitudes
> and nonaptitudes in mathematics and science that differentiate
> children at the same intellectual level. What is usually involved
> is either aptitudes or nonaptitudes to the teacher's approach.[105]

When Piaget is asked if the teacher should know what she wants the child to understand from the materials she uses, he answers in the affirmative but adds:

> as long as the child is not told. But still you should be on the lookout for the unexpected things that develop, and make sure he can pursue these, too.[106]

Repetitive behavior is helpful in satisfying children's cognitive needs. Piaget found that good devices stimulate thought in the repetitive behavior of such studies as geometry, space, and numbers. Recently he was questioned about the increasing tendency among teachers to provide the children with the same types of materials (Piagetian kits for teachers) that he uses in his own research. He says he finds this procedure rather limited indeed:

> And if the aim is to accelerate the development of these operations, it is idiotic.

> I would say that the only step in the right direction such kits represent is to provide the children with actual objects. . . . Manipulation of materials is crucial. In order to think, children in the concrete stage need to have objects in front of them that are easy to handle, or else be able to visualize objects that have been handled and that are easily imagined without any real effort.[107]

The raising of questions is just as important as knowing how to solve them. Therefore, Piaget cautions that in all stages of growth and development the materials must be:

> simple enough so that the child can indeed raise questions that he can answer for himself.

> You can facilitate it mainly through having a multitude of materials available that raise questions in a child's mind without suggesting the answers. . . . It's the materials he should learn from.[108]

For, he insists, the raising of questions on the part of the child is just as important as knowing how to answer them.

Conversation and clashes of opinions and of ideas are usually beneficial to children's mental growth, helping them to help themselves to attain the principal goal of education. Piaget sees this educational goal in the light of his own accomplishments when he declares:

> The principal goal of education is to create men who are capable of doing new things, not simply of repeating what other generations have done—men who are creative, inventive, and discoverers. The second goal of education is to form minds which can be critical, can verify, and not accept everything they are offered. The great danger today is of slogans, collective opinions, ready-made trends of thoughts. We have to be able to resist individually, to criticize, to distinguish between what is proven and what is not. So we need pupils who are active, who learn early to find out by themselves, partly by their own spontaneous activity and partly through material we set up for them; who learn early to tell what is verifiable and what is simply the first idea to come to them.[108]

To sum up, intelligence is the single most important developmental aspect in the learning process. For Piaget the aim of education is to guide the learner through the stages of intellectual growth: (a) by providing him with the appropriate organization of subject matter (curriculum), (b) through introducing information at the appropriate time levels (spacing and sequencing), (c) by introducing information in an appropriate manner (teaching strategy and methodology), thus enabling him to attain the goals of education.

Logic within Process[109]

Although the theme running through all of Piaget's studies is the developmental or process-and-response aspect, there is a trilogy in which this theme becomes operative: logic, relativity, and dialectic. Logic provides the common genotype of the mental, biological, and physical sciences and plays the central role. Piaget reasons that if logic is inherent in the mind, in biological processes, and in the laws that govern the physical world, then it must be the key to understanding nature:

The Process-and-Response Trilogy in Piaget's
Developmental Genetic Epistemology

L

O

G

RELATIVITY	I	DIALECTIC
(Subjective Element)		(Delimiting Element)
	C	

(Key)
Acting and interacting in the Knowledge Process

He believes that it is the presence of logical operations in the child that permits him to reconstruct and understand the physical, social, and biological worlds. If logic is inherent in psychic activities from the start of life, Piaget declares, how much more important is its evolution in the course of the individual's development.

Of course the logic that Piaget observes in the infant is much more primitive and much less systematic than that which he observes in the preschool and elementary school children. It is only in adolescents that he finds a true, or formal, logical system comparable to that constructed by logicians. He insists, however, that logic is taken to mean in a broad sense a set of actions that obey logiclike rules, such as transitivity. He claims to find at all age levels behavior that manifests some form of logic in the four major stages. Jerome Bruner comments as follows:

> In a word, probably the first type of acquired [logical] representation of the world the child achieves is in the form of an egocentrically oriented action schemata joint representation of action intended along with the consequences of that action, a matter to which Piaget (1954) has devoted some of his most exquisite descriptions.[110]

It is during the period of concrete operations, usually around the ages of seven (formerly known as the age of reason) to eleven, that the child's reasoning processes become logical. Prior to this development in the preoperational period, his development is termed prelogical. Bruner considers the most important development of the concrete operational period to be the attainment of logical operations for the first time.

Actually, it is internalized cognitive actions that permit the child to arrive at conclusions that are "logical." These actions are directed by comprehending activities rather than by being dominated by sense perceptions. The logical operations evolve, as do all cognitive structures, out of prior structures, as a function of assimilation and accommodation. Logical operations are means of organizing experience, called schemata, that are superior to prior organizations. According to Piaget, this logic is

> a formalized system [that] can be employed to describe the structuring spontaneously manifest in intelligent behavior. The internal consistency and necessity of logical judgments command our intellectual assent. There is a continuous genetic relation between mature logical forms and prelogical structures of early behavior.[111]

For an operation to be logical, however, Piaget says it must always possess four characteristics: (a) it is internalized or carried out in thought; (b) it is reversible; (c) it always presupposes some conservation, some invariance; (d) it never exists alone but is always related to a system of operations. The three specific types of logical operations that the child performs during the period of concrete operations are seriation, classification, and reversibility. In this period he is unable to solve hypothetical problems, problems that are entirely verbal, or other problems requiring more complex operations. In this state he remains inferior in thought to the older child (over eleven or twelve) until the attainment of formal thought indicates that the cognitive structures are complete.

Piaget's recognition of logic as the mediating factor in the construction of knowledge is attributable, at least in part, to his teacher at the University of Neuchâtel, Arnold Reymond. It was Reymond, the philosopher-logician, who pointed out to Jean Piaget as a student the relationship between Aristotelian logic and biology. This ended Piaget's attraction to the Bergsonian dualism of the vital and the logicomathematical. It was Reymond, also, who showed him the general philosophical and scientific implications that reside in any concrete issue;[112] thus, in his own works, Piaget strove to construct a logic of mental operations with psychological validity. Practically all of his writings from the 1920s on seem to reflect this "developmental" aspect, a direct influence of his doctoral studies under Reymond. It continued to grow and to be perfected to such an extent over the last fifty or more years that today he is termed a *developmentalist,* interested particularly in the human organism's adaptation to the environment through intelligence.

Piaget confronts children at different ages with tasks that require the use of reasoning for their solution. Although his genetic logic is frequently criticized by logicians, it is possibly the first successful attempt to construct a logical model of thought based upon experiment rather than on philosophical speculation. If all intelligence and thought manifest the logical structure that he claims, then they are at one with the biological and social realities that manifest a comparable structure. Logic, then, becomes the bedrock upon which any epistemology must be built.[113]

It represents the factor common to the mental, biological, and physical sciences, whereas relativity, now to be discussed, describes the relation between mind and reality.

Relativity within Process

Epistemological relativism permeates all of Piaget's thinking in the construction of reality. It is evident that the theory of relativity had a special appeal for him. If, as Albert Einstein has shown, conceptual judgments are always relative to the position of the observer making those judgments, then the observer, Piaget reasons, could never be left out in the construction of concepts. This contention reinforces a preestablished conviction of Piaget: reality always involves a subjective element, in the sense that it is always in part a projection or externalization of thought or action. Even the simplest environmental influence or stimulation is never passively received and registered by the person, but is always acted upon by him. To demonstrate, Piaget uses the example of the infant who brings everything he touches toward his mouth. Piaget interprets this as a construction of the world of reality as things to be sucked, and thus the infant's organizing the world in terms of his own actions.[114]

Piaget sees the absolute separation between mind and matter as an illusion. But he claims that such an illusion can be overcome by examining the developmental processes of thought in the child. All knowledge is mediate, or mediated, rather than immediate or copied directly. It is not difficult in this perspective to see how the copy theory dies hard. The very tendency of mental activities to become automatized, and for their results to be perceived as external to the subject, is what leads to Piaget's conviction that there is a real independence of thought. The significant point that he finds is that the older child takes as self-evident, or a priori, what only a few short years ago he did not know even existed. Once a concept is constructed, Piaget says, it is immediately externalized. It then appears to the subject as a perceptually given property of the object and independent of the subject's own mental activity. Jerome Bruner presents an appropriate case in this regard:

> In the classic experiment on the conservation of a continuous quantity (Piaget, 1952), one of two identical beakers was filled with water to a certain level. The . . . child poured an equal amount in the second beaker. Then the experimenter poured the water from one beaker into a longer, thinner beaker, causing the water level to raise. The child was then asked if the two beakers contained the same amount of water or if one had more than the other and why. He was then asked for a reason. A type of reason in support of non-conservation judgments appeared that we had not seen before among American children . . . although Piaget (1952) reports one example in a Swiss four-year-old. This was the "magical" action reason: the child would say, "It's not the same" because "you poured it." The shift from equality to "inequality" was being resolved and justified by recourse to the experimenter's action. A natural phenomena was being explained by attributing special "magical" powers to intervening human agents. More likely . . . this as well as other cases of magical causation are made possible by realism in which animate and inanimate phenomena occupy a single plane of reality. . . . Thus, "magic" only exists from the perspective of a dualistic ontology . . . [for] the child who pours on his own now uses his initial equalizing operations as the basis for his justification of conservation: "They were equal at the beginning."[115]

Like Piaget, Bruner sees the intellectual growth of the child as characterized by several major aspects. The first and most general one is that intelligence does not flow smoothly but rather in spurts of rapid growth followed by consolidation. The spurts in growth he sees as organized around the emergence of certain capacities, including intellectual ones. These have about them the character of prerequisities: one thing must be mastered before the child can go to the next, and so forth. Many of them are directed to two ends: *the maintenance of invariance* and *the transcending of momentariness in registration and response.* This is the recognition of kinship, by which the continuity in things is transformed, either in location or appearance, or in the response they evoke.[116] In his dialectics within process, Jean Piaget is in agreement with these Brunerian perspectives, for he identifies them as being operative in the critical factor of equilibration.

For both Bruner and Piaget, knowledge is not a mere imitation of reality either. To know means essentially to transform the object, the event, or the situation so as to understand it within the very personalized process involved in the tranformation. As a consequence, the person then comprehends in a highly personal manner the way the object is constituted. Actually, this understanding, as knowledge, is not over and above the internalized process, but is the very comprehending process itself, the person's knowing. The operational process constitutes the real essence of any knowledge; it must be essentially an interiorized activity that gradually modifies the object or the event of knowledge.

In claiming that a child knows, Piaget means that he has in process modified external reality. For him, knowledge always involves a personalized mental operation; it permits the person to transfer what he sees in the light of what he already knows in process. Piaget states, however, that all these functions are not identical at all ages; that they are conditioned by, and contingent upon, many factors that are themselves in process and, therefore, are characteristic of the psychology of individual differences.

The method Piaget uses to study the interiorization of the child in process through these various stages of knowledge is almost as new to psychology as his insights. By getting away from the traditional practice of applying to the child's mind the pattern of the adult, Piaget learns that "the child's mind is made up of two planes. In the early years of his life the work is done by the child himself, which attracts him pell-mell and crystallizes round his wants all that is likely to satisfy those wants." This he calls the egocentric plane. The upper plane, however, is built up by social environment. It is the plane of objectivity, speech, and logical ideas; in a word, the plane of reality, which results in the incipient cooperation level and, finally, in the genuine cooperative level of activity.[117]

In applying these two planes of action to a game of marbles, Piaget found that these workings in the child's mind could be adequately reflected because this game has rules that regulate interpersonal behavior. Then, too, since the game is played by children and the rules are made by children, the game (the response, therefore) actually reflects the workings of their minds rather than those of the adult. As Bruner remarks:

> The effective power within a particular learner's grasp is what one seeks to discover by close analysis of how in fact he is going about his task of learning. Much of Piaget's research [for example, in his book, *The Child's Conception of Number* (New York: Humanities Press, 1952)] seeks to discover just this property about children's learning and thinking.[118]

In describing the proper procedures of his clinical method as they react within the planes of the interpersonal to children's activities themselves, Piaget cautions that each child be permitted to "talk freely, without ever checking or side-tracking his utterance, and at the same time he [the observer] must constantly be on the alert for something definite. . . ."[119] Only in this manner can the listener discern how the children's thoughts originate. By looking beyond what is obviously present, while hearing what the children are revealing about their thought processes through the use of language, the inquirer can reconstruct their mental activities.

In his clinical method, Piaget discovered that:

1. Everything that the child in process is able to learn on one level is a function partly of what he has already learned within a previous level of his development.
2. Although the process is continuous, it proceeds in a discontinuous manner. The stages, therefore, are not fixed, but develop quite gradually within a plasticlike state, an outgoing process of interaction between the child and his environment.

3. As the child continues to deal with this environment, his mental processes become more and more complex, beginning with an adaptation to the social and physical environment through a set of actions and processes by which an assimilation, resulting in knowledge, makes the necessary accommodations to new knowledge.[120]
4. Language has some basis in the child out of which his symbolically organized experiences grow. Through the interaction of language and the organized activities themselves, even the child of two or three gradually entrenches himself in the realm of experience.

Piaget also discovers that in general the child receives information and fits it into the "conceptual scheme" he already possesses. When the information will not fit the child's current schema, he must proceed to alter and accommodate it to the new facts. This is termed *the fitting process* (assimilation) and the *alteration process* (accommodation).

Through very careful questioning of the children of various ages, Piaget uncovers in his progressional process how each child develops mentally, how in his view of his world he moves from a very egocentric view to a social view, accompanied by parallel progress in his conversation and reasoning. Thereby the child's belief in opinions and teachings of others develops from a sacrosanct belief to a more arbitrary one. In the same way, his respect for teaching moves from a unilateral respect to a mutual respect. It depends, however, upon the factors within process. These become the major stage or combination of stages of process in which the child finds himself.

Dialectics within Process[121]

The principle of equilibration limits the interaction of maturational and environmental influences in Piaget's theory of knowledge. The theory therefore is essentially dialectical in nature. It expresses the dynamics of mental growth and the acquisition of knowledge. Along with Bruner and his associates, Piaget considers the following to be the main factors of influence from one stage of growth and development to another:[122]

1. *Maturation:* he defines this as the ripening of neural structures in process with age, which significantly affects the transformations within mental structures. Maturation alone, however, is insufficient to account for changing mental structures; genes also influence the ripening in process.

2. *Experience* (in the broadest sense) : he maintains that this experience within process is alone not enough to accelerate logical development, particularly if experience is considered to be merely exposure to objects or events, i.e., merely extrinsic in nature. For him experience must include what he terms a total coordination of actions in process—actions of bringing things together or of ordering things about, etc., in such a way as to constitute an experiential gestalt.

3. *Social Transmission:* he considers this as the linguistic or educational transmission within the human process; for like the two preceding factors, this, too, has its essential role in logical development. This factor is not enough in itself. He cautions that linguistic transmission is possible in the full sense of process only when logical structures are present in the thinking of children; otherwise they do not comprehend the logic involved.

4. *Equilibration:* he calls this the critical factor of process. The previous factors are necessary, but it is the mental activity of the subject himself in process with which he is concerned. When confronted with a cognitive conflict and operating to compensate, the mental actually determines the development of logical structures within process. This factor is in direct opposition to those theories of learning which place the whole emphasis on mere external reinforcements.

All these factors interact in a complexity. No one of them can in itself explain the real nature of the cognitive activity. It is for this reason that Piaget introduces the fourth factor of *equilibration.* He asserts that it is the most important one and that it determines the mode of interaction of the other three.[123]

The principle of equilibration regulates the interaction within the maturational factors. It includes the activities involved in both social transmission and physical experiences in the broadest

MAJOR FACTORS IN THE DYNAMICS OF MENTAL DEVELOPMENT

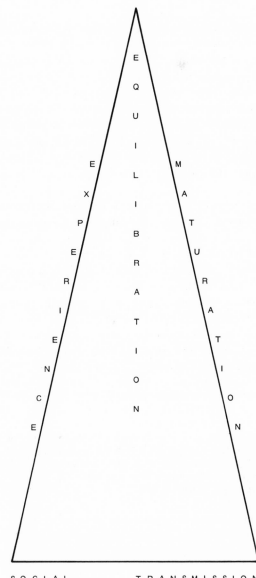

sense. At each level of the child's development there are two poles of activity—changes in the structure of the organism in response to environmental intrusions, termed accommodation, and changes in the intruding stimuli due to the existing structure, termed assimilation.[124]

These two activities constitute a sort of thesis and antithesis, whose eventual synthesis is effected through the process of equilibration. In practice, this means that a new structural system is evolving so that each new intrusion can be incorporated without either a change in the structure or a change in the stimulus. This conserves the integrity of both the internal and external systems.

As Piaget reports it, dialectical equilibration provides the dynamic principle that governs the acquisition of knowledge and the structures necessary in the acquisition of knowledge. An equilibrated system is never static and closed, but always mobile and open. Each new level of mental equilibrium prepares for a disequilibrium. Each state of biological equilibrium—for example, satiation—is preparatory to a new disequilibrium—for example, hunger. On the knowledgeable level, each new plane of conceptualization establishes a new equilibrium. It likewise opens the subject to new forms of information, but also to new possibilities of contradiction.[125] Therefore, he says:

> It is essential for teachers to know why particular operations are difficult for children, and to understand that these difficulties must be surmounted by each child in passing from one level to the next. . . . Teachers must understand, for example, why reversibility cannot be taken for granted with 4-year-olds, and why 12-year-olds have difficulty reasoning from hypotheses. What changes take place from one level to the next, and why does it take so much time?[126]

Piaget asks, "Is not the same true of science?" The notion of evolution, for example, explains the variations among species and produces a new equilibrium in biological thinking. At the same time, of course, the challenge to the established tradition creates the usual disequilibrium in the system of thought. Thus, equilibration is at all levels of analysis and is the dynamic of cognitive change; without it, the effects of maturation and physical and social experience cannot be fully understood or explained. Here is where Piaget steps into the realm of active and total awareness of the child-development process and puts his stress on the creative aspects of the learner.

Piaget has spent more than fifty years gathering an impressive mountain of research information and data pertaining to mental development in a biological context. While so doing he has been perfecting an elaborate and comprehensive theory of how intelligence develops, within process. His work is primarily concerned with describing as minutely as possible the systematic way that growth and development of intellectual structures and knowledge evolve.

It is important to understand that Piaget is not a simple maturationist. He does not believe that the infant's process unfolds solely as a result of some kind of mere biological maturation or that it is the only factor in development. He believes that the effects of the environment on development are very important, and to this extent he is in agreement with the environmentalists. "In short," he declares, "my position is somewhere between these two."[127]

Piaget is neither a maturationist nor an environmentalist, at least not in the dominant behaviorist traditions as understood today. His position is careful to incorporate basic elements from both. He elaborates on them in highly original ways. He thinks of himself as an "interactionist." In his theory he stresses intellectual development resulting largely from an interplay between both internal and external factors in the evolving process.[128] Not unlike John Dewey, he argues that the aim of "process" education is to produce people capable of re-creating and improving all that has gone before them.

From Piaget to Today[129]

Piaget is being acclaimed around the world: his books are being translated into the major languages, except in Communist countries, where he is *persona grata*. His lecturing is still remembered in Warsaw, Prague, and Moscow. He has received honorary degrees from Harvard, the Sorbonne, Rio de Janeiro, Brussels, the University of Chicago, McGill University, the University of Warsaw, the University of Manchester, the University of Oslo, Cambridge University, Brandeis University, the University of Montreal, the University of Aix Marseille, the University of Pennsylvania, and Columbia University. On June 1, 1973, he received the Kittay Scientific Foundation's First Annual Award for Research in Psychiatry. He spoke in the morning seminar of the importance of developmental studies as the major explanatory method to be utilized in psychology now and in the years ahead. This was followed by a testimonial dinner at which an award of $25,000 climaxed the honors.

In recent years he has come to the United States to address American groups on the subject of child development. For example, in November, 1971, at the University of Miami's (Florida) *International Symposium on the Ecology of Human and Child Development* he addressed a record crowd with opening words that aptly characterize his fifty or more years of epistemological insights and achievements: "In the beginning was the response . . ."

Until his retirement in the summer of 1971, he directed the International Bureau of Education of the Institute J. J. Rousseau (now the Institute of Psychology and Education), in addition to being, since 1929, professor of child psychology and history of scientific thought at the University of Geneva.

Bärbel Inhelder is replacing Piaget as professor of developmental psychology. She began her collaboration with him while still an undergraduate. Together they have written more than nine books, and she is the author of more than 50 articles. She is President of the *Association de Psychologie Scientifique de langue Française* and a past president of the Swiss Psychological Society. In 1968, with Piaget, she received the Award of the American Educational Research Association. She has been a Harvard research fellow and a Rockefeller fellow and has lectured at M.I.T., Princeton, Berkeley, Stanford, Temple, and Penn State.

In the summer of 1971, she succeeded Piaget as director of both the Bureau and the Institute. When asked to identify the nature of her approach in contrast to that of her predecessor, she replied good-naturedly: "George Miller once called himself a subjective behaviorist. If we must be labeled, you could say the same things about us."[130]

Still an indefatigable worker, Jean Piaget continues to follow a strenuous daily schedule. Up to his retirement, each summer, at the end of the school year, he would collect his research findings and head for a lone cabin in the Alps. There he would spend the months in relative isolation, thinking and writing. His whereabouts were known only to his family and a few friends. When summer ended, he would return from the mountains with a new book or two and several articles for publication.

Now, in addition to his summer retreats, he is succeeding in freeing himself to employ his retirement time exclusively in writing and lecturing on special occasions. A prolific writer even before his retirement, he published more than thirty books and hundreds of journal articles, several in conjunction with his colleagues in Geneva. He attributes much of his productivity to the group of co-workers who assisted him over the many years. This applies especially to Bärbel Inhelder, who had the good fortune to be associated with the Piagetian discovery of the conservation problem. She evaluates its effects as opening

up a whole new area of research. Conservation problems have always had a particular attraction for American psychologists, and it may be no accident that the first time Piaget referred publicly to this question was during a conference marking the third centenary of Harvard's University. Conservation problems have certainly proved to be a great source of new facets regarding both children's thinking and epistemological controversies. In Geneva we have frequently come back to conservation problems, tackling them from different angles; recently we have been studying them in experiments on the regulating mechanisms involved in cognitive development.[131]

In a memorable visit to the United States (October 17, 1972) at the City University of New York, Piaget alluded to his revolutionary experiments in how children learn conservation:

> I had the luck to be able to remark . . . that Einstein himself had advised me in 1928 to study the formation of the intuitions of velocity in order to see if they depended on those of duration, and that further, when I had the good fortune to see Einstein again at Princeton (I stayed three months at the Oppenheimer Institute, where he was permanently resident), he was quite delighted by the reactions of non-conservation of children of four to six years . . . and was greatly astonished that the elementary concepts of conservation were only constructed toward seven or eight years.[132]

Piaget stated further how he found that reflexes and other automatic patterns of behavior have a minor role in the development of human intelligence. It is not until the growing child reaches the two formal stages of process in his development that he begins to acquire the various concepts of conservation.

Piaget sheds some light on the latest research in Geneva. This is in regard to a major area concerned with the learning of abstract concepts. He illustrated by swinging a pocket watch from the end of a heavy gold chain as he said:

> A child of 5 soon learns how to let go of a swinging object so that it will land in a box. But not until about age 11 could the child grasp the fact that he lets go at the top of the circle, not the point nearest the box, and thus master the concept of a tangential trajectory.[133]

Another colleague, Piaget mentioned, had been giving similar tests to old patients suffering senile dementia. He found that they unlearned concepts in reverse order to a child's learning growth. "It's very reassuring," he stated with a smile.[134]

Piaget found that the first type of acquired representation of the world that man achieves is in the form of an egocentrically oriented action schema. It is a joint representation of action intended, along with the consequences of that action. From these concepts he has developed many of his best insights.

Harry Beilin, a leading interpreter of Piagetian works in the United States, when requested to sum up Piaget's talks at City University, acknowledged with a smile that it was not easy for a layman to do. Then he stated:

> Piaget is probably the strongest force in child psychology. Now, one school holds that language and thought are inborn. Another—take Skinner—holds that it is imposed by environment. Piaget replies that it is neither—the child is an autonomous system.[135]

He continued that Piaget emphasizes how children learn not only through intelligence and experience but also by working through successive phases; that his present argument therefore tends toward this important conclusion: the basic phases of teaching children, whether slow or fast, should remain about the same.[136]

Asked what he had got out of the Piaget sessions, Alan Reeves, an English-born graduate student at the City University, agreed that, although Piaget says that a physicist's son goes faster and a primitive slower, none goes from phase 1 to 3 to 2. Then he told what he had appreciated most:

> A chance to see Piaget. He's a fascinating mixture, to me, of this very nice, kind person and this rigorous intellect—the most rigorous in psychological research.[137]

Reflections in Conclusion[138]

When Jean Piaget was completing his interview with Eleanor Duckworth, she asked him to answer just one more question: "Admittedly it is a big one, but maybe you can give a small answer: Once a child acquires language, what part does that play in his thinking?"

"Come on! Well, I will answer you with a story I read somewhere," Piaget obliged with good humor:

> A journalist asked a physicist what he thought of interdisciplinary research, and the physicist said, "You remind me of the lady who was sitting beside a great painter at dinner and asked him, 'Master, what do you think about art?' and the painter answered, 'My dear madam, wouldn't you have one smaller question?'" As for the relationship between language and thought![139]

Reflection One. These reflections on the life and activities of Jean Piaget are pregnant with the relevance of values to the process of education today. They state his educational goals and at the same time describe his own achievements as he presents them:

> The principal goal of [process] education is to create men who are capable of doing new things, not simply of repeating what other generations have done—men who are creative, inventive, and discoverers. The second goal of education is to form minds which can be critical, can verify, and not accept everything they are offered. The great danger today is of slogans, collective opinions, ready-made trends of thought. We have to be able to resist individually, to criticize, to distinguish between what is proven and what is not. So we need pupils who are active, who learn early to find out by themselves, partly by their own spontaneous activity and partly through material we set up for them; who learn early to tell what is verifiable and what is simply the first idea to come to them.[140]

All of these insights center around the pivotal problem of intellectual development that is at the very heart of the personalization crisis itself.

Many may or may not agree with some or any of Piaget's findings, but that is not what matters. Here the constructive criticism of James Deese of the Johns Hopkins University is apropos. He asks how Piaget knows that children develop the way he claims they do? The answer, Deese declares, is obviously his personal inferences from observations and tests with which he confronts children from infancy through adolescence. Many of these conclusions are influenced by his pioneering work with his former teacher, Alfred Binet, a genuine authority in his field. That Piaget's observations and tests are ingenious cannot be denied. That they do permit him to make many surprising discoveries can hardly be discounted, but not all are acceptable.[141]

What is disturbing today is that so many professionals seem to think or even presuppose that Piaget is dealing specifically with psychological issues, philosophical discipline, and educational work. It is like approaching the author of a new book to criticize him for books he did not write instead of trying to learn about the contributions that he does present. In his new discipline, Piaget's chief concerns are not individual differences, motivation, or learning.

Reflection Two. Piaget is primarily occupied with structures in the human process of growth and development which, if they are found true for individuals, will also hold true for the species. He does not deny that individual differences, motivation, and learning affect the acquisition and perfecting of these structures. What he does deny is that such factors produce them or affect their *identification*. It is their identification that he is experimenting with. For, once identified, the successive forms of these structures during their developmental process can be compared so as to enable him to arrive at an explanation of their genesis. To achieve this objective does not require any specific reference to psychological determinants or philosophical verities. His stance resembles that of Bärbel Inhelder, who has worked so long and well in the shadow of Jean Piaget, who states:

> In effect, Piaget is quite willing to label himself a "relativist," in the non-skeptical sense of the term, because, for him, that which is knowable and that which changes during the genesis of knowledge is the relation between the knowing subject and the object known. Some commentators go further and refer to him as an "activist," reflecting Goethe's assertion that "In the beginning was the deed."[142]

Reflection Three. It is important to realize that much of Piaget's work deals with case studies. His tests, however, are not always controlled so minutely as would be desirable. The results, when analyzed carefully, reveal that his findings in many instances are based on one or two cases—barely enough evidence to decide whether he is correct in his inductions.

Many accept the main outlines of his work, but not all of its details or the inferences that he draws from his experiments. Everyone must decide for himself. It cannot be certain whether he is right or wrong, but he certainly presents much about which to inquire.

In this modern era, emerging or process education is dealing with ever-changing realities and adaptations. Piaget's profound sensitivity to knowledge within this process and its importance for man in the light of its relevance for learning become paramount. The constantly increasing knowledge explosion, which must be dealt with better and faster in terms of learning, is still one of the most important and universal occupations of man. Learning, while it is the great task of childhood and youth, remains the chief means, both individually and cooperatively, of achieving human progress at any period of life.

Piaget's insights about the personalization process—man— represent but a mere scratching of the surface in view of the great things yet to come in modern thought. Are they not a mighty leap in the right direction? Do they not add significantly to better understanding the salient features found in the traditional description of man as a "rational animal"? To Ernest Cassirer's designation of him as a "symbolic animal" in *An Essay on Man*? Does not even Boethius's (d. A.D. 524) definition of man as a person, earmarking him in all reality as "an individual substance of rational nature," find a fuller meaning in these "Piagetian" perspectives?

The accumulated concepts of rational, individual, symbolic, animal, and so on, along with the idea of substance and nature in universal processes, are uniquely different from the other realities with which man faces life. Yet Piaget is succeeding in relating and integrating these within the developmental perspective of intelligence and knowledge. Now they are influencing man more profoundly as a person. To these areas is being added a fuller understanding of how man, through evolving (process) education, can be better approached anthropocentrically.

Reflection Four. The "process" capacity to learn, which makes man truly rational and hence human, Piaget considers the most significant natural endowment of man. Precisely because rationality is the foundation of every human achievement, most psychologists and educational psychologists, along with Piaget today, are fairly well agreed that this capacity to learn constitutes the single best measure of man's intelligence. In a patterned process from infancy through adolescence, Piaget presents a blueprint of the developmental aspects of intelligence. Formerly this seemed impossible.

Piaget explicitly restricts learning to the acquisition of new knowledge derived primarily through a meaningful interaction between the personalized activities of man and his environment. His view stands in contrast to knowledge as mere maturation based on the physiological processes. Thus he probes beyond the visible.

In this probe, however, Piaget differentiates knowledge from the acquisition of general knowledge, or from intelligence, by defining it as the slowly developing sum total of action coordinations available to an organism at a given stage.[143] For him, general knowledge cannot be something merely imparted or taken from a book; rather, it is that which is actively constructed by the person himself—that is, alive within his psychological and physiological matrix, influencing his total environment.[144] It is here that Piaget discloses how knowledge is the foundation of every human act as well as of all human achievement; how it is the product of his reason for being and is the primary characteristic of his personhood; how the person is a dynamic nature in process today, rather than a mere essence from the past.

Reflection Five. In utilizing as fully as possible his powers of knowing within the various stages of mental development, each child meets his challenging opportunities to grow in excellence as a person. Piaget's theories place this emphasis on the complete nature of the child in fulfilling his potential. He stresses the how and why of knowing.

What this means is the fullest possible functioning of his intelligence. He claims that intelligence as a process is identical with learning, because to function it must be perfected by the person himself. This achievement, however, is in direct relationship to his striving to realize the process of his own development within each stage of his being.[145]

Since the major activities of any school today are learning and teaching, both must be directed toward guiding the nature of the learner into the process of meaningful self-activity; for this enables him to gain an appreciation of, and control over, the values in life. The conditions for achieving such a relevance of values are more readily understood by applying what Dr. Piaget asserts is operative within his various stages of developmental psychology. Therein he demonstrates how learning implies a self-activity in which a personal, interior change is produced; how it is the response-reaction within the thoughts, attitudes, and general conduct of the person that makes the difference.

Insights into the nature of intelligence, as manifested in man's activities, are extremely valuable. Those of Piaget, however, establish a personalistic approach to values in the process of education by which the nature of learning can be grasped in a more meaningful, "Piagetian" way. Are they not the updating and maturing of the traditional Aristotelian-Thomistic principle, *Operatio sequitur esse*? The response in process is the being in process, or more simply, the response is the person himself in process.

Reflection Six. Today Piaget's works are of sufficient scope and stature within professional circles to merit worldwide recognition and understanding among those who are functionally engaged in promoting cognitive development, especially in the areas of intelligence and perception. Each insight, as a process, is not unlike a bud which, when it unfolds in its own floral response, reveals, in all its burgeoning, a principle that has innumerable applications within the learning-teaching activities of the times.

Piaget's insights establish a flexible foundation in the process of human nature. In these perspectives, the guidance of learning and teaching becomes a reciprocal process that begets the response that has learning as its main objective. Thus learning, in its strict sense, is seen as the acquisition of knowledge due to some particular information provided by the environment of which the person himself is an active determinant. Regardless of how desirable learning may be, it is inconceivable without a theoretically prior interior structure of equilibration. It provides the capacity to learn and the structuring of the learning process to function. In the widest sense, Piaget demonstrates how equilibration includes both factors as a process-and-response.

Within learning, then, Piaget finds both the beginning and the end of all major activities of the human being to be characterized by "the response in process." The urgency of the two-fold value crisis within the schools and the intellectual revolution itself encourages a closer examination today of Piagetian theories for fostering a greater hope "in forward-looking thoughts."

Reflection Seven. Piaget's work has many important implications for philosophy, education, and psychology; yet, it is not that his works themselves are essentially philosophical, educational, or psychological. Such a contention would be tantamount to saying that Freud, for example, is an anthropologist because his works have implications for anthropology; or to assert that Darwin is a theologian because his works have implications for theology or religion. That philosophy, psychology, and education can profit much from Piaget's contributions must not demand that he *be* a psychologist, philosopher, and educator. To type Piaget as someone other than a genetic epistemologist is particularly shortsighted when one grasps that his contributions are great despite his being neither psychologist, philosopher, nor educator.

His achievements are a source of fruitfulness in process for all, but especially for those whose professional vocation and interests revolve around the activities of the person and the human mind. Whatever the final outcome of his relatively new inquiry may be, Piaget is presaging a "second spring" for a more meaningful and wholesome anthropocentric approach to the nature of knowledge-values. By establishing a sound psychological basis in cognitive functioning, he builds a bridge to unite, in a practical way, two sides of the perennial problem of values. These sides are the philosophy and psychology of essence and the philosophy and psychology of process.

Reflection Eight. In his genetic epistemology, Piaget uncovers the ontogenetic changes involving essence and response. His account of the major stages through which all normal children pass is useful not only to curriculum builders but also to teachers, whose methodology should constantly be in process, that is, adjusting to the fluctuating stages of the learner. For those concerned with subject mastery and those devoted to guiding the development and conservation of logical structures in learning, Piaget's theory of equilibration helps forcefully. It projects in proper perspective the role of external reinforcements in teaching, such as that proposed by B. F. Skinner, and the process of education in learning, as developed by Jerome Bruner.

In the present era of changing realities and personal adaptations that trigger one crisis after another, Piaget's genetic epistemology, with its process-and-response approach to knowledge, can hardly be ignored. His profound sensitivity to knowledge in the light of its relevance to learning is paramount. Learning is still the most important and universal occupation of man. It is the consuming and maturing task of childhood and youth, the chief means of achieving knowledge for progressing in understanding values during any period of life.

Piaget's works are based on fundamental insights: "In the beginning was the response . . ." and "To understand is to invent. . . ." These perspectives offer a comprehensive basis for creating effective means of educating youth today. They form the very values that are especially relevant to the *Pro Deo et Patria* aspects of the United States' 1976 bicentennial observances.

Like shadows cast before, Jerome Bruner's appreciation of Jean Piaget is now a magnificent reality:[146]

Piaget is one of the two towering figures of twentieth century psychology. . . . For Piaget, as for most of twentieth century science and philosophy, the dilemma [of values] is in the very nature and texture of our knowledge of reality. . . . His impact on psychology and pedagogy has been enormous. He has prevailed by providing a general conception of mind in growth that is so compelling that even in attacking it . . . one is inevitably influenced by it.

And so to Piaget, as to all of us, "Childhood has its own ways of seeing, thinking, and feeling. . . . Each stage [of life] has a perfection of its own. . . ."

Eh, bien!

EPILOGUE

Piaget's Triumph!

Here is a unique situation. The list of Piaget's writings below presents in capsule form the progressive steps of his achievements. Studied in sequence, the titles themselve indicate, book by book, Piaget's development in thought as he in his own consciousness experienced it—a phenomenon rarely encountered: *The Language and Thought of the Child* (1924), *Judgment and Reasoning in the Child* (1924), *The Child's Conception of the World* (1926), *The Child's Conception of Physical Causality* (1927), *The Moral Judgment of the Child* (1932), *The Origins of Intelligence in Children* (1936), *The Construction of Reality in the Child* (1937), *The Child's Conception of Number* (1941), *Play, Dreams and Imitation in Childhood* (1945), *The Child's Conception of Time* (1946), *The Child's Conception of Movement and Speed* (1946), *The Psychology of Intelligence* (1947), *The Child's Conception of Space* (with Bärbel Inhelder, 1948), *Logic and Psychology* (1953), *The Growth of Logical Thinking from Childhood to Adolescence* (with Bärbel Inhelder, 1956), *The Early Growth of Logic in the Child* (with Bärbel Inhelder, 1959), *The Child's Conception of Geometry* (with Bärbel Inhelder and Alina Szeminska, 1960), *The Mechanisms of Perception* (1961), *Six Psychological Studies* (1964), *Insights and Illusions of Philosophy*

(1965), *The Psychology of the Child* (1966, with Bärbel Inhelder), *Mental Imagery in the Child* (1966, with Bärbel Inhelder et al.), *Genetic Epistemology* (1968), *Structuralism* (1968), *Science of Education and the Psychology of the Child* (1969), *Psychology and Epistemology* (1970), *The Child and Reality* (1971), *Understanding Causality* (with the collaboration of R. Garcia, 1971), *To Understand Is To Invent: The Future of Education* (1972), *The Place of the Sciences of Man in the System of Sciences* (1974).

On the 50th anniversary of his first books, Jean Piaget's theories are readily accessible in the Piagetian Studies Center of The Jean Piaget Society at Temple University in historic Philadelphia, seat of the Bicentennial of the United States. Published first in French, these works on the mental development of the child created an impact on psychology and education in the learning-teaching process of America. Now translated, they are available in English. Certainly Americans are indebted to "the bourgeois psychologist Piaget" (the Chinese Communist compliment) for these works, which establish his presence here.

In their ensemble, Piaget's publications create a new discipline: *genetic epistemology.* The prevailing *zeitgeist,* condescending toward his methods, hostile toward his theorizing and suspicious of his results, confronts the granite strength of a great mind.

In its conception and scope, Piaget's work is both a product of the times and the source of great changes. As he himself explains, his theory is never completed, because he considers himself one of the chief "revisionists of Piaget." *Ad multos annos!*

APPENDIX

A Piagetian Note[147]

The following is a list of publications of outstanding authorities today as they interpret and apply the new discipline of Jean Piaget. They have been selected, on the basis of clarity and ease of understanding, as introductory to studying his original works mentioned in the epilogue.

Elkind, David. *Children and Adolescents: Interpretive Essays on Jean Piaget.* New York: Oxford University Press, 1974.

Pulaski, Mary Ann Spencer. *Understanding Piaget: An Introduction to Children's Cognitive Development.* New York: Harper & Row, Publishers, 1971.

Wadsworth, Barry J. *Piaget's Theory of Cognitive Development.* New York: David McKay Company, Inc., 1971.

Schwebel, Milton, and Raph, Jane, eds. *Piaget in the Classroom.* New York: Basic Books, Inc., Publisher, 1973.

Furth, Hans G., and Wachs, Harry. *Thinking Goes to School: Piaget's Theory in Practice.* New York: Oxford University Press, 1974.

Furth, Hans G. *Piaget for Teachers.* Englewood Cliffs, N. J.: Prentice-Hall, Inc., 1970.

Gorman, Richard. *Discovering Piaget: A Guide for Teachers.* Columbus, Ohio: Charles E. Merrill Books, Inc., 1972.

Isaac, Nathan. *A Brief Introduction to Piaget: The Growth of Under-*

standing in the Young Child and New Light on Children's Ideas of Numbers. New York: Agathon Press, Inc., 1972.

Ginsburg, Herbert, and Opper, Sylvia. *Piaget's Theory of Intellectual Development: An Introduction.* Englewood Cliffs, N. J.: Prentice-Hall, Inc., 1969.

Brearley, Molly, ed. *The Teaching of Young Children: Some Applications of Piaget's Learning Theory.* New York: Schocken Books, Inc., 1970.

————, and Hitchfield, Elizabeth. *A Guide to Reading Piaget.* New York: Schocken Books, Inc., 1973.

Flavell, John H. *The Developmental Psychology of Jean Piaget.* New York: D. Van Nostrand Co., 1963.[148]

NOTES

Preface

1. Jean Piaget, *Science of Education and the Psychology of the Child,* trans. from the French by Derek Coltman (New York: Orion Press, 1970), p. 7.

Prologue

1. This view is clearly substantiated by Robert B. Mellert, *What Is Process Theology?* (New York: Paulist Press, 1975), pp. 7–19.

2. Matthew 16:25, *The New American Bible* © 1970, used here by permission of the Confraternity of Christian Doctrine, copyright owner.

1 Dynamics of Process-and-Response

1. Eleanor Duckworth, "Piaget Takes a Teacher's Look," *Learning* (October, 1973), p. 22.

2. John F. Emling, "In the Beginning Was the Response," *Religious Education* (January–February, 1974), pp. 53–71.

3. Duckworth, "Piaget Takes. . . ," p. 22.

4. Such as a toy, a doubt, a question, a guess, a noise, a meaning, an enlightenment, a desire, a prayer, an image, an idea, a precept, etc.—anything.

5. Duckworth, *Piaget Takes. . . ,* pp. 22–27.

6. *Dynamics* refers to the energies, the competences, and the predominance of all the personalized powers of the individual.

7. D. Bess, *The Nation,* February 20, 1967.

8. Internalized dynamics relate to that totality which makes each person what he really is as a person: his uniqueness.

9. It seems reasonable to describe this fusion of the personal and the objective as *personal knowledge*. Michael Polanyi, *Personal Knowledge* (New York: Harper & Row Publishers, 1962), p. xiv.

10. Externalized dynamics concern the individual's activating his own value as he comprehends it and as society acknowledges it.

11. These graphic views epitomize the functional interrelationship between the person's maximum objective worth (internalized dynamics) and his objective and subjective worth (externalized dynamics), i.e., the interaction among his personalized achievements and how his public views them.

12. From *Living in Hope* by Ladislaus Boros © 1969 by Burns and Oates Ltd., p. 15. Used by permission of the publisher, The Seabury Press, Inc.

13. Jeremy Zwelling, "Religion in the Department of Religion," *Religious Education* (Special Edition, May–June 1974), p. S-137.

14. C. Mead, *The American Scholar Today* (New York: Dodd, Mead and Co., 1970), pp. 24–25.

15. Maurice Merleau-Ponty, *The Structure of Behavior* (Boston: Beacon Press, 1963), quoted in James E. Royce, *Man and Meaning* (New York: McGraw-Hill Book Company, 1969), p. 3.

16. James C. Coleman, *Personality Dynamics and Effective Behavior* (Chicago: Scott, Foresman and Company, 1960), p. 70.

17. Gordon W. Allport, *Becoming: Basic Considerations for a Psychology of Personality* (New Haven, Conn.: Yale University Press, 1955), pp. 82–88.

18. M. I. Berger, "Existential Criticism in Educational Theory: A Subjective View of a Serious Business," *Proceedings of the Nineteenth Annual Meeting of the Philosophy of Education Society, Sir Francis Drake Hotel, San Francisco, Cal., April 7–10, 1963,* edited by Martin Levit (Lawrence, Kansas: Ernest E. Bayles, University of Kansas, 1963), pp. 93–98.

19. Hugh C. Black, Kenneth V. Lottich, and Donald S. Seckinger, eds., *The Great Educators* (Chicago: Nelson-Hall Co., 1972), pp. 69–70. Copyright by Hugh C. Black, Kenneth V. Lottich, and Donald S. Seckinger.

20. Ibid., p. 70.

21. Ibid.

22. Jerome A. Shaffer, *Reality, Knowledge, and Value* (New York: Random House, Inc. © 1971), pp. 95–96.

23. Hadley Cantril, *The "Why" of Man's Experience* (New York: The Macmillan Company), p. 37. © Copyright 1950 by The Macmillan Co.

24. Will Durant, "What Education Is of Most Worth," *The Saturday Evening Post* (April 11, 1936), p. 14. Reprinted with permission from THE SATURDAY EVENING POST © 1936, The Curtis Publishing Company.

25. Robert H. Finch, "That Question of Relevancy," *The School and the*

Democratic Environment, Danforth Foundation and Ford Foundation (New York: Columbia University Press, 1970) , p. 18.

26. Edith Hamilton, "Adventures of the Mind II," *The Saturday Evening Post,* September 27, 1958, pp. 114–17. Reprinted with permission from THE SATURDAY EVENING POST © 1958, The Curtis Publishing Company.

27. Ibid.

28. Ibid.

29. Ibid.

30. William H. Boyer, "Education for Survival," *Phi Delta Kappan* (January 1971) , p. 258.

31. Sir Richard Livingstone, *Portrait of Socrates* (New York and Oxford: Oxford University Press, 1938) , p. v.

32. Adapted from the Task Force's rewrite of the paper "Crises in Values," *1970 White House Conference on Children* (U.S. Govt. Printing Office, 1970).

33. *Report of the Invitational Conference on Values in Education* (Sponsored on April 13, 1972 by the Commission on Education, Ohio Council of Churches, Columbus, 1972) , p. 4.

34. W. D. Ross, ed., *The Works of Aristotle* (Oxford: Clarendon Press, 1921) , 10. 8. 1337a.

35. John Henry Cardinal Newman, *The Idea of a University* (New York: Longmans, Green and Co., 1947) , p. 97.

36. Zwelling, "Religion in the Department. . . ," pp. S-136, S-137.

37. Ibid., p. S-137.

38. Hugh C. Black, "Values, Philosophy, and Education," *Progressive Education* 32 (1955) : 109–16.

39. Quoted in James H. Breasted, *The Dawn of Conscience* (New York: Charles Scribner's Sons, 1950) , from Ralph Waldo Emerson, *Essays* (Boston: Houghton, Mifflin and Company, 1903) , Second Series, pp. 216–17.

40. Carlton E. Beck, Normand R. Bernier, James E. MacDonald, Thomas W. Walton, and Jack C. Willers, *Education for Relevance* (New York: Houghton Mifflin Company, 1968) , p. viii.

41. Alexander Meiklejohn, *Education Between Two Worlds,* 2d ed. (New York: Harper & Bros., 1942) , p. 289.

42. Ibid., p. 291.

43. Edmund Sullivan, "Piaget and the School Curriculum: A Critical Appraisal," Bulletin No. 2 of the Ontario Institute for Studies in Education (Toronto, 1967) , Foreword.

2 *Evolving Value Perspectives*

1. Jean Piaget, *Science of Education and the Psychology of the Child,* trans. from the French by Derek Coltman (New York: Orion Press, 1970),

pp. 12f.; Mary Ann Spencer Pulaski, *Understanding Piaget* (New York: Harper & Row, 1971) , chap. 18.

2. Andrew L. Seebold, *Social-Moral Reconstruction* (Washington, D.C.: The Catholic University of America Press, 1946) , p. 1.

3. Carlton J. H. Hayes, *A Political and Social History of Modern Europe* (New York: The Macmillan Company) , 1: 465. © Copyright, 1926 by The Macmillan Company.

4. Wilbert C. Lepkowski and Gilbert R. Parker, "The Search for Relevance," *Chemical & Engineering News* (March 10, 1969) , p. 4a.

5. Piaget, *Science of Education. . .* , pp. 139–40; Jean Piaget, *To Understand Is To Invent* (New York: Grossman Publishers, 1973) , pp. 47f.

6. Piaget, *Science of Education. . .* , p. 140. In his recent book, *Understanding Causality* (New York: W. W. Norton & Company, Inc., 1974) , Jean Piaget, with the collaboration of R. Garcia, discusses important conclusions with regard to mental development as affected naturally by constant laws within human development. Although the entire book is apropos, pp. 112–38 are especially pertinent.

7. Piaget, *Science of Education. . .* , p. 140.

8. Ibid.

9. Ibid., pp. 140–41.

10. John D. Redden and Francis A. Ryan, *A Catholic Philosophy of Education* (Milwaukee, Wis.: Bruce Publishing Company, 1942) , p. 60.

11. Ibid., pp. 60ff., chap. 13; Carroll Atkinson and Eugene T. Maleska, *The Story of Education* (New York: Chilton Books 1965) , pp. 45f.

12. Piaget, *Science of Education. . .* , p. 139.

13. Ibid., p. 141; idem, *To Understand Is To Invent,* pp. 46–48.

14. Atkinson and Maleska, *Story of Education,* p. 64.

15. When our forefathers came to America they brought Old-World patterns with them. James Keller, *All God's Children—What Your Schools Can Do for Them* (Garden City, N.Y.: Hanover House, 1953) , p. 258. Used with the permission of The Christophers.

16. As quoted from Horace Mann, *The Massachusetts System of Common Schools*; Being an Enlarged and Revised Edition of the Tenth Annual Report of the First Secretary of the Massachusetts Board of Education [Dec. 3, 1846] (No. 37 Congress Street, Boston: Dutton and Wentworth, State Printers, 1849) , pp. 7f. in *The Great Educators* by Hugh C. Black, Kenneth V. Lottich, and Donald S. Seckinger, eds., (Chicago: Nelson-Hall Co., 1972) , p. 557. Copyright © by Hugh C. Black, Kenneth V. Lottich, and Donald S. Seckinger.

17. Ibid.

18. Ibid.

19. Ibid.

20. Keller, *All God's Children*, p. 258.

21. During the first half of the nineteenth century, although most schools were established by religious denominations, they commonly had some share in the public funds. William F. Cunningham, *The Pivotal Problems of Education* (New York: Macmillan Co.), p. 524. © Copyright, 1940 by William F. Cunningham, renewed 1968 by Zita Sullivan.

22. From the beginning our system was pluralistic, consisting of public, private, and church schools. Keller, *All God's Children*, p. 258.

23. Ibid., p. 260.

24. Ibid.

25. This first period of educational development is entitled "Education for Salvation" in *Education for Relevance* by Carlton E. Beck, Normand R. Bernier, James B. MacDonald, Thomas W. Walton, and Jack C. Willers (New York: Houghton Mifflin Co., 1968), pp. 10–17.

26. Keller, *All God's Children*, p. 258.

29. Ibid., pp. 260–61.

30. Cf. William F. Cunningham, *The Pivotal Problems of Education* (New York: The Macmillan Co.), p. 523. © Copyright, 1940, by William F. Cunningham, renewed 1968 by Zita Sullivan.

31. In a series of seventeen essays, the impact of universal concern for the relevance of American values is carefully explained and developed in *Values and the Future*, ed. Kurt Baier and Nicholas Rescher (New York: The Free Press, 1969).

32. Keller, *All God's Children*, p. xix.

33. Quoted from Horace Mann, *The Massachusetts System of Common Schools*, in *The Great Educators*, p. 558.

34. James Monroe Hughes, *Education in America* (New York: Harper & Row, Publishers, 1970), p. 240.

35. Quoted from Horace Mann, *The Massachusetts System of Common Schools*, in *The Great Educators*, p. 558.

36. The Puritans believed that the principal reason why education was necessary was that one should learn to read the Bible. Hughes, *Education in America*, p. 234.

37. Ibid., p. 240.

38. Keller, *All God's Children*, p. 262. In the book *Democratic Legacy in Transition*, ed. John E. Sturm and John A. Palmer (New York: Van Nostrand Reinhold Co., 1971), pp. 19f., there is another perspective: that from the very beginning in America education was a function of the government.

39. Massachusetts Bay towns sent deputies to represent them in the General Court, as the legislature was called. This General Court, which met in Boston in 1642, enacted what is probably the first school law to be passed

in what afterwards became the United States. Hughes, *Education in America*, p. 240.

40. In the original spelling the "Old Deluder Satan Act" is quoted in its entirety by Hughes, *Education in America*, p. 304.

41. Quoted from Horace Mann, *The Massachusetts System of Common Schools*, in *The Great Educators*, p. 561.

42. Ibid., p. 560.

43. Keller, *All God's Children*, p. 257.

44. Ibid., p. 264.

45. Ibid., p. 261.

46. Ibid., pp. 261–62.

47. Atkinson and Maleska, *Story of Education*, p. 100.

48. When he set up his academy in Philadelphia in 1751, he declared that education ideally should include "all that is ornamental and all that is useful." Beck, Bernier, MacDonald, Walton, and Willers, *Education for Relevance*, pp. 18–19.

49. Keller, *All God's Children*, p. 262.

50. Ibid., p. 261.

51. Henry P. Van Dusen, *God in Education* (New York: Charles Scribner's Sons, 1951), p. 43.

52. Keller, *All God's Children*, p. 261.

53. Ibid., p. 259. For a more complete development of this pioneer stage in public education see Ellwood P. Cubberley, *Public Education in the United States* (Boston: Houghton Mifflin Co., 1934); R. Freeman Butts and Lawrence A. Cremin, *A History of Education in American Culture* (New York: Henry Holt and Co., 1953); B. A. Hinsdale, *Horace Mann and the Common School Revival in the United States* (New York: Charles Scribner's Sons, 1900).

54. A most important step toward the building of state school systems was made while the country was still operating under the Articles of Confederation. Two ordinances were passed covering disposition of the vast public lands in the West, claims that the various states had surrendered to the federal government. The Ordinance of 1785: Income from the sale of the sixteenth section, located in the center of each township, was to be used for common schools when land was sold or rented. . . . The Ordinance of 1787 confirmed this land policy and set forth the governmental principles to be followed, including establishment of common schools, when the Northwest Territory was settled. These two ordinances marked the establishment of a new principle of federal aid to education—they represented the eighteenth century's greatest legacy to American free public education in the centuries to follow. Atkinson and Maleska, *Story of Education*, pp. 101–2.

55. "The most unfortunate law on the subject of Common Schools, ever enacted in the State." Horace Mann, *Tenth Annual Report of the Secretary of the Board Covering the Year 1846* (Washington, D.C.: National Education Association of the United States, facsimile ed., 1952), p. 130.

56. Arnold Toynbee, "Education: The Long View," *Saturday Review* 43, no. 47 (November 19, 1960): 60–62, 76–81.

57. Hughes, *Education in America,* p. 241.

58. Piaget, *Science of Education. . . ,* p. 139.

59. Ibid., p. 69.

60. Ibid., pt. 1, chap. 1; Piaget, *To Understand Is To Invent,* pp. 21f.; Atkinson and Maleska, *Story of Education,* pt. 1; Robert Ulich, ed., *Three Thousand Years of Educational Wisdom* (Cambridge, Mass.: Harvard University Press, 1971), pp. 250f., 287f., 355f., 383f., 480f., 508f., 523f., 615f.; Black, Lottich, and Seckinger, *The Great Educators,* chaps. 18, 37, 43, 44, 45, 46, 47, 48, 49, 50, and 52; Robert R. Rusk, *Doctrines of the Great Educators* (New York: St. Martin's Press, 1969), chaps. 7, 8, 9, 10, 11, 13, 14; Cunningham, *Pivotal Problems. . . ,* pp. 18–21.

61. Genetic epistemology is explained by Piaget as "the study of the process of learning as it develops." Jean Piaget, *The Place of the Sciences of Man in the System of Sciences* (New York: Harper Torchbooks, Harper & Row, Publishers, 1974), p. 11.

62. Robert H. Finch, "That Question of Relevancy," *The School and the Democratic Environment,* Danforth Foundation and Ford Foundation (New York: Columbia University Press, 1970), p. 16.

63. Beck, Bernier, MacDonald, Walton, and Willers, *Relevance of Education,* Preface.

64. Piaget, *Science of Education. . . ,* chaps. 1, 2; idem, *To Understand Is To Invent,* pp. 3–37.

65. Piaget, *Science of Education. . . ,* p. 51.

3 Horace Mann's Nonsectarian Education

1. Neal Gerard McCluskey, *Public Schools and Moral Education* (New York: Columbia University Press, 1958), pp. 11–98; Hugh C. Black, Kenneth V. Lottich and Donald S. Seckinger, eds., *The Great Educators* (Chicago: Nelson-Hall Company, 1972), pp. 557–76.

2. Jean Piaget, *Science of Education and the Psychology of the Child,* trans. from the French by Derek Coltman (New York: Orion Press, 1970), pp. 3–4.

3. McCluskey, *Public Schools and Moral Education,* p. 15.

4. James K. Morse, *Jedidiah Morse: A Champion of New England Orthodoxy* (New York: Columbia University Press, 1939), p. 121.

5. *Laws of Massachusetts,* March 10, 1827, chap. 143, sec. 3.

6. James Monroe Hughes, *Education in America* (New York: Harper & Row, Publishers, 1970), pp. 241–42.

7. Ibid., p. 242.

8. McCluskey, *Public Schools and Moral Education*, p. 15.

9. Ibid., p. 22.

10. Ibid., pp. 22–23, quoted from *Journal* (June 30, 1837).

11. Ibid., p. 33.

12. But there existed a dilemma, one that would plague him all through his career. We have a statute, he recalls, which makes special provision that no school books should be used in any of the public schools "calculated to favor any particular religious sect or tenet." This measure was provided in 1826, he wrote, "to prevent the school from being converted into an engine of religious proselytism; to debar successive teachers in the same school from successively inculcating hostile religious creeds, until the children in their simple-mindedness should be alienated, not only from creeds, but from religion itself." McCluskey, *Public Schools and Moral Education*, pp. 32–33; Mary Peabody Mann and George Combe Mann, eds., *Life and Works of Horace Mann* (Boston: Lee and Shepard, 1891), 2: p. 385.

13. McCluskey, *Public Schools and Moral Education*, p. 54.

14. William F. Cunningham, *The Pivotal Problems of Education* (New York: The Macmillan Co.), p. 524. © Copyright, 1940, by William F. Cunningham, renewed 1968 by Zita Sullivan.

15. McCluskey, *Public Schools and Moral Education*, pp. 23–31.

16. Piaget, *Science of Education. . . ,* p. 141.

17. Ibid., p. 30.

18. Hugh C. Black, "Pestalozzi and the Education of the Disadvantaged," *The Educational Forum* 33, no. 4 (May 1969): 511–22.

19. McCluskey, *Public Schools and Moral Education*, p. 31.

20. Piaget, *Science of Education. . . ,* p. 10.

21. Carroll Atkinson and Eugene T Maleska, *The Story of Education* (Philadelphia: Chilton Co., 1965), p. 72.

22. After Mann's death the distinguished French educator and historian François Pecault made an observation that is peculiarly significant for the present study: "He [Mann] had hoped, with other generous spirits, that the doctrine of Combe—a doctrine both scientific and religious, speculative and practical—might serve as a basis of moral education in the public schools, and that all the churches of the country would rally to this common ground. To this was to be added the reading of some beautiful passages from the Scriptures." McCluskey, *Public Schools and Moral Education*, pp. 24–25.

23. Black, Lottich, and Seckinger, *The Great Educators*, pp. 474–95; Hughes, *Education in America*, pp. 202–7: Robert Ulich, ed., *Three Thousand Years of Educational Wisdom* (Cambridge, Mass.: Harvard University Press, 1971), pp. 480f.; Atkinson and Maleska, *The Story of Education*, pp.

62, 71–72, 79–80, 142–43.

24. Black, "Pestalozzi and the Education. . . ," pp. 511–21.

25. Pestalozzi's account of his work in Stanz, which appeared as a letter in *Wochenschriften* (1807), as quoted in Appendix I to J. A. Green, *The Educational Ideas of Pestalozzi* (London: W. B. Clive, University Tutorial Press, 1911), pp. 186–87. Baron Roger De Guimps, *Pestalozzi: His Aim and Work*, translated from the 1874 ed. by Margaret Cuthbertson Crombie (Syracuse, N.Y.: C. W. Bardeen, 1889), p. 92.

26. Piaget, *Science of Education*. . . , p. 70.

27. McCluskey, *Public Schools and Moral Education*, p. 30.

28. Black, "Pestalozzi and the Education. . . ," pp. 511–21.

29. Piaget, *Science of Education*. . . , pp. 142–43.

30. McCluskey, *Public Schools and Moral Education*, p. 52. A comparatively recent publication by Dietrich von Hildebrand and Alice von Hildebrand, *The Art of Living* (Chicago: Franciscan Herald Press, 1965), treats in detail the essence of this natural-moral education espoused by Horace Mann for the public schools in his nonsectarian response-process approach to values, without, however, making any specific references to him or his works. In an earlier book by Hildebrand, *Fundamental Moral Attitudes*, trans. from the German by Alice C. Jourdan, lecturer at Hunter College (New York: Longmans, Green and Co., 1950), the first five chapters of *The Art of Living*, dealing with reverence, faithfulness, awareness of responsibility, veracity, and goodness, are presented as natural basic attitudes within their original response perspectives, and therefore indispensable to the human maturing process of value relevance.

31. Edward A. Newton, Esq., editor of the Christian Witness, *The Common School Controversy* (Boston: J. M. Bradley and Co., 1844), p. 12.

32. McCluskey, *Public Schools and Moral Education*, p. 94.

33. Ibid., p. 79.

34. As quoted from Horace Mann, *The Massachusetts System of Common Schools* in *The Great Educators*, pp. 575–76.

35. Mann gave to the new work all his tremendous energy, lecturing passionately, issuing voluminous reports, and publishing his views in the *Common School Journal*, which he created. He won friends to his cause but he also stirred up enemies. Property owners contested his pleas for higher taxes; religious denominations called his schools "godless." Even the Boston schoolmasters were peeved by the aspersions he cast on their efficiency. Mann's twelve years in office produced terrific agitation, but the battle was being won. The school fund was doubled, teachers' salaries were raised, new hygienic schoolhouses erected, school terms lengthened, high schools established, three normal schools opened, and teaching methods improved. His

crusade for public education spread to almost every other American site. McCluskey, *Public Schools and Moral Education*, chap. 4.

36. William F. Cunningham, *The Pivotal Problems of Education* (New York: The Macmillan Co.), p. 524. © Copyright, 1940 by William F. Cunningham, renewed 1968 by Zita Sullivan.

37. McCluskey, *Public Schools and Moral Education*, chap. 3.

38. T. Brosnahan, "The Education Fact," *Catholic Quarterly Review* 30: 515.

39. Payson Smith, A. E. Winship, and W. T. Harris, *Horace Mann and Our Schools* (New York: American Book Co., 1937), p. 24.

40. After serving (12 years as head of the state board of education in Massachusetts) two terms in Congress, Mann finished his career as the president of Antioch College (Ohio). Horace Mann, some historians claim, is the foremost educational statesman that America has ever produced. Certainly it can be said that he played a most important role in the establishment of nonsectarian school systems under state control. McCluskey, *Public Schools and Moral Education*, chap. 2.

41. Edmund Sullivan, "Piaget and the School Curriculum: A Critical Appraisal," Bulletin No. 2 of the Ontario Institute for Studies in Education (Toronto, 1967), Foreword.

42. McCluskey, *Public Schools and Moral Education*, p. 98.

43. McCluskey, *Public Schools and Moral Education*, p. 277.

44. Ibid., pp. 277–78.

4 William T. Harris's Secularization of Education

1. Neil Gerard McCluskey, *Public Schools and Moral Education* (New York: Columbia University Press, 1958), pp. 99–176; Hugh C. Black, Kenneth V. Lottich, and Donald S. Seckinger, eds., *The Great Educators* (Chicago: Nelson-Hall Company, 1972), pp. 577–602. Copyright © by Hugh C. Black, Kenneth V. Lottich, and Donald E. Seckinger.

2. As quoted in McCluskey, *Public Schools and Moral Education* p. 126, n25.

3. Jean Piaget, *Science of Education and the Psychology of the Child* (New York: Orion Press, 1970), pp. 12f.

4. Merle Curti, *Social Ideas of American Educators* (New York: Charles Scribner's Sons, 1935; renewal copyright © 1965), pp. 310f.

5. Ibid., pp. 310f.

6. As quoted from William T. Harris, *The Philosophy of Education*, in *The Great Educators*, p. 577.

7. William T. Harris, "Social Culture in the Form of Education and Religion," *Educational Review* 29 (January 1905).

8. Eleanor Duckworth, "Piaget Takes a Teacher's Look," *Learning* (October 1973), pp. 22–23.

9. William T. Harris, "What Shall We Study?" Reprint from *American Journal of Education* 2 (September 1869): 1–3.

10. *A Statement of the Theory of Education in the United States by Many Leading Educators* (Washington, D.C., 1874), pp. 34–35.

11. *Education* 9 (December 1888): 215.

12. *N.E.A. Proceedings,* 1894, p. 59. For the opposition of Harris to the demands of organized labor in the Bureau of Engraving, see *Education* 19 (February 1899): 377f.

13. William T. Harris, "The Kindergarten as a Preparation for the Highest Civilization," *Atlantic Educational Journal* 6 (July–August 1903): 35ff.

14. Ibid.; *Report of the Commissioner of Education,* 1896–97, 1: 903.

15. The [kindergarten] movement came to America during the wave of immigration from Germany following the Prussian Revolution in 1848. Mrs. Carl Schurz (1834–1879), a student of [Friedrich] Froebel (1782–1852), in 1856 started in Watertown, Wisconsin, the first kindergarten in this country. The language used was German, and several other German-speaking communities followed suit. The movement in America owed its development not to those German kindergartens but to the work of Elizabeth Peabody (1804–1894), who in 1860 established in Boston the first English-speaking kindergarten, Of some significance was the fact that she had become acquainted with the idea in England, where the concept had been considerably changed from the original German model. Miss Peabody's school was a private enterprise, as were others that followed shortly thereafter. Carroll Atkinson and Eugene T. Maleska, *The Story of Education* (Philadelphia: Chilton Books, 1965), p. 127.

16. William F. Cunningham, *The Pivotal Problems of Education* (New York: The Macmillan Co.), p. 351. © Copyright, 1940 by William F. Cunningham, renewed 1968 by Zita Sullivan.

17. *Annual Report of the St. Louis Public Schools* (19th), 1872–73, p. 110.

18. William T. Harris, "Observations on Physical Training in and out of School," *Recess* (Popular Education Document No. 20, St. Louis, 1884), p. 8.

19. *N.E.A. Proceedings,* 1891, p. 141; *Report of the Commissioner of Education,* 1893–94, 1: 618–19.

20. *Education* 17 (June 1897): 583.

21. William T. Harris, "The Use of the Higher Education," *Educational Review* 16 (September 1898), pp. 147–61.

22. Harris to Wheeler, August 23, 1897 (*Harris MSS.* no. 855).

23. William T. Harris, "The Place of University Extension in American Education," *Report of the Commissioner of Education*, 1891–1892, 2: 743–51; *N.E.A. Proceedings*, 1894, pp. 133–34.

24. *Educational Review* 3 (February 1892) : 169.

25. *Education* 12 (December 1891) : 194.

26. William T. Harris, "The Future of Teachers' Salaries," *Independent* 59 (August 3, 1905) : 255–58.

27. Edgar B. Wesley, *NEA: The First Hundred Years* (New York: Harper and Brothers, 1957) , p. 48.

28. Curti, *Social Ideas*. . . , pp. 310f.

29. *N.E.A. Proceedings*, 1880, p. 108; *ibid.*, 1898, pp. 127–28.

30. William T. Harris, "Herbart's Doctrine of Interest," *Educational Review* 10 (June 1895) : 71–80; cf. also *North American Review* 160 (May 1895) : p. 542; *N.E.A. Proceedings*, 1910, p. 193.

31. William T. Harris, "Fruitful Lines of Investigation in Psychology," *Educational Review* 1 (January 1891) : 8–14; "The Old Psychology versus the New," *Report of the Commissioner of Education*, 1893–1894, 1: 433–47.

32. William T. Harris, "The Pendulum of School Reform," *Education* 8 (February 1888) : 347–50; cf. also *St. Louis Report* (20th) , 1873–1874, p. 121; *N.E.A. Proceedings*, 1900, p. 336.

33. Piaget, *Science of Education*. . . , pp. 74–75.

34. William T. Harris, "The Study of Arrested Development in Children as Produced by Injudicious School Methods," *Education* 30 (April 1900) : 453–66.

35. Curti, *Social Ideas*. . . , pp. 310–47.

36. *Newark Evening News*, May 2, 1890 *(Harris MSS. No. 787)* .

37. *St. Louis Report*, 20th, 1893, p. 171.

38. "Immigration and Rural Problems," Address before the American Defense Association, December 1890 *(Harris MSS. No. 855)* .

39. *Proceedings of the 13th Annual Meeting of the Lake Mohawk Conference on the Indian*, 1895, pp. 33–38; *N.E.A. Proceedings*, 1902, p. 876; "A Definition of Civilization," *Report of the Commissioner of Education*, 1904, 1: 1129–39.

40. William T. Harris, "The Education of the Negro," *Atlantic Monthly* 69 (June 1892) : 720–36; "Normal School Training for the Negro," *Harris MSS. No. 866*. Harris supported the Blair Educational Bill, Harris to J. R. Preston, 1889 *(Harris MSS. No. 519)* .

41. Curti, *Social Ideas*. . . , pp. 310f.

42. Piaget, *Science of Education*. . . , p. 178.

43. Ibid., pp. 178f.

44. Ibid., p. 180.

45. McCluskey, *Public Schools and Moral Education,* p. 99.

46. Harris to S. S. McClure, September 7, 1887 (Harris MSS. No. 863); "Books That Have Helped Me," *The Forum* 3 (April 1887) : 142f.

47. D. H. Harris, "A Brief Report of the Meeting Commemorative of the Early St. Louis Movement in Philosophy, Psychology, Literature, Art and Education" (St. Louis: Privately published by D. H. Harris, 1922) , p. 26.

48. McCluskey, *Public Schools and Moral Education,* p. 113.

49. "The Metaphysical Assumptions of Materialism" in the April 1882 issue, and "The Pantheism of Spinoza" in the July 1882 issue. George Dykhuizen, *The Life and Mind of John Dewey* (Carbondale, Ill.: Southern Illinois University Press, 1973) , pp. 22–24.

50. Curti, *Social Ideas. . . ,* pp. 311f.

51. For an expansion of Harris's philosophy see John S. Roberts, *William T. Harris, A Critical Study of His Educational and Related Philosophical Views* (Washington, D.C.: National Education Association, 1924) ; William T. Harris, "Social Culture in the Form of Education and Religion," *Educational Review* 29 (January 1905) : 18–37.

52. McCluskey, *Public Schools and Moral Education,* p. 113, n47.

53. Jean Piaget, *Insights and Illusions of Philosophy,* translated by Wolfe Mays, pp. 220–21. © by The World Publishing Company from *Insights and Illusions of Philosophy* by Jean Piaget, translated by Wolfe Mays with permission of Thomas Y. Crowell Co., Inc.

54. The high school of those days was commonly the cultural hub of the community. Colleges were few in number, and a high school diploma was entrée enough to cultivated society. McCluskey, *Public Schools and Moral Education,* p. 112.

55. Ibid., p. 279.

56. Curti, *Social Ideas. . . ,* pp. 312f.

57. William T. Harris, "Social Culture in the Form of Educational Religion," *Educational Review* 29 (January 1905) : 18–37.

58. "On the Significance of Peace," *The Western,* September 1873 (Harris MSS. No. 800) .

59. William T. Harris, "The Church, the State, and the School," *North American Review* 133 (September 1881) : 215.

60. Piaget, *Science of Education. . . ,* p. 151.

61. William T. Harris, "Thoughts on the Basis of Agnosticism," *Journal of Speculative Philosophy* 15 (April 1881) : 114.

62. *St. Louis Report,* 17th, 1870–71, p. 173.

63. Believing that reality unfolds according to an inevitable design of spiritual unity, he insisted that education's chief task is to acquiesce in this process. . . . Like Spencer and Sumner, who argued from the premises of scientific realism, Harris, the idealist, concluded that on the whole "what-

ever is, is right." The school, in short, is dedicated to preserving inherited values and adjusting man to society. . . . this obligation accords with absolute ontological law. Theodore Brameld, *Patterns of Educational Philosophy* (New York: Holt, Rinehart and Winston, Inc., 1971) , pp. 214–15.

64. William T. Harris, "The Intellectual Value of Tool Work," *Scientific American*, Supplement, No. 1598 (August 18, 1906) .

65. William T. Harris, "The Printing Press as an Instrument of Education," *Education* 1 (March 1881) : 371–83; "What Shall the Public Schools Teach?" *Forum* 4 (February 1888) : 573–81.

66. William T. Harris, "Philosophy Made Simple," *Chautauquan* 6 (May 1886) : 440.

67. Dykhuizen, *The Life and Mind. . .* , p. 92.

68. Piaget, *Science of Education. . .* , p. 59.

69. *Education* 102 (December 1891) : 197; Harris, in *A Memorial of the Life and Services of John Philbrick*, pp. 60–61; *N.E.A. Proceedings*, 1896, p. 196.

70. Piaget, *Science of Education. . .* , p. 151.

71. Harris was still fully committed to the value of universal free public education. He firmly believed that "only a people with universal education can sustain a republican form of government." William T. Harris, "Our Educational System: What it is; Why it is; What it accomplishes," *Chautauquan* 15 (April 1892) : 17.

72. Harris repeats the philosophy of Horace Mann: "Where the people are to obey the laws made for them by an hereditary ruling class, it may be necessary that the people shall be taught in the schools so much as will enable them to read and understand those laws. But where the people are to make the laws as well as obey them, what limit can there be to the school education required except the full preparation of the individual citizen to carry on his education for himself?" McCluskey, p. 126, n25.

73. William T. Harris, "The Church, the State, and the School," *North American Review* 133 (September 1881) : 216–17.

74. William T. Harris, "The Aesthetic Element in Education," *N.E.A. Proceedings*, 1897, pp. 330–38; "The Study of Art and Literature in the Schools," *Report of the Commissioner of Education*, 1898–1899, 1: 687f.

75. Harris advised his teachers to "educate toward a knowledge of truth, a love of the beautiful, a habit of doing good, because only through these forms can the self-activity continue to develop progressively in this universe. These forms—the true, the beautiful, and the good—will lead the individual into union with his fellow-man through all eternity, and make him a participator in the divine-human work of civilization and culture and the perfection of man in the image of God." William T. Harris, "Psychological Inquiry," *Education* 6 (November 1885) : 157–58.

76. Piaget, *Science of Education. . . ,* p. 153.

77. *North American Review* 133 (September 1881) : 216.

78. Curti, *Social Ideas. . . ,* pp. 310–47.

79. Hans G. Furth, "The Problem of Piaget," *Commonweal,* April 4, 1969, p. 69. Used with permission of Commonweal Publishing Co.

80. "The Relation of Women to the Trades and Professions," Smith College Anniversary, 1900 (Harris MSS. No. 719) ; Address at the Women's Educational Association, Boston, April 18, 1872, ibid.; *St. Louis Report,* 16th, 1869–1870, pp. 18f.

81. *Pall Mall Gazette,* May 14, 1894 (Harris MSS. No. 219–334) ; *Report of The Commissioner of Education,* 1900–1901, pp. xli-xliii. The committee appointed by President Nixon to study the drug problem reported in 1973 that alcoholism is the number-one drug problem in the nation.

82. McCluskey, *Public Schools and Moral Education,* p. 131 (quoting from Harris's *Eighteenth Annual Report,* pp. 141–42) .

83. Curti, *Social Ideas. . . ,* pp. 310–47.

84. *N.E.A. Proceedings,* 1898, pp. 49–51; "An Educational Policy for Our New Possessions," *ibid.,* 1899, pp. 69–79.

85. *Report of the Commissioner of Education,* 1902, 1: 959.

86. *Educational Review* 16 (September 1898) : 205.

87. Curti, *Social Ideas. . . ,* pp. 310–47.

88. Mary Ann Spencer Pulaski, *Understanding Piaget* (New York: Harper & Row, Publishers, 1971) , pp. 4–5.

89. William T. Harris, "Professor John Dewey's Doctrine of Interest as Related to Will," *Educational Review* 11 (May 1896) : 488.

90. William T. Harris, "The Relation of Religion to Art," *Journal of Speculative Philosophy* 10 (April 1876) : 207.

91. John W. Gardner, *Self-Renewal* (New York: Harper & Row, Publishers, 1964) , p. 12.

92. William T. Harris, "Moral Education," *American Journal of Education* 9 (January 1876) : 4.

93. McCluskey, *Public Schools and Moral Education,* p. 148 (quoting from Harris's *Seventeenth Annual Report,* p. 26) .

94. Pulaski, *Understanding Piaget,* pp. 77, 84; Jean Piaget, *Six Psychological Studies* (New York: Random House, 1968) , pp. 56f. © 1967 by Random House, Inc.

95. *Ibid.,* p. 88.

96. Jean Piaget, *The Moral Judgment of the Child* (New York: Free Press, 1965) , pp. 319–20.

97. William T. Harris, "The Separation of the Church from the Tax-Supported School," *Educational Review* 26 (October 1903) : 226.

98. R. J. Gabel, *Public Funds for Church and Private Schools* (Washington, D.C.: The Catholic University of America, 1937) , p. 699.

99. McCluskey, *Public Schools and Moral Education,* pp. 163–71.

100. Ibid., p. 170.

101. William T. Harris, "The Philosophic Aspects of History," *Papers of the American Historical Association* (1891) , 5: 247–54; Thomas Davidson, *The Education of the Greek People* (New York, 1903) , Preface, pp. v–viii; *The Arena* 17 (February 1897) : 354; *N.E.A. Proceedings,* 1891, p. 72; "The Practical Lessons of History," (Harris MSS. No. 804) .

102. Furth, "The Problem of Piaget," p. 69.

103. *American Review of Reviews* 34 (August 1906) : 164–66. For further evidence of the influence of Harris, see *Journal of Education* 61 (February 21, 1895) ; *ibid.* 70 (December 16, 1907) : 1881; *The Nation* 83 (July 5, 1906): 8–9; *Outlook* 93 (November 20, 1909) : 61–62; *Education* 30 (December, 1909) : 247; *Educational Review* 39 (March 1910) : 229–308; *ibid.* (January 1910) , pp. 1–12; *ibid.* (February 1910) , pp. 120–43; *Ibid.* 40 (September 1910) : 173–83; *N.E.A. Proceedings,* 1910, pp. 185–98; *Life and Confessions of a Psychologist* (New York, 1923) , pp. 496–97. Additional evidence of this influence of Harris can be found in Roberts, *William Torrey Harris,* chaps. XI–XII. Henry Ridgley Evans, *A List of the Writings of William Torrey Harris* (Washington, 1908) , contains 479 titles, but is incomplete.

104. Albert Camus, *The Rebel,* trans. Anthony Bower (New York: Alfred A. Knopf, Inc., Vintage Books © 1956) , p. 194.

105. McCluskey, *Public Schools and Moral Education,* p. 279.

106. Ibid., pp. 279–84.

5 *John Dewey's Democracy for Education*

1. Neal Gerard McCluskey, *Public Schools and Moral Education* (New York: Columbia University Press, 1958) , pp. 177–258; Hugh C. Black, Kenneth V. Lottich, and Donald S. Seckinger, eds., *The Great Educators* (Chicago: Nelson-Hall Company, 1972) , pp. 613–31; George Dykhuizen, *The Life and Mind of John Dewey* (Carbondale, Ill.: Southern Illinois University Press, 1973) ; John D. Redden and Francis A. Ryan, *A Catholic Philosophy of Education* (Milwaukee, Wis.: The Bruce Publishing Co.) © Copyright 1942, 1956 by The Bruce Publishing Co., pp. 476–586.

2. Black, Lottich, and Seckinger, *The Great Educators,* chap. 50; William Torrey Harris has been called the "Conservator." In the sense that he fought to preserve what he considered the hard-won heritage of humanity, this is preeminently just. The number of his opponents, far from thinning with the years, has increased as the decades rolled by. At one or another interval Harris challenged the tenets, in whole or in part, of Rousseau, Pestalozzi, Spencer, Herbart, Froebel, Darwin, Parker, Stearns, the McMurrys, DeGarmo, James, and Dewey. McCluskey, *Public Schools and Moral Education,* p. 128.

3. McCluskey, *Public Schools and Moral Education,* p. 178.

4. Edmund Sullivan, "Piaget and the School Curriculum: A Critical Appraisal," Bulletin No. 2 of the Ontario Institute for Studies in Education (Toronto, 1967), pp. 1–2.

5. Dewey wrote in *Democracy and Education,* the most-used text for courses in Philosophy of Education: "One of the fundamental problems of education . . . is set by the conflict of a nationalistic and a wider social aim. In Europe . . . the new idea of the importance of education for human welfare and progress was captured by national interests and harnessed to do a work whose social aim was definitely narrow and exclusive. The social aim of education and its national aim were identified, and the result was a marked obscuring of the meaning of a social aim. . . . Science, commerce, and art transcend national boundaries. They are largely international in quality and method. They involve interdependencies and cooperation among the peoples inhabiting different countries." John Dewey, *Democracy and Education* (New York: The Macmillan Co., 1916), p. 97. © Copyright, 1916, by The Macmillan Co.

6. John Dewey, "Ethics and Physical Science," *Andover Review* 7 (June 1887): 576. This same view has been carefully analyzed existentially for values process education by John A. Stoops in *Religious Values in Education* (Dansville, Ill.: The Interstate Printers & Publishers, Inc., 1967).

7. Sullivan, "Piaget and the School. . . ," p. 2.

8. Since growth is the characteristic of life, education is all one with growing; it has no end beyond itself. The criterion of the value of school education is the extent to which it creates a desire for continued growth and supplies means for making the desire effective in fact. John Dewey, *Democracy and Education* (New York: The Macmillan Co.), p. 62. © Copyright, 1916, by The Macmillan Co.

9. Dewey, *Reconstruction in Philosophy* (New York: Henry Holt and Co., 1920), pp. 84–87.

10. Strictly speaking, Dewey understood pragmatism to be a theory of logic, which "means only the rule of referring all thinking . . . to consequences for final meaning and test." John Dewey, *Essays in Experimental Logic* (Chicago: University of Chicago Press, 1916), p. 330. Reprinted from *Experimental Logic* by John Dewey by permission of The University of Chicago, owner of the copyright.

11. According to Dewey, "The most penetrating definition of philosophy which can be given is, then, that it is the theory of education in its most general phases." John Dewey, *Democracy and Education* (New York: The Macmillan Co.), p. 386. © Copyright, 1916, by The Macmillan Co.

12. Jean Piaget, *Science of Education. . . ,* p. 174.

13. McCluskey, *Public Schools and Moral Education,* p. 184 (quoting from John Dewey's letter of January 17, 1884, addressed to William T. Harris).

14. Dewey, *Reconstruction in Philosophy,* pp. 84–87.

15. McCluskey, *Public Schools and Moral Education*, pp. 184f.

16. Piaget, *Science of Education. . .* , p. 19.

17. McCluskey, *Public Schools and Moral Education*, pp. 188–89.

18. Originally a neo-Hegelian, Dewey abandoned this philosophical viewpoint after publishing his text on *Psychology* in 1886. This was followed by a struggle toward a new unity of thinking in the next decade. The shift is evident in his book *Outline of Ethics*, published in 1891, and became definitely established in his moral philosophy with his publication of *The Study of Ethics* in 1897. Edwin A. Burtt, "The Core of Dewey's Way of Thinking," *The Journal of Philosophy* 57, no. 13 (June 23, 1960) , pp. 402–7. Though Hegelianism faded out of Dewey's life during the next fifteen years, it left a permanent deposit in his mind. The rigid structuring in Hegel, the formal schematism that Dewey came to find artificial, eventually turned him away from the System. McCluskey, *Public Schools and Moral Education*, p. 185.

19. Black, Lottich, and Seckinger, *The Great Educators*, pp. 613–31; Sullivan, "Piaget and the School. . . ," pp. 1–2; Dykhuizen, *The Life and Mind. . .* , pp. 96–98; McCluskey, *Public Schools and Moral Education. . .* , pp. 177–258; Dewey, *Democracy and Education;* Robert Ulich, ed., *Three Thousand Years of Educational Wisdom* (Cambridge, Mass.: Harvard University Press, 1971) , pp. 615–40.

20. George Plimpton Adams and William Pepperell Montague, eds., *Contemporary American Philosophy: Personal Statements*, vol. 2 (1930) (New York: Russell & Russell, 1962) . Dewey, "From Absolutism to Experimentalism," p. 22; John Gouinlock, *John Dewey's Philosophy of Values* (New York: Humanities Press, 1972) , chap 7.

21. John Dewey, *Education Today*, edited and with a foreword by Joseph Ratner (New York: G. P. Putnam's Sons, 1940) , p.v.

22. Dewey, *Reconstruction in Philosophy*, p. 186.

23. As Dewey wrote in 1897: "Education is the fundamental method of social progress and reform. All reforms which rest simply upon the enactment of law, or the threatening of certain penalties or upon changes in mechanical and outward arrangements, are transitory and futile." Democracy as a way of life, as Dewey conceived it, is essentially a life of social progress and reform. Dewey, *Education Today*, p. v.

24. Piaget, *Science of Education. . .* , p. 174.

25. Dewey, *Education Today*, p. v; McCluskey, *Public Schools and Moral Education*, p. 191.

26. *Ibid.*

27. Adams and Montague eds., *Contemporary American. . .* , p. 23.

28. Piaget, *Science of Education. . .* , p. 160.

29. Jean Piaget, *To Understand Is To Invent* (New York: Grossman Publishers, 1973) , pp. 46–52.

30. He implies this when he states that the process of growth, of improvement and progress, rather than the static outcome and result, becomes the significant thing. Not health as an end fixed once and for all, but the needed improvement in health—a continual process—is the end and goal (sic). The end is no longer a terminus or limit to be reached. It is the active process of transforming the existing situation. Not perfection as the final goal, but the ever-enduring process of perfecting, maturing, refining, is the aim of living. Honesty, industry, temperance, and justice, like health, wealth, and learning, are not goods to be attained. They are directions of change in the quality of experience. Dewey, *Reconstruction in Philosophy*, p. 177.

31. William F. Cunningham, *The Pivotal Problems of Education* (New York: The Macmillan Co.) , p. 38. © Copyright, 1940 by William F. Cunningham, renewed 1968 by Zita Sullivan.

32. John Dewey, *How We Think* (Boston: Heath, 1910) , p. 11.

33. In John Dewey's *Democracy and Education* (New York: The Macmillan Co., © Copyright, 1916 by The Macmillan Co.) , p. 143, this concept of education comes to full bloom: "Education is such a life. To maintain capacity for such education is the essence of morals. For conscious life is a continual beginning afresh."

34. Herbert Ginsburg and Sylvia Opper, *Piaget's Theory of Intellectual Development: An Introduction* (Englewood Cliffs, N.J.: Prentice-Hall, Inc., 1969) , pp. 218f. © 1969, by Prentice-Hall, Inc.

35. Piaget, *Science of Education*. . . , p. 152.

36. John Dewey, *Experience and Nature* (Chicago: Open Court Publishing Co., 1925) , p. 443. Permission granted by the Center for Dewey Studies, Southern Illinois University, Carbondale, Illinois.

37. Burtt, "The Core of Dewey's. . . ," pp. 402f. In this regard, Dewey admits that "upon the whole, the forces that have influenced me have come from persons and from situations more than from books." Adams and Montague, eds. *Contemporary American*, p. 22.

38. Burtt, "The Core of Dewey's. . . , pp. 402f.

39. John Dewey, *The Study of Ethics: A Syllabus* (Ann Arbor, Mich: Register Publishing Co., 1894) , pp. 22f.

40. "To learn from experience," Dewey says, "is to make a backward and forward connection between what we do to things and what we enjoy or suffer from things in consequence. Under such conditions, doing becomes a trying, an experiment with the world to find out what it is like; the undergoing becomes instruction—discovery of the connection of things. . . . Experience is primarily an active-passive affair; it is not primarily cognitive." Dewey, *Democracy and Education*, p. 140. Dewey has influenced one of the most important documents on value relevance: *Moral and Spiritual Values in Public Schools*, published by the Educational Policies Commission

of the National Education Association and the American Association of School Administrators in 1951. Even the description of these values as presented in the publication is that of John Dewey (p. 4). McCluskey, *Public Schools and Moral Education,* pp. 4–7.

41. This is so, Dewey claims, because "Education is by its nature an endless circle or spiral. It is an activity which includes science within itself. In its very process, it sets more problems to be further studied, which then react into the educative process to change it still further, and thus demands more thought, more science, and so on, in everlasting sequence." John Dewey, *The Sources of a Science of Education* (New York: Horace Liveright, 1929), p. 77.

42. Dewey, *The Study of Ethics,* pp. 402–7.

43. Dewey asserts that "education is a process of living and not a preparation for future living. . . . Education must be carried on in forms worth living for their own sake." Dewey, *Education Today,* p. x.

44. Ginsburg and Opper, *Piaget's Theory. . . ,* pp. 107–9.

45. Henry P. Cole, in *Process Education* (Englewood Cliffs, N.J.: Educational Technology Publications, 1972), pp. 30, 37, 43, lists Dewey and Piaget as among those who have contributed to process education today.

46. John Dewey, *Experience and Education,* The Kappa Delta Pi Lecture Series, pp. 23–52. Copyright, 1938 by Kappa Delta Pi. Used by permission of Kappa Delta Pi, an Honor Society in Education.

47. Ibid.

48. John Dewey, *The Logical Conditions of a Scientific Treatment of Morality.* University of Chicago Decennial Monograph (Chicago: University of Chicago Press, 1903), 1st s. 3: 113–39.

49. Dewey's instrumentalism purported to slash away all . . . cultural tendrils by adhering to the principle that "life is development, and that development, growing, is life." Translating this into its educational components, Dewey says: "This means (i) that the educational process has no end beyond itself; it is its own end, and that (ii) the educational process is one of continual reorganizing, reconstructing, transforming." John Dewey, *Democracy and Education* (New York: The Macmillan Co.), p. 59. © Copyright, 1916 by The Macmillan Co.

50. Hugh C. Black, "The Learning-Product and the Learning-Process Theories of Education: An Attempted Synthesis," Dissertation, University of Texas, 1949, pp. 179–91.

51. David Elkind, *Children and Adolescents: Interpretative Essays on Jean Piaget* (New York: Oxford University Press, 1970), pp. 82–85.

52. Cole, *Process Education,* pp. 42–43.

53. Ibid., p. 37.

54. In Dewey's educational philosophy *experimentation* is not a loose term

used to denote any kind of novel, spontaneous, or random departure from habitual ways. For him it is a precise term, denoting the way of thinking and doing that is exemplified, in its most highly developed form, in modern science. Within science, experimentation is not a blind reaction against the old or habitual, against the knowledge and techniques that have already been developed. It is a way of creatively reconstructing the old. Dewey, *Education Today*, p. xi.

55. Piaget, *To Understand Is To Invent*, p. 56.

56. Democracy as a way of life, as Dewey conceives it, is essentially a life of social progress and reform. Dewey, *Education Today*, p. v.

57. John Dewey, "The Relation of Science and Philosophy as the Basis of Education," *School and Society*, April 9, 1938, pp. 471–73.

58. John Dewey, "The Liberation of Modern Religion," *Yale Review*, n.s. 23 (June 1934) : 764.

59. Piaget, *Science of Education. . .* , p. 159.

60. Ibid.

61. Douglas E. Lawson and Arthur E. Lean, eds., *John Dewey and the World View* (Carbondale, Ill.: Southern Illinois University Press, 1964) , p. v.

62. James E. Royce, *Man and Meaning* (New York: McGraw-Hill Book Co., 1969) , p. 13. Used with the permission of McGraw-Hill Book Company, owner of the copyright.

63. Piaget, *Science of Education. . .* , p. 146.

64. John Dewey, *Individualism, Old and New* (New York: Minton, Balch & Co., 1930) , pp. 176, 178.

65. Carroll Atkinson and Eugene T. Maleska, *The Story of Education* (New York: Chilton Books, 1965) , p. 289; James Monroe Hughes, *Education in America* (New York: Harper & Row, 1970) , p. 123.

66. John Dewey, *Logic: The Theory of Inquiry* (New York: Henry Holt, 1938) , p. 9N.

67. Hughes, *Education in America*, p. 123. Nominalism teaches that only *words* are universal, that there are no universal concepts, and that reality is utterly singular. It holds that ideas are mere group names. Royce, *Man and Meaning*, p. 101. Denotationalism teaches that extension is the only reality in human thought. Vincent Edward Smith, *Idea-Men of Today* [Milwaukee, Wis.: Bruce Publishing Co., 1950], pp. 122, 134, 143.

68. As quoted by Edward C. Moore and Richard S. Robin, eds., *Studies in the Philosophy of C. S. Peirce* (Amherst: University of Massachusetts Press, 1964) , p. 243, in *Collected Papers of Charles Sanders Peirce*, ed. Charles Hartshorne and Paul Weiss, vol. 5 (Cambridge, Mass.: The Belknap Press of Harvard University Press, 1963) : 402.

69. Hughes, *Education in America*, pp. 123, 125.

70. Robert S. Ehrlich, *Twentieth Century Philosophers* (New York: Monarch Press, Inc., 1965) , pp. 34–35.

71. Horace Kallen, "Dewey and Pragmatism," in *John Dewey, Philosopher of Science and Freedom: A Symposium,* ed. Sidney Hook (New York: Dial Press, 1950) , pp. 34–35.

72. McCluskey, *Public Schools and Moral Education,* part four.

73. The most extended development of the value relevance of religion in process education from Dewey's perspective is the work first published in 1908 in the *Hibbert Journal* and later reprinted both in *Characters and Events* (1929) and in *Intelligence in the Modern World* (1939) . Compare "Religion and Our Schools," *Hibbert Journal* 6 (July 1908) : 796–809 with *Characters and Events* 2: 504–16 and *Intelligence in the Modern World,* and you find that not only are the principles set forth in the 1908 article unchanged but many of them are repeated in *A Common Faith* (1934) ; in "Religion, Science and Philosophy," in *Southern Review* 1, 2d s. (Summer 1936) : 53–62; and in the reprints of *Credo* (1939) and *My Pedagogic Creed* (1944) . McCluskey, *Public Schools and Moral Education,* p. 246.

74. George R. Geiger, *John Dewey in Perspective: A Reassessment* (New York: McGraw-Hill Book Co., 1964) , p. v. During his ninetieth year, as a kind of valedictory, Dewey addressed himself to the value crisis that science was provoking—how it can now destroy man as well as save him—declaring that: ". . . the one thing of prime importance today is development of methods of scientific inquiry to supply us with the humane or moral knowledge now conspicuously lacking." John Dewey, "Philosophy's Future in our Scientific Age," *Commentary* (October 1949) , p. 391. Reprinted from *Commentary,* by permission; copyright © 1949 by the American Jewish Committee.

75. Redden and Ryan, *Catholic Philosophy. . . ,* pp. 488–91.

76. This challenge becomes evident when analyzing *Proceedings Fourth Interdisciplinary Seminar: Piagetian Theory and Its Implications for the Helping Professions.* In that publication interdisciplinary approaches now opening areas and professions vulnerable to Piagetian insights for education are presented as the new humanizations of Piagetian theory. John F. Emling, "Book Reviews," review of *Proceedings Fourth Interdisciplinary Seminar: Piagetian Theory and Its Implications for the Helping Professions,* ed. Gerald I. Lubin, James F. Magary, and Marie K. Poulsen, in *Religious Education* 71, no. 2 (March–April 1976) : 220–23.

77. Hans G. Furth and Harry Wachs, *Thinking Goes to School: Piaget's Theory in Practice* (New York: Oxford University Press, 1974) , p. 281.

78. McCluskey, *Public Schools and Moral Education,* pp. 284f; Dykhuizen, *The Life and Mind. . . ,* pp. 329–403.

6 After Dewey, What?

1. J. A. St. John, ed., *The Prose Works of John Milton,* vol. 1 (London: Henry G. Bohn Ltd, 1848) , p. 276.

2. Jean Piaget, *Science of Education and the Psychology of the Child*, trans. from the French by Derek Coltman (New York: Orion Press, 1970), p. 3.

3. These values summarize those of the triumvirate. They are treated in detail in chapter 2 of *Moral and Spiritual Values in the Public Schools* (Washington: Educational Policies Commission of the National Education Association of the United States and the American Association of School Administrators, 1951), pp. 17–34. The selection of these three men as the triumvirate, however, hardly requires justification. The first United States Commissioner of Education, Henry Barnard, could have been chosen; but so much of his career parallels that of Mann's and his ideas and ideals of the common school are so similar to those of his Massachusetts colleague that his inclusion would entail considerable overlapping and repetition. Neil Gerard McCluskey *Public Schools and Moral Education* (New York: Columbia University Press, 1958), p. 6.

4. Douglas E. Lawson, and Arthur E. Lean, eds., *John Dewey and the World View* (Carbondale, Ill.: Southern Illinois University Press, 1964), pp. vf. In their book, *Models of Teaching*, Joyce and Weil note that the dominating classic in the study of developing models for democratic process is still John Dewey's work: *How We Think* (Boston: Heath, 1910), without its advocates', however, emphasizing directly or indirectly the same procedures (cf. *Models of Teaching*, p. 33).

5. George Dykhuizen, *The Life and Mind of John Dewey* (Carbondale, Ill.: Southern Illinois University Press, 1973), p. 178.

6. Polanyi is severely misinterpreted in his critique of science by Theodore Roszak, *The Making of a Counter-Culture* (Garden City, N.Y.: Doubleday, 1969, ch. vii). Polanyi's critique in his book, *Personal Knowledge* (Chicago: Press, 1958, Torchbook edition 1962, ch. vi, sec. 8) is not as Roszak claims of science but of scien*tism*, not of scientific objectivity, but of "objectivism": of the kind of "logical reconstruction" of science which cuts out from it the heuristic passion of the scientist himself as well as his rootedness in the intellectual and institutional traditions of his particular branch of science. Were science what Roszak and his followers believe it to be, it would never have come into existence nor could it have survived. Nor, as Polanyi clearly explains, is the logical structure of scientific research identifiable with the very different structure of engineering or invention. Jose A. Arguelles, "The Believe-In-An Aquarian Age Ritual," *Main Currents in Modern Thought*, 26 (No. 26, May–June, 1970), pp. 24–26, as cited by Hugh C. Black, Kenneth V. Lottich, and Donald E. Seckinger, eds., *The Great Educators* (Chicago: Nelson-Hall Co., 1972), pp. 757f. Copyright © by Hugh C. Black, Kenneth V. Lottich, and Donald E. Seckinger.

7. Mary Harrington Hall, "A Conversation with Michael Polanyi, "*Psychology Today* 1 (May 1968): 23.

8. In this regard Dewey says: "What the best and wisest parent wants for his own child, that must the community want for all its children. Any other ideal for our schools is narrow and unlovely; acted upon it destroys our democracy." John Dewey, *Education Today,* ed. and with a foreword by Joseph Ratner (New York: G. P. Putnam's Sons, 1940) , p. iii.

9. Ibid., pp. ix–x.

10. Ibid., pp. ix–x.

11. Basic to Dewey's philosophy of education is his conception of learning as a social process. Traditional education, institutionalized in the grade school, with its system of credits, promotions, and physical, vindictive punishment, conceived of education as a one-way procedure of handing down above to below. Ibid., pp. vii–viii; Dykhuizen, *The Life and Mind. . . ,* pp. 96f., 178f.

12. Lawson and Lean, *John Dewey and the World View,* pp. vf. As Dewey says: "If there is one conclusion to which human experience unmistakably points it is that democratic ends demand democratic methods for their realization." John Dewey, *Freedom and Culture* (New York: G. P. Putnam, 1939) , p. 175.

13. For Whitehead's rejection of pragmatism and Deweyism see *Dialogues of Alfred North Whitehead as recorded by Lucien Price* (London: Max Reinhardt 1954) , pp. 173, 251, 234; Whitehead's challenge is of great significance today because of the great importance of process philosophy. Cf. Robert B. Mellert, *What Is Process Theology?* (New York: Paulist Press, 1975) , pp. 11f.

14. Robert R. Rusk, *Doctrines of the Great Educators* (New York: St. Martin's Press, 1969) , pp. 328–29. Nevertheless, Piaget points out in his *Understanding Causality* (New York: W. W. Norton & Company, 1974) , p. 156, that Whitehead tried to return to a dualism, structured space-matter, within the relativistic context.

15. Alfred North Whitehead, *Adventures of Ideas* (Gretna, La.: Pelican Books, 1948) , p. 226. © Copyright, 1948, by The Macmillan Co.

16. Ibid., p. 335.

17. Black, Lottich, and Seckinger, *The Great Educators,* pp. 651f., 86f.

18. John Dewey, "The Need of a Philosophy of Education," *The New Era* (London) (November 1934) , pp. 214f.

19. *The Unique Function of Education in American Democracy* (Washington, D.C.: The Educational Policies Commission of the National Education Association, 1937) , p. 71.

20. Alfred North Whitehead, *The Aims of Education* (London: Ernest Benn Ltd., 1962) , p. 23.

21. See, for example, that curious book by H. G. Wells, *The Anatomy of Frustration*; it bears witness to the faith and misgivings of modren man.

22. Black, Lottich, and Seckinger, *The Great Educators,* p. 651.

23. Romano Guardini, *The End of the Modern World,* trans. Joseph Theman and Herbert Burke, ed. with an introduction by Frederick D. Whilhelmsen (New York: Sheed & Ward, Inc.), p. 4. Copyright 1956.

24. Ibid., p. 5.

25. Ibid.

26. According to Guardini, the alternatives are neither reaction nor progress: we cannot go back nor can we advance. Man can never retreat in history, but today he is also blocked from advancing into the future. The new age is precisely that—something absolutely *new* and therefore not a development of what has gone before it. Guardini, *The End of. . . ,* p. 12. The technological aspects of value relevance are treated in great detail in *Values and the Future,* ed. Kurt Baier and Nicholas Rescher (New York: The Free Press, 1969).

27. Guardini says that this new man will soon supplant modern man altogether, and that the new man is Mass man. Guardini, *The End of. . . ,* p. 9.

28. John Dewey, *Democracy and Education* (New York: The Macmillan Co.) © Copyright, 1916 by The Macmillan Co., p. 143; "Actually, everything is [in] process. . . ." Dykhuizen, *The Life and Mind. . . ,* p. 211.

29. Dewey claimed that the increased interdependence of men in our civilization calls for a new type of individuality, one in which "the balance of the individual and the social will be organic." John Dewey, *Individualism, Old and New* (New York: Minton, Balch and Co., 1930), p. 50; quoted in McCluskey, *Public Schools and Moral Education. . . ,* p. 256.

30. As quoted in Black, Lottich, and Seckinger, *The Great Educators,* p. 651.

31. Sidney Hook, ed., *Philosopher of Science and Freedom: Symposium* (New York: Dial Press, 1950), p. 37.

32. Jonas F. Soltis, "Analysis and Anomalies in Philosophy of Education," *Educational Philosophy and Theory* 3, no. 2 (Oct. 1971), pp. 34–50.

33. Ibid.

34. Bruce Joyce and Marsha Weil, *Models of Teaching* (Englewood Cliffs, N.J.: Prentice-Hall, Inc.), pp. 180–98.

35. Piaget used these memorable words in his opening address at the International Symposium on the Ecology of Human and Child Development in 1971 sponsored by the University of Miami, Miami, Florida. John F. Emling, "In the Beginning Was the Response." *Religious Education* 69 no. 1 (Jan.–Feb. 1974): p. 55.

36. Quoted by Molly Brearley and Elizabeth Hitchfield in *A Guide to Reading Piaget* (New York: Schocken Books, 1973), p. x, from *The Language and Thought of the Child* (London: Routledge & Kegan Paul, Ltd., 1926), introduction.

37. B. Claude Mathis, John W. Cotton, and Lee Sechrest, *Psychological*

Foundations of Education (New York: Academic Press, 1970) , p. 195.

38. Elizabeth Hall "A Conversation with Jean Piaget and Barbel Inhelder," *Psychology Today* 3, no. 12 (May 1970) : 27.

39. Bruner remarks, in this regard, that "most psychologists who work on development are strongly influenced by Piaget. But although Piaget has given us our richest picture of cognitive development, it is one that is based almost entirely on experiments in which age alone is varied. While he admits that environment influences play a role, the admission is *pro forma,* and inventive experiments remain confined to Western European children, usually middle-class children at that. Where Piaget's work has been extended to non-Western societies, the emphasis has been almost entirely quantitative." Jerome S. Bruner, *Relevance of Education* (New York: W. W. Norton & Co., 1971) , p. 24.

40. Frank Jennings, "Jean Piaget: Notes on Learning," *Saturday Review,* May 20, 1967, p. 81. Used with the permission of the author.

41. C. F. Nodine, J. M. Gallagher, and R. D. Humphreys, eds., "Piaget and Inhelder: On Equilibration," Proceedings of the First Annual Symposium of the Jean Piaget Society, May, 26, 1971 (Philadelphia: The Jean Piaget Society, 1972) , pp. 1f.

42. Ibid., p. 17.

43. Ibid., pp. 17–18.

44. Ibid., p. 18.

45. Joyce and Weil, *Models of Teaching,* pp. 183–84.

46. Hans G. Furth, *Piaget and Knowledge* (Englewood Cliffs, N.J.: Prentice-Hall, Inc., 1969) , p. 261; Jean Piaget, *Six Psychological Studies* (New York: Random House, 1968) , pp. 2–3; "Piaget and Inhelder: On Equilibration," pp. 1f; David Elkind, *Children and Adolescents: Interpretive Essays on Jean Piaget* (New York: Oxford University Press, 1970) , pp. 17f; David Elkind and John H. Flavell, eds., *Studies in Cognitive Development: Essays in Honor of Jean Piaget* (New York: Oxford University Press, 1969) , pp. 145f.

47. Mary Ann Spencer Pulaski, *Understanding Piaget* (New York: Harper & Row, Publishers, 1971) p. 16; Piaget, *Six Psychological Studies,* p. 9.

48. Eleanor Duckworth, "Piaget Takes a Teacher's Look," *Learning* (October 1973) , pp. 22–27.

49. John F. Emling, "Book Reviews," review of *Piaget In the Classroom,* ed. Milton Schwebel and Jane Raph, in *Religious Education* 69, no. 6 (November–December 1974) : 734; Piaget *Six Psychological Studies,* pp. 8–17; Pulaski, *Understanding Piaget,* pp. 207–8; Jean Piaget, *Science of Education. . . ,* p. 30.

50. John F. Emling, "Jean Piaget's Concepts of the Nature of the Learner," *The University of Dayton Review* 7, no. 2 (Spring 1971) : 57.

51. Piaget, *Six Psychological Studies,* pp. 17–38; idem, *Science of Education. . . ,* pp. 30–32.

52. Ibid., pp. 38–69; Pulaski, *Understanding Piaget,* pp. 26–27, 56–65; Piaget, *Science of Education. . . ,* pp. 32–33.

53. J. Piaget and A. Szeminska, *The Child's Conception of Numbers* (New York: W. W. Norton & Co., Inc., 1965), p. 161.

54. Furth, in his *Piaget and Knowledge,* pp. 29–32, gives only three major stages by combining the first two. In his recent article, "Piaget's Theory of Child Development and Its Implications" (*Phi Delta Kappan* 55, no. 1 [Sept. 1973]: 20–25), Robbi Case explains the four major stages in terms of their practical application to equilibration.

55. Piaget, *Six Psychological Studies,* p. 93. Edmund V. Sullivan, "Piaget and the School Curriculum–A Critical Appraisal," Bulletin No. 2 of the Ontario Institute for Studies in Education (Toronto, 1967), p. 9.

56. Emling, "Jean Piaget's Concepts of the Nature of the Learner," pp. 56–57; Pulaski, *Unstanding Piaget,* pp. 66–76, 208; Piaget, *Science of Education. . . ,*" p. 33; Sullivan, "Piaget and the School. . . ," pp. 8–10.

57. Piaget, *Six Psychological Studies,* p. 60.

58. Ibid., pp. 60–70; Pulaski, *Understanding Piaget,* pp. 93–95; Elkind, *Children and Adolescents. . . ,* pp. 50–80.

59. Piaget, *Six Psychological Studies,* pp. xiv–xv.

60. Pulaski, *Understanding Piaget,* pp. 89–95; Elkind, *Children and Adolescents,* p. 80.

61. Piaget, *Six Psychological Studies,* pp. 68–70.

62. Emling, "Jean Piaget's Concepts. . . ," p. 57.

63. John H. Flavell, *The Developmental Psychology of Jean Piaget* (New York: Van Nostrand Reinhold Co., 1963), pp. 1, 6; Herbert Ginsburg and Sylvia Opper, *Piaget's Theory of Intellectual Development: An Introduction* (Englewood Cliffs, N.J.: Prentice-Hall, Inc. © 1969), pp. 1, 12. Reprinted by permission of Prentice-Hall, Inc.

64. Emling, "Jean Piaget's Concepts. . . ," p. 58.

65. Emling, "In the Beginning. . . ," pp. 64–65.

66. Piaget, *Six Psychological Studies,* p. v.

67. E. Hall, "A Conversation. . . ," p. 26.

68. John L. Hess, "Piaget Sees Science Dooming Psychoanalysis," *The New York Times,* October 19, 1972, p. 45M. © 1972 by The New York Times Company. Reprinted by permission.

69. Ibid. In his recent book, *The Quest for Mind* (New York: Alfred A. Knopf, 1973), pp. 56f., Howard Gardner notes how Einstein analyzed the basic concepts of Piaget as being so simple that "only a genius" could have thought of them.

70. Hess, "Piaget Sees Science. . . ," pp. 27–28.

71. Ibid., p. 28.

72. Ibid., pp. 28–30.

73. E. Hall, "A Conversation. . . ," p. 31.

74. Ibid.

75. Ibid., p. 27.

76. Ibid.

77. Ibid., p. 30.

78. Ibid., pp. 26f.; Pulaski, *Understanding Piaget,* p. 205; Sullivan, *"Piaget and the School. . . ,"* Foreword.

79. Ibid., pp. 26f. Many decades ago, Dr. Dewey in his philosophical experimentalism encouraged the schools to develop a lifelike situation within the learning-teaching process. Piaget has aided them greatly along this path through his insights into and explanations of how the child utilizes his own experience in learning. Herbert Ginsburg and Sylvia Opper, *Piaget's Theory. . . ,* p. 231.

80. Hans G. Furth, "The Problem of Piaget," *Commonweal,* April 4, 1969, p. 69. Used with permission of Commonweal Publishing Co.

81. Ibid., pp. 69f.; Jean Piaget, *Insights and Illusions of Philosophy,* trans. Wolfe Mays, © 1971 by The World Publishing Company from *Insights and Illusions of Philosophy* by Jean Piaget, trans. by Wolfe Mays with permission of Thomas Y. Crowell Co., Inc., pp. xii–xvii.

82. John B. Watson *Behaviorism* (New York: W. W. Norton, 1930) , p. 82. Copyright 1924, 1925, by W. W. Norton & Co., Inc. Copyright Renewed 1952, 1953 by John B. Watson; Elkind and Flavell, *Studies in Cognitive. . . ,* pp. 13–14.

83. E. Hall, "A Conversation. . . ," p. 32.

84. Among the arguments used by so-called materialists, prominence is given to that known as *evolution,* or *transformism of living species.* In the eighteenth century Denis Diderot (1713–1784) and Jean Baptiste Robinet (1735–1820) taught a sort of evolutionary monism, but offered no theory of the manner in which one species is changed into another. Such an explanation was offered by Jean Baptiste Lamarck (1744–1829) in his *Philosophie Zoologique,* which he published in 1809. He asserted that the organism of a living thing takes on new and external elements in a very gradual but continuous manner, and, adapting itself to these new "parts" or elements of structure, is slowly changed into a new species. Paul J. Glenn, *History of Philosophy* (St. Louis, Mo.: B. Herder Book Co., 1929) , p. 351.

85. E. Hall, "A Conversation. . . ," p. 32.

86. Hess, "Piaget Sees Science. . . ," p. 45M.

87. Ibid.

88. Ibid.

89. Ibid.

90. Furth, "The Problem of Piaget," p. 69; Piaget, *Insights and Illusions of Philosophy,* pp. 16–17.

91. An excellent example of B. F. Skinner's influence in this regard is his most recent book, *Beyond Freedom and Dignity* (New York: Alfred L.

Knopf © 1971) , in which he proposes a technology of behavior in attempting to help solve the terrifying problems involving process-and-response education for values.

92. Furth, "The Problem of Piaget," p. 69.

93. Piaget, *Insights and Illusions of Philosophy*, p. xii.

94. Thus Piaget sees the value relevance as not in "the difference between the nature of the problems but in the limited scope and in the increasing technicality of methods of verification"; Furth, "The Problem of Piaget," pp. 69-71; Piaget, *Insights and Illusions of Philosophy*, pp. 3-77.

95. E. Hall, "A Conversation. . . ," p. 27. In Jean Piaget, *The Place of the Sciences of Man in the System of Sciences* (New York: Harper & Row, Publishers, first Harper Torchbook edition, 1974) , pp. 4-87, these same perspectives in philosophy are presented in relation to psychology by appropriate applications to the work of UNESCO.

96. Furth, "The Problem of Piaget," p. 69.

97. On the contrary, Piaget considers the formation of a scientific epistemology, independent from philosophical opinions, as his chief and lasting contribution. Ibid., p. 70.

98. Joyce and Weil, *Models of Teaching*, chap 6.

99. E. Hall, "A Conversation. . . ," pp. 52, 32.

100. Arthur W. Foshay, "How Fare the Disciplines?" *Phi Delta Kappan* 51, no. 7 (March, 1970) : 359-62. In his work *Process Education* (Englewood Cliffs, N.J.: Educational Technology Publications, 1972) , Henry P. Cole cites Jerome Bruner frequently for his process perspectives.

101. E. Hall, "A Conversation. . . ," p. 32.

102. Hess, "Piaget Sees Science. . . ," p. 45M.

103. Ibid.

104. Elizabeth Hall, "Bad Education—A Conversation with Jerome Bruner," *Psychology Today* 4, no. 7 (December 1970) : 52.

105. Bruner states it this way: "Each generation gives new form to the aspirations that shape education in its time. . . . We have reached a level of public education in America where a considerable portion of our population has become interested in a question that until recently was the concern of specialists: 'What shall we teach and to what end?' Jerome S. Bruner, *The Process of Education* (Cambridge: Harvard University Press, 1961) , p. 1. Copyright © 1960 by the President and Fellows of Harvard College.

106. Jerome S. Bruner, *Toward a Theory of Instruction* (New York: W. W. Norton & Co., Inc., 1968) , pp. viif.

107. Bruner, *The Process of Education*, Preface; Ronald T. Hyman, ed., *Contemporary Thought on Teaching* (Englewood Cliffs, N.J.: Prentice-Hall, Inc., 1971) , pp. 152-60.

108. Hall, "Bad Education. . . ," p. 53.

109. Ibid.

110. Ibid., p. 57.

111. Bruner, *The Process of Education*, p. xiii.

112. Five more recent publications have done a great deal to stimulate effort in America toward overcoming the linguistic barriers: *Piaget and Knowledge* and *Piaget for Teachers*, both by Dr. Hans G. Furth; *Thinking Goes to School: Piaget's Theory in Practice* by Hans G. Furth and Harry Wachs (1974), a valuable book with additional insights first proposed in Furth's *Piaget for Teachers*; *Piaget's Theory of Cognitive Development* by Barry J. Wadsworth; and *A Brief Introduction to Piaget* by Nathan Isaacs. This last publication, first printed in England (1960), is now reprinted in the United States (1973). It is understood best in its relationship to the other four and, as stated in the foreword, is especially helpful for teachers: "The two essays [The Growth of Understanding in the Young Child and New Lights on Children's Ideas of Number] reprinted here were the result of great effort on his [Isaacs'] part to put the case in a form which he found logically satisfactory while at the same time rendering Piaget's difficult thought and vocabulary into a form easily assimilated by teachers." Two other books, *Understanding Piaget* by Mary Ann Spencer Pulaski (1971) and *Piaget in the Classroom*, ed. Milton Schwebel and Jane Raph (1973), are also highly recommended. However, *Children and Adolescents* by David Elkind remains about the best introduction for the general reader.

113. Hall, "Bad Education. . . ," p. 56.

114. Bruner, *The Relevance of Education*, pp. ix–xvi.

115. Hall, "Bad Education. . . ," p. 51.

116. Ibid., p. 53.

117. Ibid., pp. 57, 74, 70, 52.

118. Ibid., pp. 54, 56.

119. David F. Feldman, "Bruner Collects Nine Essays—'Great Synthesis' Yet to come," *Phi Delta Kappan* 52, no. 3 (Nov. 1971): 196–97.

120. Daniel Sargent, "A Word About Maritain," *Commonweal* 19 (March 1934): 567. (Maritain's publications include more than 50 books.) Reprinted with permission of Commonweal Publishing Co.

121. Raissa Maritain, *Adventures in Grace*, trans. Julie Kernan (New York: Longmans Green and Co., 1945), p. 216. One of the finest process treatises about current educational problems regarding religious values within this humane context proposed by Maritain is discussed in John A. Stoop, *Religious Values in Education* (Danville, Ill.: The Interstate Printers & Publishers, Inc., 1967).

122. Maritain significantly claims that his outlook on education [in process] agrees in many respects with the practical ways and methods of progressive education, when such an education is not led astray by prejudice or ide-

ological intemperance. Jacques Maritain, "Thomist Views on Education," *The Fifty-Fourth Yearbook of the National Society for the Study of Education*, Part I, ed., Nelson B. Henry (Chicago, 1955), p. 57.

123. Theodore Brameld, *Patterns of Educational Philosophy* (New York: Holt, Rinehart, Winston, Inc., 1971), p. 285.

124. Maritain is aware that the word *humanism*, as a general term in process, lends itself to many different interpretations. With regard to a general definition, he says, let us say simply that "humanism tends essentially to render man more truly human and to manifest his original greatness by enabling him to partake of everything in nature and in history capable of enriching him. It requires both that man develop the latent tendencies he possesses, his creative powers and the life of reason, and that he work to transform into instruments of his liberty the forces of the physical universe." Jacques Maritain, *The Twilight of Civilization*, trans. Lionel Landry (New York: Sheed & Ward, Inc., 1943), p. 3. Copyright 1943.

125. Ibid., pp. 10–11. Maritain feels that anthropocentric humanism "walls the creature up in the abyss of animal vitality, [and warns us against] . . . excluding all reference to the superhuman and . . . foreswearing all transcendence." Jacques Maritain, "Integral Humanism and the Crisis of Modern Times," in *The Image of Man*, ed. Matthew A. Fitzsimons, Thomas T. McAvoy, and Francis Malley (South Bend, Ind.: University of Notre Dame Press, 1959), pp. 5–6.

126. St. John, ed., *The Prose Works of John Milton*, 1: 276.

127. Maritain is fond of calling such an integrality "integral humanism." Ellis A. Joseph, "The Practical Attitude of Jacques Maritain Toward the Problems of Education," *The University of Dayton Review*, 1, no. 1 (Spring 1964): 47, n45. In his value perspectives Jacques Maritain's "integral humanism" is similar to that of Joseph Sarto (Pius X) in his encyclical *Acerbo Nimis*. John F. Emling, "Exceedingly Harsh Beyond Measure," *Journal of Religious Instruction* 16 (November 1945): 298–302.

128. Maritain feels that if such evils are to be prevented, the school has three major tasks. The first task is to end the rift between the social claim and the individual claim [of value relevance] within man himself. The second task is to bring to an end the cleavage between religious inspiration and secular activity [in its domain of value relevance]. The third task is to bring to an end the cleavage between work and useful activity and the blossoming of spiritual life and disinterested joy in knowledge and beauty [within its value relevance]. Ellis A. Joseph, *Jacques Maritain on Humanism and Education* (Fresno, Calif.: Academy Guild Press, 1966), p. v.

129. Maritain characterizes the twentieth century as that period of process in which a revolution has occurred by a materialist reversal of all values. Jacques Maritain, *True Humanism*, trans. M. R. Adamson (New York: Geoffrey Bles, 1938), p. xii.

130. As recorded in the Bible, Matt. 16:25: "What profit would a man show if he were to gain the whole world and destroy himself in the process?" Excerpt from the *New American Bible* © 1970 used here by permission of the Confraternity of Christian Doctrine, copyright owner.

131. Joseph, *Jacques Maritain on Humanism and Education,* pp. 22–24. In *Building a Philosophy of Education,* Part 2, (Englewood Cliffs, N.J.: Prentice-Hall, Inc., 1961), pp. 125–279, Harry S. Broudy has presented a classification and description of values that should be the warp and woof of the reciprocal-interaction process described by Maritain.

132. Maritain, *The Twilight of Civilization,* p. viii. Jacques Maritain died April 28, 1973, after developing a values-process philosophy that he termed, "a philosophy of personal humanism." His publications include more than 50 books, the last of which, *The Peasant of the Garonne,* was published in 1968. His teachings have influenced generations, including philosophers, scholars, and religious leaders, not least of which is Pope Paul VI, who has said, "I am a disciple of Maritain; I call him my teacher."

133. John W. Gardner, *Self-Renewal* (New York: Harper & Row, Publishers, 1964), p. 12.

134. John Dewey, *Reconstruction in Philosophy* (New York: Henry Holt, 1920), p. 177. We have become primarily oriented to process. In educational philosophy this orientation reached its highest expression in John Dewey, and perhaps its most straightforward application to educational practice presented by [his colleague at Teachers College] William Heard Kilpatrick (1871–1965). John A. Stoops, *Religious Values in Education* (Danville, Ill.: The Interstate Printers & Publishers, Inc., 1967), p. 134; Dykhuizen, *The Life and Mind. . . ,* p. 264.

135. Peter Drucker, *Landmarks of Tomorrow* (New York: Harper & Brothers, 1959), chaps. i, ii.

136. Nietzsche, as quoted in Harry Slochower, *No Voice Is Wholly Lost* (New York: Giroux, Farrar and Straus, 1945), p. 378.

137. Black, Lottich, and Seckinger, *The Great Educators,* pp. 121, 133, 163, 120, 195f., 316f., 340f., 382, 409f., 416f., 452f., 474f., 496f., 503f., 517f., 557f., 577f., 563f. Piaget, *Science of Education. . . ,* Part 1, chap. 1; Piaget, *To Understand Is To Invent,* pp. 21f; Atkinson and Maleska, *The Story of Education,* Part One; Robert Ulich, ed., *Three Thousand Years of Educational Wisdom* (Cambridge: Harvard University Press, 1971), pp. 250f., 287f., 355f., 383f., 480f., 508f., 523f., 615f.; Robert R. Rusk, *Doctrines of the Great Educators* (New York: St. Martin's Press, 1969), chaps. 7, 8, 9, 10, 11, 13, 14; Cunningham, *The Pivotal Problems. . . ,* pp. 18–21.

138. In his preface to *Children and Adolescents. . . ,* David Elkind states that in 1952 Piaget was made Professor of Child Psychology at the Sorbonne, the first non-Frenchman to be given a chair at that University since Desiderius Erasmus.

139. R. Maritain, *Adventures in Grace*, p. 216.

140. Alfred North Whitehead, *Process and Reality: An Essay in Cosmology* (New York: Harper & Row, Harper Torchbooks, The Academy Library, 1957) , p. 14.

7 Further Significant Piagetian Insights

1. The developmental changes that occur within the individual. Among these are understanding and inventing, for Piaget writes: "To understand is to invent." Jean Piaget, *To Understand Is To Invent*, trans. George-Anne Roberts (New York: Grossman Publishers, 1973) , p. viii; Edmund Sullivan, "Piaget and the School Curriculum: A Critical Appraisal," Bulletin no. 2 of the Ontario Institute for Studies in Education (Toronto, 1967) , p. 3.

2. Jean Piaget, *Six Psychological Studies,* trans. Anita Tenzer with an Introduction, Notes and Glossary by David Elkind (New York: Random House, 1969) , p. v.

3. Robert Williams, S.M., "Piaget's Theory of Thought Activity as Related to an Arithmetic Achievement Test Battery," Dissertation, School of Education, University of Dayton, July 23, 1971, p. 1.

4. Elton Mayo, "The Work of Jean Piaget," *Proceedings of the Ohio State Educational Conference* (Columbus, Ohio: The Ohio State University, 1930), p. 146.

5. Intelligence consists in a comprehensive process-perspective of personalization, according to Jean Piaget. It is contingent upon the growth and developmental maturing of the child from birth through adolescence, involving a dynamic form of adaptation in adjustment. It strives through self-activity for equilibrium in mental organization that possesses content, function, and structure as components. The latter, termed "schemata," which are particularly studied in Piaget's conceptualization of the psychology of intelligence, are developmental in format, substantive in content, and operational in behavior (cf. Hans G. Furth, *Piaget and Knowledge,* Englewood Cliffs, N.J.: Prentice-Hall, Inc., © 1969, pp. 243–52; Sullivan, "Piaget and the School. . . ," p. 33.

6. Herbert Ginsburg and Sylvia Opper, *Piaget's Theory of Intellectual Development* (Englewood Cliffs, N.J.: Prentice-Hall, Inc. ©, 1969) , p. vii. Reprinted by permission of Prentice-Hall, Inc.

7. John H. Flavell, *The Developmental Psychology of Jean Piaget* (New York: D. Van Nostrand Co., Inc., 1963) , pp. 50f.

8. Jean Piaget, *Six Psychological Studies,* p. v. Scientific concepts are similar to those of language and mathematics and involve a developmental perspective. Philip H. Phenix, *Realms of Meaning* (New York: McGraw-Hill Book Co., 1964) , p. 299. Copyright © 1964 by Philip H. Phenix. Used with permission of McGraw-Hill Book Company.

9. Eleanor Duckworth, "Piaget Takes a Teacher's Look," *Learning*, October 1973, p. 22.

10. Elizabeth Hall, "A Conversation with Jean Piaget and Bärbel Inhelder," *Psychology Today*, May 1970, p. 26.

11. John L. Hess, "Piaget Sees Science Dooming Psychoanalysis," *The New York Times*, October 17, 1972, p. 54M. "© 1972 by The New York Times Company. Reprinted by permission."

12. Ibid.

13. Ibid.

14. Ibid.; David Elkind and John H. Flavell, *Studies in Cognitive Development: Essays in Honor of Jean Piaget* (New York: Oxford University Press, 1969) , pp. 28–30.

15. Hess, "Piaget Sees Science. . . ," p. 54M.

16. Ibid.

17. Ibid.

18. Ibid.

19. Ibid.

20. Ibid. The contributions of Dr. Piaget's research to new areas of normal and abnormal psychology both for children and for adults were recognized in March 1973, when he was proclaimed winner of the first Kittay International Award of $25,000, the largest for psychiatry in the world. The honor bestowed on June 1, at a full day's program in New York City, included a morning seminar by Dr. Piaget and a testimonal dinner. "The Jean Piaget Society Newsletter" 3, nos. 3 & 4 (Summer & Fall 1973) , p. 6.

21. James Monroe Hughes, *Education in America* (New York: Harper & Row, Publishers, 1970) , p. 544.

22. B. F. Skinner, "Teaching Machines," *Scientific American*, November 1961, p. 97; Piaget, *To Understand is to Invent*, p. 7.

23. B. F. Skinner, "Why Teachers Fail," *Saturday Review*, October 16, 1965, pp. 80, 102.

24. Ibid.

25. Michael Christopher, "Behaviorism and Belief," *U. S. Catholic*, March 1972, p. 43.

26. T. George Harris, "All the World's a Box, An Introduction," *Psychology Today*, August 1971, p. 35.

27. B. F. Skinner, "Freedom and the Control of Men," *American Scholar* 25 (1955–56) : 47–65.

28. B. F. Skinner, *Walden Two* (New York: The Macmillan Co., 1948) , as quoted in *Humanistic Viewpoints in Psychology*, ed. Frank T. Severin (New York: McGraw-Hill Book Co., 1965) , p. 393.

29. Ibid., p. 394. The possibilities for controlling behavior through reinforcement are, according to Skinner, extensive. He refers to this process as *the shaping of behavior*. B. Claude Mathis, John W. Cotton, and Lee

Sechrest, *Psychological Foundations of Education* (New York: Academic Press, 1970) , p. 55.

30. B. F. Skinner, *Beyond Freedom and Dignity* (New York: Alfred A. Knopf, © 1971) , pp. 3f. In his work "B. F. Skinner and Religious Education," *Religious Education* 69, no. 5 (September–October 1974) : 558–67, John L. Elias emphasizes that Skinner should not be ignored by educators today, for he represents in many ways the scientific and technological culture within which religion is taught.

31. Ginsburg and Opper, *Piaget's Theory. . .* , p. vii.

32. James E. Royce, *Man and Meaning* (New York: McGraw-Hill Book Co., 1969) , p. 93. Used with permission of McGraw-Hill Book Company.

33. Hans G. Furth, "The Problem of Piaget," *Commonweal,* April 4, 1969, p. 69. Used with permission of Commonweal Publishing Co., Inc.

34. Jerome S. Bruner, *Toward a Theory of Instruction* (New York: W. W. Norton & Co., Inc., 1968) , pp. 6–7.

35. Jean Piaget, *Insights and Illusions of Philosophy,* translated by Wolfe Mays © 1971 by The World Publishing Company from *Insights and Illusions of Philosophy* by Jean Piaget, translated by Wolfe Mays with permission of Thomas L. Crowell Co., Inc., p. xvi. Furth, "The Problem of Piaget," p. 69.

36. Ibid., p. 4.

37. Flavell, *The Developmental Psychology. . .* , pp. 1f.; Furth, "The Problem of Piaget," pp. 69–70; idem, *Piaget and Knowledge,* p. 253; Piaget, *Insights and Illusions of Philosophy,* p. 4; idem, *Six Psychological Studies,* p. 170.

38. Piaget, *Insights and Illusions of Philosophy,* pp. 4f.

39. Ibid., p. 5.

40. Ibid., p. 6.

41. Henri Bergson, *Creative Evolution* (New York: Henry Holt Co., 1911), pp. 303f.

42. Ibid., p. 7.

43. Piaget, *Insights and Illusions of Philosophy,* p. 4; Ginsburg and Opper, *Piaget's Theory. . .* , p. 2; Furth, "The Problem of Piaget," p. 70.

44. Piaget, *Insights and Illusions of Philosophy,* p. 8

45. Ibid., pp. 9–10.

46. James Deese, *General Psychology* (Boston: Allyn and Bacon, Inc., 1967), pp. 383f.

47. Piaget, *Insights and Illusions of Philosophy,* p. 10.

48. Flavell, *The Developmental Psychology. . .* , pp. 1f.

49. Piaget, *Insights and Illusions of Philosophy,* pp. vii–viii.

50. Jean Piaget, quoted by Frank Jennings in "Jean Piaget: Notes on Learning," *Saturday Review,* May 20, 1967, p. 81. Used with the Permission of the author.

51. Furth, *Piaget and Knowledge,* pp. 18, 264.

52. Ibid., p. 19.

53. Furth, "The Problem of Piaget," p. 71.

54. Piaget, *Insights and Illusions of Philosophy,* pp. xiii–xiv.

55. Furth, "The Problem of Piaget," p. 69.

56. Ibid.; Piaget, *To Understand Is To Invent,* pp. 32–33.

57. Piaget, *Insights and Illusions of Philosophy,* p. 12.

58. Ibid., p. 45.

59. Furth, "The Problem of Piaget," pp. 69f.; Piaget, *Insights and Illusions of Philosophy,* p. xiii.

60. Furth, "The Problem of Piaget," pp. 69f.; Piaget, *Insights and Illusions of Philosophy,* chap. 2.

61. Furth, "The Problem of Piaget," p. 70.

62. Piaget, *Insights and Illusions of Philosophy,* p. 51.

63. Furth, "The Problem of Piaget," p. 70.

64. Ibid., pp. 69–72.

65. Ibid., p. 70.

66. Piaget, *Insights and Illusions of Philosophy,* p. 28.

67. Furth, "The Problem of Piaget," p. 69.

68. Ibid.

69. Ibid., p. 72.

70. Ibid.

71. Ibid., p. 71.

72. Ibid., p. 72.

73. Piaget, *Insights and Illusions of Philosophy,* pp. 28–29.

74. Furth, "The Problem of Piaget," p. 71. Evidence of this interdisciplinary nature of Piaget's genetic epistemology was presented in the Fourth Interdisciplinary Seminar: Piagetian Theory and Its Implications for the Helping Professions, held February 15, 1974, at the University of Southern California and co-sponsored by University Affiliated Program Childrens Hospital of Los Angeles and the USC School of Education. John F. Emling, "Book Reviews," review of *Proceedings Fourth Interdisciplinary Seminar: Piagetian Theory and Its Implications for the Helping Professions,* ed. Gerald I. Lubin, James F. Magary, and Marie K. Poulsen, in *Religious Education* 71, no. 2 (March–April 1976) : 220–23.

75. Ibid., pp. 71–72.

76. Piaget, *Insights and Illusions of Philosophy,* pp. 29–30; Barry J. Wadsworth, *Piaget's Theory of Cognitive Development* (New York: David McKay Company, Inc., 1971) , p. 5.

77. Piaget, *Six Psychological Studies,* pp. v–xiv; David Elkind and John H. Flavell, eds., *Studies in Cognitive Development: Essays in Honor of Jean Piaget* (New York: Oxford University Press, 1969) , pp. 4–11.

80. R. E. Ripple and V. N. Rockcastle, eds., *Piaget Rediscovered: A report of the Conference on Cognitive Studies and Curriculum Development, March 1964.* (Ithaca, N.Y.: School of Education, Cornell University, 1964).

81. Piaget, *Six Psychological Studies*, pp. 25–27, 42.

82. Ibid., p. 158 n3; Jerome Bruner, *The Relevance of Education* (New York: W. W. Norton & Co., 1971), pp. 138–39.

83. Piaget, *Six Psychological Studies*, p. viii.

84. Robert Oppenheimer, "Analogy in Science," *American Psychologist* 11 (1956): 135.

85. John F. Emling, "In the Beginning Was the Response," *Religious Education* 69, no. 1 (January–February 1974): 62–63.

86. Ginsburg and Opper, *Piaget's Theory. . .* , pp. 23f.

87. Bruner, *The Relevance of Education*, p. 60.

88. Piaget, *Six Psychological Studies*, p. ix and chap. 1.

89. Bruce Joyce and Marsha Weil, *Models of Teaching* (Englewood Cliffs, N.J.: Prentice-Hall, Inc., 1972), pp. 193–98; Mary Ann Spencer Pulaski, *Understanding Piaget* (New York: Harper & Row, 1971), chap. 9; Thomas D. Yawkey, "Overview of Moral Development of Children From the Writings of Jean Piaget and Lawrence Kohlberg," in Presentation entitled "Piaget's Child: A View of Moral Development and Religious Education," at the National Catholic Education Association in Cleveland, Ohio, on April 17, 1974 at the Cleveland Civic Arena (Madison, Wis.: Early Childhood Education Division, The University of Wisconsin-Madison, The Child and Family Studies Program Area, Wisconsin Early Childhood Study Center), pp. 1–12; Ronald Duska and Mariellen Whelan, *Moral Development: A Guide to Piaget and Kohlberg* (New York: Paulist Press, 1975); Edmund V. Sullivan, *Moral Learning: Findings, Issues and Questions* (New York: Paulist Press, 1975).

90. Yawkey, "Overview of. . . ," pp. 1–12.

91. Robert Williams, "A Theory of God-Concept Readiness: From the Piagetian Theories of Child Artificialism and the Origin of Religious Feeling in Children," *Religious Education* 66 (January–February 1971): 62–66.

92. Yawkey, "Overview of. . . ," pp. 1–12; Duska and Whelan, *Moral Development. . .* , chaps. 1 and 2.

93. Lawrence Kohlberg, "Moral Education in the Schools," *School Review* 74, no. 1 (1966): 1–30.

94. Yawkey, "Overview of. . . ," pp. 1–12.

95. Ibid.

96. Ibid.

97. Ibid.

98. Lawrence Kohlberg, "The Child as a Moral Philosopher," *Psychology*

Today (September 1968), p. 28; J. H. Krahn, "Comparison of Kohlberg's 2nd Piaget's Type 1 Morality," *Religious Education* (September 1971), pp. 373–75.

99. Elizabeth Monroe Drews and Leslie Lipson, *Values and Humanity* (New York: St. Martin's Press, 1971), p. 67.

100. Yawkey, "Overview of. . . ," pp. 1–12.

101. The following applications to the learning-teaching process are logical deductions drawn from the many Piagetian principles explained and demonstrated in the thirteen letters addressed to teachers by Hans G. Furth in his *Piaget for Teachers* (Englewood Cliffs, N.J.: Prentice-Hall, Inc., 1970); Pulaski, *Understanding Piaget.* . . , chap. 18; Sullivan, "Piaget and the School. . . ," pp. 17–33; Emling, "In the Beginning. . . ," pp. 67–68; Joyce and Weil, *Models of Teaching*, pp. 180–98; Hans G. Furth and Harry Wachs, *Thinking Goes to School: Piaget's Theory in Practice* (New York: Oxford University Press, 1974), pp. 3–30; Yawkey "Overview of. . . ," pp. 1–12; David Elkind, *Children and Adolescents: Interpretive Essays on Jean Piaget* (New York: Oxford University Press, 1970), pp. 3–103; Elkind and Flavell, *Studies in Cognitive.* . . , pp. 465–88. Duska and Whelan, *Moral Development.* . . , pp. 80–123.

102. Yawkey, "Overview of. . . ," pp. 1–12.

103. Duckworth, "Piaget Takes a. . . ," p. 25.

104. Ibid., p. 24.

105. Ibid., p. 26.

106. Ibid., p. 23.

107. Ibid., p. 22.

108. Ibid., p. 23.

108. Ripple and Rockcastle, *Piaget Rediscovered.* . . , p. 5.

109. Piaget, *Six Psychological Studies*, pp. ixf.; Piaget, *To Understand Is To Invent*, p. 10. Furthermore, Piaget writes in this regard: "If we can say today that it is as much as demonstrated that language is not the source of logic, that Chomsky is right in grounding logic in reason, it must nevertheless also be said that the detailed study of their interaction has only begun." Daniel Yergin, "The Chomskyan Revolution," *The New York Times Magazine*, December 3, 1972, p. 127. "© 1972 by The New York Times Company. Reprinted by permission."

110. Bruner, *The Relevance of Education*, p. 139.

111. Furth, *Piaget and Knowledge*, p. 262.

112. Piaget, *Six Psychological Studies*, p. x.

113. Ibid.

114. Ibid., pp. xif.

115. Bruner, *The Relevance of Education*, pp. 28f.

116. Ibid., pp. 12f.

117. Jean Piaget, *The Language and Thought of the Child* (New York: Harcourt, Brace and Co., 1926), p. xii.

118. Bruner, *Toward a Theory of Instruction*, p. 48.

119. Jean Piaget, *The Child's Conception of the World* (New York: Harcourt, Brace and Co., 1929), p. 9.

120. Jean Piaget, *Psychology of Intelligence* (Totowa, N.J.: Littlefield, Adams, 1963), p. 157.

121. Piaget, *Six Psychological Studies*, pp. xiif.

122. Emling, "In the Beginning. . . ," pp. 65–66; Sullivan, "Piaget and the School. . . ," pp. 10–12; Jean Piaget, *Science of Education. . .* , pp. 36–40.

123. Ibid.; C. F. Nodine, J. M. Gallagher, and R. H. Humphreys, eds., "Piaget and Inhelder: On Equilibration," Proceedings of the First Annual Symposium of the Jean Piaget Society (May 26, 1971), The Jean Piaget Society, Philadelphia, Pa., pp. 1–20.

124. Ibid.

125. Ibid.; Piaget, *Six Psychological Studies*, pp. xiif.

126. Duckworth, "Piaget Takes a. . . ," p. 25.

127. Ibid., p. 26.

128. Ginsburg and Opper, *Piaget's Theory. . .* , p. 70; Furth and Wachs, *Thinking Goes to School*, pp. 13f.

129. Elkind, *Children and Adolescents. . .* , Preface; Emling, "In the Beginning. . . ," pp. 54–55; Wadsworth, *Piaget Theory. . .* , pp. 4–5; On January 18, 1971, The Jean Piaget Society was founded and on May 26 of the same year its First Annual Symposium began. Piaget was present to address over 3,000 participants and to encourage the founders of the society that bears his name. This society is the nucleus of Piagetian studies in the United States (cf. Nodine, Gallagher, and Humphreys, "Piaget and Inhelder on Equilibration," pp. vii–xiii).

130. Hall, "A Conversation with Jean Piaget. . . ," p. 56.

131. Irving E. Sigel and Frank H. Hooper, eds., with Foreword by Bärbel Inhelder, *Logical Thinking in Children* (New York: Holt, Rinehart and Winston, Inc., 1968), p. vi.

132. Hess, "Piaget Sees Science. . . ," p. 45M.

133. Ibid.

134. Ibid.

135. Ibid., pp. 45M, 86M.

136. Ibid., p. 86M.

137. Ibid.

138. Emling, "In the Beginning. . . ," pp. 68–71.

139. Duckworth, "Piaget Take a. . . ," p. 27.

140. Ripple and Rockcastle, *Piaget Rediscovered. . .* , p. 5.

141. Deese, *General Psychology*, p. 329; Sullivan, "Piaget and the

School. . . ," pp. 12–34. Other recent evaluations may be found in Barry Hill, "Piaget's Theories Undermined," *Times Educational Supplement* 2936 (Aug. 27, 1971), p. 6; David Cohen, "Piaget and His Critics: Part 1," *Times Educational Supplement* 2937 (Sept. 3, 1971), pp. 4 and 53; Geoffry Matthews, "Piaget and His Critics: Part 2," *Times Educational Supplement* 2938 (Sept. 10, 1971), p. 4; E. A. Limez, "Piaget Controversy," *Times Educational Supplement* 2960 (Feb. 11, 1972), p. 18; P. Bryant, "Reply," *Times Educational Supplement* 2962 (Feb. 25, 1972), p. 4; N. Jordan, "Is There an Achilles' Heel in Piaget's Theorizing?" *Human Development* 15, no. 6 (1972): 379–82. Regardless of how the matter is resolved, the point to be made here is that since the meaningfulness of scientific ideas is affected by the child's development, the teacher needs to know what can and what cannot be usefully introduced at any given level of maturity. Philip H. Phenix, *Realms of Meaning* (New York: McGraw-Hill Book Co., 1964), p. 299. Copyright © 1964 by Philip H. Phenix. Used with permission of McGraw-Hill Book Company.

142. Furth, *Piaget and Knowledge,* p. 24.

143. Ibid., p. 262.

144. Ibid., pp. 20f.

145. Ibid., pp. 175f.; In this relationship, Piaget insists that development explains learning achievements and not vice versa. Sullivan, "Piaget and the School. . . ," pp. 30f.

146. Quoted from *New York Times Book Review* in Jean Piaget's *Six Psychological Studies,* rear cover. "© 1972 by The New York Times Company. Reprinted by permission."

147. John F. Emling, "Jean Piaget's Concepts of the Nature of the Learner," *The University of Dayton Review,* 7, no. 2 (Spring 1971): 64.

148. To this list of books must be added "Piaget Takes a Teacher's Look," *Learning,* October, 1973, pp. 18–23, by Eleanor Duckworth of the Atlantic Institute of Education, Nova Scotia, a longtime associate of Piaget. It consists of a personal interview with Jean Piaget in October 1972, when he visited the United States and spoke at the City University of New York.

INDEX

and Socrates, 76; Sorbonne, 324, 371; stages of process, 279; stability of motion, 237; summary, 31, 78, 241, 336, 337; system of, 274; teacher training, 121; Temple University, 277; topological intuitions, 219; truth, 274; UNESCO, 104, 132; University of Chicago, 324; University of Geneva, 104, 324; University of Neuchatel, 104, 196, 260, 263; University of Pennsylvania, 324; variability of age-stage, 279; and Whitehead, 190; wisdom, 224, 265, 267, 272. *See also* Beilin, Harry; Bergson, Henri; Binet, Alfred; Bruner, Jerome S.; Bruner and Piaget; Burt, Cyril; Dewey, John; Education; Einstein, Albert; Genetic epistemology; Harris, William T.; Hegel, Georg Wilhelm Friedrich; Jean Piaget Society; Kohlberg, Lawrence; Mann, Horace; Mann and Piaget; Mays, Wolfe; Moral development; Philosophy; Science; Skinner, B. F.; Socrates; Watson, John B.; Whitehead, Alfred North; Whitehead and Piaget

Pilgrims, 28, 60, 61, 62, 72, 85, 116

Plato, 268; and Dewey, 154; and education, 238; Platonic idealism, 157. *See* Dewey, John

Polanyi, Michael, 188; *Personal Knowledge,* 362

Positivism, 271

Pragmatism, 47, 189; and Bruner, 227; and Dewey, 153, 164, 168–69, 170; and James, 170; and Peirce, 170

Present, importance of, 190

Pre-Socratics, 278

Problem solving, 159. *See* Dewey, John; Piaget, Jean

Process perspectives, 31, 33, 39, 40, 43, 46, 47, 188, 190, 240; relevance of, 131, 158, 172; and Dewey, 194

Process philosophy, father of, 78. *See*

Whitehead, Alfred North

Process-and-Response, 27, 40, 43, 47, 48, 59, 198; dynamics of, 32–53, 213, 214; perspectives, 27, 28, 30, 31, 33, 42, 43, 46, 49, 50, 51, 172

Psychology, 92, 159, 172, 225, 227, 270; as new science, 152, 170, 260; philosophical vs. scientific, 276. *See* Dewey, John; Piaget, Jean

Psychology, educational, 92

Psychology, genetic epistemological, 248. *See* Piaget, Jean

Quintilian, 238. *See* Education

Relevance, 28, 30, 31, 37, 39, 41, 49, 50, 54, 56, 69, 97; individual, 56, 64, 66, 68, 73, 83, 85, 90, 93; of process, 158; pragmatic, 190

Religion, 28, 29, 62, 63, 64, 66, 67, 69, 70, 72, 73, 74, 75, 98, 106, 112, 133, 134, 135, 138, 171, 225; and Piaget, 266; value relevance of, 361. *See* Harris, William T.; Mann, Horace

Renaissance, 46

Responsibility, 161, 162, 163

Reverence, 348

Revolution, 195, 370; American, 55; French, 55; and learning, 195, 200; sexual, 209. *See* Education; Learning

Reymond, Arnold, 314

Robinet, Jean Baptiste, 367

Roszak, Theodore: criticism of Polanyi, 362

Rousseau, Jean Jacques: 56, 57, 59, 77, 103, 192, 355; and education, 239; his three principles of natural law for education, 77. *See* Piaget, Jean

Sargent, Daniel, 233. *See* Maritain, Jacques

Sartre, Jean Paul, 272, 275

School and Society, 155–58. *See* Dewey, John